Relating Work
and
Education

Dyckman W. Vermilye, EDITOR

1977

CURRENT ISSUES IN HIGHER EDUCATION

ASSOCIATE EDITOR, *William Ferris*

RELATING WORK
AND
EDUCATION

Jossey-Bass Publishers

San Francisco • Washington • London • 1977

RELATING WORK AND EDUCATION
    Dyckman W. Vermilye, Editor

Copyright © 1977 by: American Association for Higher Education

                        Jossey-Bass, Inc., Publishers
                        615 Montgomery Street
                        San Francisco, California 94111

                        Jossey-Bass Limited
                        28 Banner Street
                        London EC1Y 8QE

Library of Congress Catalogue Card Number LC 77-80065

International Standard Book Number ISBN 0-87589-345-7

Manufactured in the United States of America

JACKET DESIGN BY WILLI BAUM

FIRST EDITION

Code 7744

THE JOSSEY-BASS SERIES IN HIGHER EDUCATION

 A publication of the

AMERICAN ASSOCIATION FOR HIGHER EDUCATION
National Center for Higher Education
One Dupont Circle, Northwest
Washington, D.C. 20036

DYCKMAN W. VERMILYE, *Executive Director*

The American Association for Higher Education, AAHE,
seeks to clarify and help resolve critical issues
in postsecondary education through conferences,
publications, and special projects. Its membership
includes faculty, students, administrators, trustees,
public officials, and interested citizens from all
segments of postsecondary education. This diversity
of membership reflects AAHE's belief that unilateral
solutions to problems are not as sound as those arrived
at through a coming together of all who are affected
by a problem.

Preface

In Washington, D.C., many of the busboys and waiters are from underdeveloped countries in Latin America and other parts of the world. Waiting on tables and clearing them off is hard work and the wages are usually low. Picking grapes is also hard, low-paying work. There is not much competition among Americans for jobs like these, but the foreigners are grateful to have them. What we think of as drudgery, many of them think of as opportunity.

The observation that what we call problems in America are solutions in some other parts of the world is not original, but it is useful. It can help us distinguish a crisis from a concern. To need work in order to eat is a crisis. To want work that is interesting or personally satisfying is a concern. At this moment in the history of the United States it would be an exaggeration to say that we have a work crisis. It would be an insult to all of the people in the world who do have one—most people according to demographers. But we have a concern, and it is probably fair to say that we have a *potential* economic crisis that could, if we do not take steps to avoid it, shake us to our roots.

The concern is with the quality of worklife. As noted, when people move beyond a certain level of prosperity, they become less willing to perform drudgery. They come to regard work time

ix

as an integral part of living time. It occurs to them that work itself —and not just the paycheck from it—should be life-enhancing. Several chapters of this book trace the development of this concern and describe efforts here and abroad to respond to it. In Europe, the term used to describe these efforts is *industrial democracy.* It is a term aptly chosen to convey a central idea of the movement—the idea that workers have human rights. If, as Hazel Henderson suggests, industrial societies have cast workers in the role of "industrial peasants," then industrial democracy can be understood as an effort to grant them first-class citizenship in the world of work.

Years ago John Dewey, who is quoted frequently in this book, fought a lonely battle against the trend toward industrial peasantry. For Dewey, the purpose of work in a democratic society was not simply efficient production but personal growth for the worker. E. F. Schumacher restates the case succinctly in this volume. Good work, he says, "ennobles the product as it ennobles the producer." In the salad days of the industrial age few were inclined to listen. Now we have ears. Dewey lost the battle but maybe not the war.

The potential crisis is a much larger matter, and work is only a part of it. Even to try to give this potential crisis a name is risky because it does not loom before us as a single problem but as a confluence of trends in demography, ecology, and energy. For Americans, the energy member of this triad has already caused a tremor or two. Many remain unconvinced that the tremors are a prelude to the big shock, but the experts say it is coming. The tank that fuels our economy is nearing empty—America is running out of gas.

We are told that we have thirty years, maybe. And during that maybe thirty years, we are told, if our dependence on fossil fuels does not decrease, each year will put a greater strain on our economy than the one before. Unemployment, by this scenario, could run as high as 25 percent in ten years according to one Congressional study group. That qualifies as a depression. Ten years is not much time to turn the tide. This is not a potential crisis, some would say. This is the thing itself.

In the most general terms, we seem to have only three choices: keep the same old economy we have been driving all these years and try to develop new fuels for it; trade it in on a new model that uses less fuel; or do a little of both. In the chapters of this book that offer scenarios for the future, the weight of the argument falls on the second of these choices—changing the vehicle, not the fuel. Over the years we have become increasingly dependent on increasingly centralized, capital-intensive systems that have become increasingly vulnerable. Now, according to people like Schumacher, Henderson, and to an extent Willard Wirtz, we have to move the other way: to decentralize and become more labor-intensive and self-sufficient. The new direction is captured in the title of Schumacher's captivating book, *Small Is Beautiful: Economics as if People Mattered*—a book that shares about equal footnote space with John Dewey in this volume.

Stated most fearsomely, then, the potential crisis goes something like this: The industrial age is on the verge of collapsing around our ears. We will not likely be able to shore it up much longer and we would be wise to begin preparing ourselves for a new era that is more closely aligned with present and projected realities. If one accepts this assessment of our predicament—and many thoughtful people do—then the question is: How can we bring about the kind and magnitude of change that is called for? This question is picked up by several authors—Howard R. Bowen and Willard Wirtz in particular—and none believes the impetus for change will come from the government, or even that it should. In a democracy that is functioning right, the government responds to and reflects the will of the people. Even when government leads, it does so from the will of the people. And so, in America, the people will have to decide. Would we have it any other way?

As Howard Bowen points out in this book, the choice that presents itself is a value choice. In other words, we are not going to change our way of life *voluntarily* until we change our values. There are signs that such a change of values is occurring. Hazel Henderson catalogues a number of them: alternative media, the ecology movement, cooperatives, the growing number of people committed to a lifestyle of "voluntary simplicity," the proliferation of small, craft-oriented enterprises, and other manifestations of concern about the quality of life. But whether these new lifestyles can spread and become the dominant lifestyles of industrial societies in two or three decades is uncertain at best and probably unlikely without an added stimulus. That stimulus could come in the form of a sudden shockwave of adversity—not an energy tremor but an energy quake. Or it could come from education, and the authors of this book are explicit in hoping it will.

For a long time now, educators have shied from the question of values. Those who have touched it have burned their hands. Their caution is understandable. They have learned from experience that when you take up the question of values in education you run almost immediately into another question: Whose values, yours or mine? Now, it seems, we are learning something else—that values are implicit in education whether we want them there or not. Ted Mills, another contributor to this book, makes some interesting observations in this regard. Education, he suggests, never really turned its back on ethics. It just swapped human ethics for merchant ethics. To educators, that may seem like an inflammatory way to draw the issue, but it does cast it in debatable terms. In any event, at this late stage, few would argue that we can afford to put off the question of values. We might even find, if we confront it sincerely and with good will, that the related question—yours or mine?—can be resolved in one word: ours.

As usual, I want to thank several people who helped put this book together. The first, and properly so, is James O'Toole. It would be enough to say that he did a remarkable job heading the planning group responsible for the conference from which the chapters in this book were developed—the thirty-second National Conference on Higher Education. But, characteristically, he did more than that. He helped select the papers to be included in the book and wrote a very thoughtful introductory chapter as well. Thanks also to Sister Joel Read, president of the American Association for Higher Education at the time of the conference. She was greatly helpful in both the planning of the conference and the selection of the papers. And finally, thanks to William Ferris of the AAHE staff, whose hard work, remarkable editorial skills, and sensitivity to the issues discussed here are largely responsible for getting this book to the printer.

Washington, D.C.   Dyckman W. Vermilye
September 1977

Contents

Preface   ix

Contributors   xvii

The Purposes of Higher Learning: An Introduction   1
     James O'Toole

ONE: MEANINGS

1. The Philosophical Split   12
     Arthur G. Wirth

2. Values, the Dilemmas of Our Time, and Education   22
     Howard R. Bowen

3. Ironies and Paradoxes   36
     Thomas F. Green

4. Work, Education, and Leisure   46
     Mortimer J. Adler

5.   Good Work   55
       E. F. Schumacher

TWO: RELATING WORK TO EDUCATION

6.   The Current State of Recurrent Education   65
       Stanley D. Nollen

7.   Education in Industry   79
       Seymour Lusterman

8.   Work as a Learning Experience   87
       Ted Mills

9.   Three Factors of Success   102
       George O. Klemp, Jr.

THREE: RELATING EDUCATION TO WORK

10.   Education, Work, and FIPSE   110
        Russell Edgerton

11.   Vocations and the Liberal Arts   125
        Arthur W. Chickering

12.   Reassessing General Education   141
        Burton J. Bledstein

13.   The Core of Learning   148
        Ernest L. Boyer

14.   Continuing Education and Licensing   154
        Benjamin S. Shimberg

15.   Licensure: A Critical View   167
        Daniel M. Kasper

FOUR: THE MARKETPLACE

16. Too Many College Graduates? 172
Lewis C. Solmon

17. College and Jobs: International Problems 182
Beatrice G. Reubens

18. Successful Careering 195
Adele M. Scheele

19. The Company and the Family 206
Jean R. Renshaw

FIVE: MAKING PEOPLE MATTER

20. Breaking Down Bureaucracy 218
Einar Thorsrud

21. A New Economics 227
Hazel Henderson

22. Future Work, Future Learning 236
Willis W. Harman

23. Cyclic Life Patterns 250
Barry Stern and Fred Best

24. Education for What? 268
Willard Wirtz

Index 277

Contributors

Mortimer J. Adler, director, Institute for Philosophical Research, Chicago

Fred Best, special assistant to the deputy assistant secretary for economic development, U.S. Department of Commerce

Burton J. Bledstein, professor of history, University of Illinois, Chicago Circle

Howard R. Bowen, R. Stanton Avery professor of economics and education, Claremont Graduate School

Ernest L. Boyer, commissioner of education, Office of Education, U.S. Department of Health, Education and Welfare

Arthur W. Chickering, vice-president for policy analysis and evaluation, Empire State College, State University of New York

Russell Edgerton, senior program analyst, Fund for the Improvement of Postsecondary Education, U.S. Department of Health, Education and Welfare

Thomas F. Green, acting director, Division of Education and Social Policy, School of Education, Syracuse University

Willis W. Harman, professor, Department of Engineering—Economic Systems, Stanford University

Hazel Henderson, co-director, Princeton Center for Alternative Futures, Inc. (Note: no affiliation with Princeton University)

Daniel M. Kasper, professor, Graduate School of Business Administration, Harvard University

George O. Klemp, Jr., director of research, McBer and Company,
Boston

Seymour Lusterman, senior research associate, The Conference
Board, New York

Ted Mills, director, National Quality of Work Center, Washington,
D.C.

Stanley D. Nollen, assistant professor, School of Business Administration, Georgetown University

James O'Toole, associate professor of management, Graduate
School of Business Administration, University of Southern
California

Jean R. Renshaw, organization consultant, Mathematical Bio-
sciences, School of Engineering, University of Southern
California

Beatrice G. Reubens, senior research associate, Conservation of
Human Resources, Columbia University

Adele M. Scheele, vice-president, Social Engineering Technology,
Los Angeles

E. F. Schumacher, chairman, Intermediate Technology Development Group, Ltd., London

Benjamin S. Shimberg, associate director, Center for Occupational and Professional Assessment, Educational Testing Service, Princeton, N.J.

Lewis C. Solmon, executive officer, Higher Education Research Institute, Inc., Los Angeles

Barry Stern, policy analyst, office of the assistant secretary for education, Office of Education, U.S. Department of Health, Education and Welfare

Einar Thorsrud, professor, Work Research Institutes, Oslo

Arthur G. Wirth, professor, Graduate Institute of Education, Washington University

Willard Wirtz, president, National Manpower Institute, Washington, D.C.

Relating Work
and
Education

The Purposes
of Higher Learning:
An Introduction

James O'Toole

For the first time in decades, American society lacks a sense of purpose. It almost seems that there are no wars to be won, no crises to be resolved, no missions to be accomplished, no new worlds or moons to be conquered. It is not that the nation is smug and complacent. America faces serious problems—energy availability, poverty, pollution, inflation, unemployment, crime, the deterioration of the great cities—but there is no overriding sense of urgency about these or other manifest domestic ills. In part, this is because there is no consensus on the priorities among these challenges. But, most important, there is no conviction that solutions exist. Thus, the moral condition of the nation is not apathy. Rather, this appears to be a time for taking stock, for

1

changing gears, and, above all, for questioning—processes complicated by an underlying mood of cynicism, helplessness, drift, and
even futility.

Higher education, as usual, *mirrors* these changing conditions of the greater society. Indeed, among the community of educators, there is even a scarcely concealed penchant for *magnifying*
these oscillations. A small blip on a national monitor translates
into an enormous upswing in activity in institutions of higher
learning. For example, in the 1950s and 1960s, when the nation's
economy was expanding steadily, higher education grew exponentially; when the nation was breaking down discriminatory race and
sex barriers, higher education escalated the process with affirma-
tive action and open admissions; when the nation sought to meet
the Soviet challenge in science and technology, higher education
raced headlong to turn out qualified brain power; when the country grew uneasy about the Vietnam war, higher education erupted
in protest; when the nation recently grew tired of social protest
and reform, higher education seemingly went fast to sleep. And
now that the nation is mildly depressed about its prospects, higher
education is downright psychotic about its *own* future.

But even hypochondriacs can catch cold. There *is* real reason to worry about the future of higher education. For example, it
does seem clear that America's love affair with education has
terminated. Symptoms of estrangement abound. In 1976, one
searched in vain for concern about higher education in the campaign pronouncements of either President Gerald Ford or candidate Jimmy Carter. In California, whenever Governor Jerry
Brown's popularity dips a bit, he restores his "credibility" with
the electorate by lashing out at the state's university system.
Throughout the nation, the prestige of education and educators
continues to fall in public opinion polls; voters refuse to support
community college bond issues; and state governments have become increasingly parsimonious about supporting educational
institutions.

A three-word question on a recent cover of *Newsweek* neat-
ly summed up the depressed state of higher education: "Who
Needs College?" Significantly, the question was not "Who should
go to college?" but who *needs* it, a question in tone and inflection
that is colloquially akin to "Who needs a Jewish mother?"

The answer *Newsweek* gave to its own question was simple.

Drawing on some controversial findings by a Harvard economist, the magazine concluded that most college-age youth should stay home and save their money. Since plumbers, bricklayers, and auto workers with high school educations earn more than college-educated schoolteachers, secretaries, and bank clerks, it was abundantly obvious to Harvard economists and *Newsweek* editors that college is a waste of money for anyone but preprofessional undergraduates.

During the last three years, higher education has been bombarded with such neat feats of reductionist logic. These growing pressures, as irrational as they sometimes are, compelled the theme of this book. Significantly, however, the overarching question its authors address is not "Is college a good investment?" or "Why has the value of the credential plummeted?" or even "Is vocational training driving liberal education out of college?" Rather, the question is a far more fundamental one: "What are the *purposes* of higher education?" Admittedly, this question is old hat. It lacks glamour and pizzazz. But has it been seriously raised in recent years by the higher education community? There is evidence that it has not. For example, recall that all those excellent volumes produced by the Carnegie Commission during the last decade thoroughly questioned the programs, policies, and processes of higher education but seldom, if ever, systematically questioned its purposes.

But now *society* is questioning the purposes of higher learning. The question on the lips of students, parents, employers, and government officials is "What has higher education done for me lately?" Put thus, the question is crude and misdirected. But it cannot be ignored. Just as society is now demanding accountability from institutions of government, business, and labor, it is rightly also demanding accountability from educational institutions. For a concatenation of reasons (supply your own lists), educators are now being asked to calculate and justify the payoff of higher learning to the individual, the society, and the economy. "What have you done for me lately?" is a legitimate question unfortunately made difficult to answer by the myopic insistence of economists that the payoff be demonstrated in dollar terms only. (Apparently these influential scholars have a trained incapacity to use any other standard of measurement.) But, whatever the measure, society has made continued support of higher education contingent on a cost-benefit analysis of its value. And here is the rub. Just when society is putting pressure on education to justify its costs, educators are less clear about its benefits than at any recent time. (As an anonymous British mathematician put it, "The only advantage of a classical brain is that it will enable you to despise the wealth it will prevent you from earning.")

Significantly, society has chosen to question the value of higher education in terms of its relationship to work. This is, perhaps, not the way in which educators would have chosen to undertake such an important reckoning. Nevertheless, work may not be a totally inappropriate measure for analyzing the purposes of education. After all, work is of cross-cutting and transcendent concern, important to all institutions of higher learning (universities, colleges, and community colleges alike), to all interest groups, and to minorities, men and women, liberals and conservatives, old and young. Work probably encompasses most of the basic questions that need to be analyzed in exploring the purposes of higher education. Some of these questions, which are explored in this volume, are as follows:

- Should universities serve as society's credentialers, sorters, and certifiers? If not, what are the alternative ways to allocate status in a meritocracy?
- What can or should education do to meet the increasing desires for social mobility and equality?
- Can education compensate for the deficiencies of family, church, community, and other social institutions?
- Are there some social functions that should legitimately remain outside of the domain of higher education, for example, training people for specific jobs or attacking the problem of unemployment?
- Is there such a thing as overeducation? Or is it more accurate to say that college graduates are underemployed? That is to say, should education be reformed or jobs be redesigned?
- What should be the relationship between employers and educators? Who should serve whom, or should there be an equal partnership?
- What is the proper relationship between education and the trade union movement?
- Does liberal education have any value in people's working careers?

- Is a career just a job, or does it include a series of jobs in life (and even leisure and voluntary activities)?
- What can higher education do to meet the differing needs of youth and adults for individual growth and self-actualization?
- How can education and work patterns be made more flexible, to allow for easier access to both activities and for smoother transitions between the two?
- Should work be made into learning experiences, or should education be made more like work?
- Can or should education provide work skills, labor market information, and job experience? If so, for whom, when, where, how, and in what amounts?

These are merely some of the practical questions with which educators are grappling. That the questions have not been fully and finally answered is indicative of their importance, complexity, and controversial nature. More basically, perhaps, they have not (and cannot) be finally answered because they are dependent on a series of prior and even *more* fundamental questions. These are the questions raised here by Hazel Henderson, E. F. Schumacher, Mortimer J. Adler, and Thomas F. Green: What are the proper relationships among work, leisure, and learning? What is the proper relationship between humans and machines? Basically, these questions deal with the kind of a society we want in the future. With a vision of what we are trying to achieve in this broader context, the practical "how-to" questions of educational process and programs that we have raised would probably answer themselves.

In a democratic society it is not the prerogative of educators alone to decide what future is desirable for the nation. Nevertheless, the failure to think at this level of basic purposes will condemn educators to prolonged and futile squabbles over the means to get we know not where. Thus, it is probably worth the effort to recast, at a higher level, the question about the role of education in preparation for work. In short, all of society can benefit if higher education takes the initiative in defining its benefits.

Fortunately, some educators—represented in this book by Howard R. Bowen, Russell Edgerton, and Arthur W. Chickering— have worked to raise the debate about work and education to a higher level. They and a growing number of others like them are asking an imaginative set of questions about the value of higher education to the work world: "What is it that students will need to cope with work and life in the future?" and "What competencies will they need to succeed in such central activities as those related to work, leisure, and family?" There are no right answers to these questions, but partial answers to the right questions will be more important than complete answers to the inconsequential and misinformed questions about work and education that are being raised in the popular press.

Now, finally, we are asking the right questions. Alas, the answers that are coming back are quite conventional. Those of us who take pride in being nontraditionalists are arriving at anachronistic answers to up-to-date questions. To find out why, we invited E. F. Schumacher, Hazel Henderson, Willis W. Harman, Willard Wirtz, Ted Mills, and other outsiders to the world of higher education to contribute chapters to this book. Where we see only *one* future for education, they see many. Where we see only constraints and limitations, they see scores of opportunities. They have provided us not only with alternative visions of work but also, and more importantly, with an alternative paradigm for analyzing the purposes of higher education. They show us that our progressive and nontraditional ideas of the 1960s are now the conventional and outdated wisdoms of our profession.

For example, progressive educators now argue that one of the most important work skills or competences that can be conveyed in higher learning is "problem solving." This conclusion seems quite reasonable, given the list of national problems the nation and private employers face. Moreover, *problem solving* has a nice, nontraditional ring to it, in that it is transdisciplinary and not oriented to any specific job, ideology, or method of instruction. Unfortunately, this new common wisdom may be incompatible with the realities of the future social, political, and economic environment. As it is traditionally conceived and taught, problem solving may actually be an anachronistic skill for the world of work. Isn't that remarkable? But let us think about it for a moment. Do the problems that bedevil society have a solution or even solutions? What is the solution to racial segregation, deteriorating cities, or starvation in Bangladesh? To even phrase questions like these in terms of solutions is patently naive.

Yet, it is believed by those in traditional academic depart-

ments—and the rest of us who have been trained by these economists, physicists, engineers, and the rest—that young people can
be taught unidimensional problem-solving methods ranging from
cost-benefit analysis to statistical regression and can then be sent
into the real world equipped to tackle the intransigent systemic
problems faced by private corporations and public agencies. Ironi-
cally, higher education already does a fair job in preparing people
to be good, solid, traditional problem solvers. Unfortunately, the
most pressing social problems—energy, food availability, unemployment, urban decay—are not traditional problems. They cannot
be solved by empirical trial and error or reduced to mathematical
precision. Today's problems are no longer solvable in the old sense
because they are not discrete or isolated from each other; they
interact aggressively with each other—food shortages compound
energy shortages, energy shortages compound unemployment, and
so on. Some of the issues facing decision makers in industry and
government *do* have clearly defined alternative solutions, but these
alternatives are highly incompatible, and there is no objective or
scientific way to resolve these differences of ideology or values.
More often, however, no course of action at all has been advanced
to resolve the new, interactive issues of the age.

Let me offer a few examples of the kinds of answers that
traditional problem solvers advance for complex issues: They propose public service jobs for unemployment; income maintenance
for poverty; nuclear fusion for energy—all good, solid, traditional
*non*solutions. Each of these "correct" answers entails negative, un-
intended, or indirect consequences, or unacceptable economic
trade-offs. We keep rearriving at these same old nonsolutions because we are trained to solve problems that are well structured,
easily definable, amenable to standard methods or solutions, and
neutral as to value. But the problems that have led society to the
point of futility are hard to define, poorly structured, and not
amenable to standard procedures or methods.[1] Moreover, there is
no value consensus about the nature of the problems, let alone
agreement about what course of action should be pursued.

So when progressive educators say that problem solving is
the most important work-oriented competence an individual can

[1] I. Mitroff and R. Kilmann, "Teaching Managers To Do Policy Analysis—The Case of Corporate Bribery," *California Management Review*, in press.

have in the future, we should ask, "What *kind* of problem solving?" Perhaps it is not problem solving at all that is needed in business, government, and academia, but problem identification and definition. Employers may need individuals who can think holistically, creatively, and nonideologically and who can see interrelationships and interactions among nonrecurrent events. Even the so-called interdisciplinary studies fail to teach these skills. (Instead of teaching just the ideology of economics, they teach the ideology of economics *plus* the ideology of sociology, engineering, or whatever.) Moreover, they only teach how to solve *recurrent* problems. But these routine problems—the ones for which there are formula solutions—can be fed into a computer. And, what is frightening to those worried about the employment prospects of college graduates, these problems will be fed *exclusively* into computers in the future. There will simply be no demand in coming decades for traditional problem solvers.

In this regard, Schumacher gives an interesting twist to his critique of the track record of formal education. He argues that education is irrelevant for life and work not because it fails to teach what it promises but because it succeeds so well. He argues that formal education successfully induces "convergent" thinking—an artificial, reductionistic process of abstraction that permits people to write down the solution to a problem and then to pass it on to others "who can apply it without needing to reproduce the mental effort needed to find it."[2] Unfortunately, the real problems of life are divergent. That is, there is more than one response to family, political, economic, and other real problems.

My colleague, Selwyn Enzer, has illustrated the insidious and counterproductive way in which education produces convergent thinking among those who would naturally think in a divergent way. Enzer recalls finishing a calculus problem in a high school examination and, in the time remaining, coming up with an alternative way of arriving at the same solution. Not surprisingly, he was marked down by his teacher for offering two methods of solution when she asked for only one. Unfortunately, most of us can find similar examples, from our own experience as students and teachers, of the ways in which young people are guided to

[2] E. F. Schumacher, *Small Is Beautiful: Economics as if People Mattered* (New York: Harper & Row, 1973).

think not in terms of alternatives but in terms of single, right answers.

Our system does not teach young people to search for alternative ways to think about technology, ecology, or the other baffling, open-ended -ologies of the era. Instead, the discipline-bound, pedantic system closes minds to the new and untried, while focusing attention solely on the safe solutions of the past. When presented with a new idea, the college-educated mind is trained to reject it reflexively. Indeed, a major accomplishment of academic training is to provide young people with a series of devices for nit-picking divergent ideas to death: "Where is your data?" "That has never been tried." "That won't work because. . . ." The opportunity costs of such thinking are enormous. It brands as "unscholarly" the individual who greets a new idea by saying, "That sounds fascinating, tell me more." It provides *dis*incentives for the kind of divergent thinking that is needed for an unpredictable future—the kind of thinking that could be the foundation for institutional flexibility and change. It provides negative sanctions to those with the creativity and innovative spirit required to find appropriate approaches to the new breed of social problems.

Most dangerously, convergent thinking leads individuals and society to frontal attacks on complex problems. But it is now becoming increasingly clear that societal problems must be attacked indirectly, peripherally, and systemically. For example, educational researchers have for years unsuccessfully tried to improve the effectiveness of teachers through such direct means as improved teacher training, new curricula, audiovisual aids, team teaching, and individualized instruction. Sociologists Alice and Melvin Seeman have recently discovered that teacher effectiveness may be improved through indirect institutional changes.[3] They found that teacher participation in school-wide decision making is highly correlated with student attitudes toward school and learning and with positive student self-concepts. Teachers with favorable attitudes toward their own jobs make school fun for their students. Teachers who are actively involved in the management processes of their schools generate an attitude of commitment that

---

[3] A. Z. Seeman and M. Seeman, "Staff Processes and Pupil Attitudes: A Study of Teacher Participation in Educational Change," *Human Relations,* 1976, *29* (1): 25-40.

is infectious and is more important to their effectiveness than such direct, traditionally measured factors as years of teaching experience or pedagogical style. Alienated teachers apparently produce alienated students; *engagé* teachers produce willing learners. Significantly, the Seemans are not educational researchers. It probably would have been unprofessional or heretical for someone in the field to address the problem of teacher effectiveness from such a divergent perspective.

What does all this have to do with defining the basic purposes of higher education and with documenting its benefits to society? A great deal, I suggest. While there can be no doubt that the ultimate purpose of higher education must be to serve society, at issue are competing concepts of what that service should entail. It is my personal conclusion, from reading the papers included here, that the purpose of higher education should be to prepare people to work on the emerging, systemic problems that beset society. At all levels of public and private institutions, there is a growing need for people capable of divergent and holistic thinking about alternative solutions to the problems of the future. Higher education will have to find ways to train young people to meet these problems if it is to be perceived as providing a necessary function.

Traditional vocational and liberal approaches to higher education are inappropriate to this challenge, because they are based on outmoded assumptions about the nature of the tasks that need to be done in the world. Higher educators—traditionalists, nontraditionalists, vocationalists, whoever—have often gone wrong in their attempts to prepare youth for employment. They have gone wrong in that they have prepared young people for the jobs and tasks of the past. Even competency-based education, mastery learning, individualized instruction in problem solving, and all the other avant-garde processes and programs will lead to the same disappointing outcomes as did the nontraditional reforms of the 1960s *if* they are predicated on inappropriate assumptions.

If higher education were to set as its goal the provision to society of the talent needed to deal with the complex, nonrecurrent, interactive social and economic problems of the future, it is highly probable that the programs, processes, pedagogy, and curricula for achieving this could be found. Setting the right goals— defining the right purposes for education—is the critical first step.

In this regard, the late Robert Hutchins offered some advice about the future for which young people should be prepared: "If I had a single message for the younger generation I would say, 'Get ready for anything, because anything is what's going to happen.' We don't know what it is, and it's very likely that whatever it is it won't be what we now think it is."[4]

Accordingly, higher education should prepare young people to work on the unpredictable, complex, dynamic problems of the future. If it could successfully provide such a preparation, I suggest that it would have no difficulty in justifying whatever support it required from society.

[4]R. Hutchins, "A Center Conversation, 'Get Ready for Anything,' " *Center Report*, Center for the Study of Democratic Institutions, June 1975.

The Philosophical Split

Arthur G. Wirth

The thinking of E. F. Schumacher and others like him is forcing us to face bedrock issues about the relationship between education and work. We can expect tensions to run high, because beyond the pedagogical issues the debate is about what kind of society we want. Fundamentally, what is at issue is the relation of democratic values to our economic system. Put another way, the question is whether we can continue to give priority to what Max Lerner called the faith in America as a business civilization—the unfettered pursuit of profits as the unquestioned engine for progress—or whether we are facing new circumstances where a concern about the quality of our relatedness to nature, to our fellows, and to ourselves will force us to reexamine our priorities.

Two other contemporary ways of clarifying the nature of these tensions are found in the writings of Daniel Bell and Thomas F. Green. Bell argues that there is a widening tension between the values of our economic, technical order, which is oriented to func-

tional rationality and organized on the simple principle of econo-
mizing—of least costs and optimization of production and profits
—and a counter set of values concerned with the wholeness of persons and self-realization. Bell sees hedonism in the latter view,
while I see it as part of the democratic ethos that insists on treating people as ends rather than means. Bell points out that the
structural principle of the utilitarian efficiency system is bureau-
cratization. "You divide people into roles, you segment them, you
specialize them. People then become subordinated within the
structure so as to facilitate the greater output of goods and greater
efficiency in the use of resources."[1] There is a growing tension between this structure and aspirations to redesign institutions to promote wholeness of persons.

The issue is reflected in another way in the distinction
Thomas Green makes between *job* and *work*. In his analysis, job
and work become two models for society and education. According to Green, it is useful to distinguish job or labor from work. A
job is what most people do to make a living in the corporate society. If the living is made by *labor* alone, it includes doing tasks
that fail to provide a sense of completion or fulfillment. The labor
is separate from the personal purposes of the laborer, and it involves low engagement of self. Its goal is merely income for consumption. Green argues that "in the modern world the sphere of
labor has been enlarged and the sphere of work diminished."[2]

Work, as Green describes it, is quite different. It includes
the production of persistent stable products that enrich or sustain
life and in which the worker's purposes and meanings are involved.
A job becomes work when performance includes the "exercise of
judgment, sense of style, and the practice of a sense of craft." The
quest for work is related to the human quest for potency in which
the person may explore his potential, test his limits, be in touch
with his powers, and discover his human dignity and worth.

We can gain perspective on the value tensions described by
Schumacher, Bell, and Green if we understand that the philosophical issues they describe have roots in earlier American experience.

---

[1] D. Bell, "Schools in a Communal Society," in L. Rubin (Ed.), *The
Future of America: Perspectives on Tomorrow's Schooling* (Boston: Allyn &
Bacon, 1975), p. 44.

[2] T. F. Green, *Work, Leisure and the American Schools* (New York:
Random House, 1968), p. 44.

They were foreshadowed in the early debate about the relation of
education and industry when we were first confronted with the
realities of large-scale corporatism. This debate took place in the
early 1900s between John Dewey and the philosophers of social
efficiency.[3] Since it pointed to a basic split in American culture
that has never been resolved, it is a useful starting point for considering presently emerging tensions about education-work relations.

In its early form, the debate centered around the defense by
vocationalists of Social Darwinist economic philosophy and
Dewey's defense of what Paul Goodman later came to call "our
libertarian, pluralist, and populist experiment."

The vocationalists enunciated a social efficiency philosophy
which favored school policies that would support the values and
job needs of the industrial corporate system. Dewey challenged
the priorities of the system and called for institutional redesigns in
both work and education.

One of the early proponents of vocational education in the
1890s was the National Association of Manufacturers (NAM),
founded in 1895. Its leaders were motivated in part by the need to
increase their share of foreign markets to overcome the woes of
the depression of 1893. They found it difficult to meet the challenge of their chief competitor, imperial Germany. When they
investigated the sources of German achievement, they found
highly differentiated vocational training programs geared precisely
to the needs of German industry. These programs were part of a
system that was separate from the general schools and was administered by the Ministry of Commerce.

The American businessmen, as revealed in their speeches at
NAM conventions, believed that the Social Darwinist philosophy
of William Graham Sumner explained the source of human progress. This ideology assumes that society consists of isolated individuals of varying abilities and capacities. When left to pursue their
self-advantage in rugged competition, they will bring forth the
promise of ever-increasing material prosperity for all. From this
wellspring of increased production and consumption flow all other
goods: home ownership, more education, and support for religion
and the arts.

[3] For elaboration, see A. G. Wirth, *Education in the Technological
Society: The Vocational Liberal Studies Controversy in the Early Twentieth
Century* (New York: Crowell, 1972).

The logic of Social Darwinism for vocational education was quite clear. Its tasks were to increase material productivity as vocationalism had in Germany, to give priority to meeting hierarchical skill needs, and to preserve the dominant values of Social Darwinist ideology. Social efficiency and social control were the watchwords.

The manufacturers found two proficient articulators of a social efficiency philosophy to support the German idea. David Snedden was a pioneer professor of educational sociology, a Massachusetts commissioner of education who introduced large-scale vocational education programs, and the first editor of *The American Vocational Journal.* Charles Prosser, a colleague, became executive secretary of the National Society for the Promotion of Industrial Education and was principal author of the Smith-Hughes Act of 1917.

Snedden confidently viewed the growth of the burgeoning corporate-urban-industrial phenomenon as the foremost means for human progress. He called those who bemoaned the mechanization and depersonalization of work "simple-lifers" or "romantic impracticalists" who yearned for times that were gone forever. Modern people might be subjected to fragmented, routine job tasks, but production specialization and differentiation enabled them to live longer, more comfortably, and with the leisure to consume the arts. Moreover, the application of mass production methods to school life could bring about even more advances. As Snedden put it, "Quantity production methods applied in education speedily give us school grades, uniform textbooks, promotional examinations . . . strictly scheduled programs, mechanical discipline, and hundreds of other mechanisms most of which are unavoidably necessary if our ideals of universal education are to be realized."[4]

In Snedden's view, scientific testing instruments combined with vocational guidance would make it possible for educational institutions at all levels to do what Charles Eliot had suggested in 1907—separate American youth into programs according to their "probable destinies" based on heredity plus economic and social factors. The nature of the jobs to be planned for youth in school

[4]D. Snedden, *Toward Better Education* (New York: Bureau of Publications, Teachers College, 1931), pp. 330-331.

was roughly to parallel the design of jobs in the work world. Quantitative measurement of outcomes could increase efficiency in both realms. The question of whether or not such arrangements would help people find "work" in Green's sense could not be seen as a serious question or could be dismissed as the talk one might expect from "easy-lifers."

Snedden's philosophy sets forth in stark outline a concept of society and of schooling based on a Social Darwinist job-efficiency model. The task of schooling is to help the student fit an efficiently functioning society. The school in both its vocational and liberal aspects is modeled on the job archetype. Schooling will sort us out according to our various capacities. As we become more efficient in the slots that are right for us, we help increase the size of the pie to be consumed. The tasks we perform for our teachers may not engage our personal selves, but so what? If schooling does its job—provides access to higher income—then we can find personal sustenance in our private lives, families, churches, and fraternal organizations. Meanwhile, we can learn in school how to cope with or con the system. Score high and you are on your way. It's the ticket to the promised land.

John Dewey, the philosopher of democracy, also was seriously involved with the policy issues of vocationalism. But he brought a very different perspective to the topic: "All social institutions have a meaning, a purpose," he said. "That purpose is to set free and to develop the capacities of human individuals without respect to race, sex, class or economic status. . . . [The] test of their value is the extent to which they educate every individual into the full stature of his possibility. Democracy has many meanings, but if it has a moral meaning, it is found in resolving that the supreme test of all political institutions *and* industrial arrangements shall be the contribution they make to the all-around growth of every member of society."[5]

To Snedden, this kind of talk sounded like the language of "romantic impracticalists," and he confessed to a difficulty in understanding Dewey's position. When he found Dewey opposing the German model of vocationalism, he expressed his hurt in a letter to *The New Republic*. Dewey replied sharply that his differ-

[5] J. Dewey, *Reconstruction in Philosophy* (New York: New American Library, 1950), p. 147.

ences with Snedden were profoundly social and political as well as educational: "The kind of vocational education in which I am interested is not one which will 'adapt' workers to the existing industrial regime; I am not sufficiently in love with the regime for that. . . . The business of all who would not be educational time-servers is to resist every move in this direction, and to strive for a kind of vocational education which will first alter the existing industrial system and ultimately transform it."[6] Thus Dewey was taking direct issue with the assumptions of Social Darwinist economic doctrine. A few years later, in *Individualism Old and New,* Dewey held that the basic problem for the new industrialized United States was a qualitative one: "Can a material, industrial civilization be converted into a distinctive agency for liberating the minds and refining the emotions of all who take part in it?"[7]

Dewey was blunt about what he held to be the "the fundamental defect of our civilization." He noted that Americans now had available more power over nature and more intellectual resources than were available to classical Athenians or to the people of the Renaissance. Why, he asked, has this collective enrichment not operated more to elevate the quality of our lives? The reason, he said, was that we live in a culture where technique and technology are controlled too exclusively by our interest in private profit.[8] Economic enterprises, he said, are fixed in ways that exclude most workers from taking part in their management. The subordination of enterprises to pecuniary profit makes workers only "hands." "Their hearts and brains are not engaged." They execute plans that they do not form and of whose meaning they are ignorant beyond the fact that these plans make profits for others and secure a wage for themselves.[9]

As long as priority is given to pecuniary gain rather than social utility, Dewey said, the intellectual and moral development of both workers and management will be one-sided and warped. "It is impossible for a highly industrialized society to attain a widespread excellence of mind when multitudes are excluded from occasion for the use of thought and emotion in their daily occupa-

[6] J. Dewey, Letter to *The New Republic*, 1915, 3: 42.
[7] J. Dewey, *Individualism Old and New* (New York: Capricorn Books, 1962), p. 124.
[8] Dewey, *Individualism Old and New*, pp. 30-31.
[9] Dewey, pp. 131-132.

tions."[10] Industry itself must become a primary educative and cultural force for those engaged in it. Science, industry, and technology should be redirected to assure "an ordered expression of individual capacity and for the satisfaction of the needs of man."[11] And, said Dewey, "If a system of cooperative control of industry were generally substituted for the present system of exclusion, there would be enormous liberation of mind, and the mind set free would have constant direction and nourishment! Desire for related knowledge, physical and social, would be created and rewarded; initiative and responsibility would be demanded and achieved."[12]

Dewey's central concern was with the problems of persons and of democratic traditions in the industrial society. He rejected the image of isolated individuals moved by the play of natural forces in the marketplace. He took the social psychology position of his colleague George H. Mead in which the self was seen as the result of both the patterning of culture and the value choices of the individual. According to this view, persons capable of sustaining democratic values had to be nourished in communities marked by such values. As Dewey saw it, people were beginning to repeat the rhetoric of democratic values while living in daily contradiction of them.

When Dewey was at the University of Chicago, he created the elementary Laboratory School where he put his ideas about education into practice. He conceived the school as a small collaborative learning-work community. Studies were organized around "occupations" such as weaving, gardening, cooking, and constructing. Studies in the sciences, history, language, mathematics, and the arts were related to these activities. Children, for example, could see how science and technology had affected a basic process such as the turning of raw wool into clothing by first trying the process by hand and then observing factory methods. They could study also the social and human effects of moving from handicraft to corporate industrial modes of production. As students grew older, activities and studies could be extended to the community beyond the school.

[10]Dewey, p. 133.
[11]J. Dewey, *Liberalism and Social Action* (New York: Capricorn Books, 1963), p. 89.
[12]Dewey, *Individualism Old and New*, pp. 132-133.

Dewey deliberately designed the school as a small learning community in order to preserve collaborative working relations. When William Rainey Harper, president of the University of Chicago, put pressure on Dewey to expand enrollments in order to increase revenue, Dewey resisted the pressure on the grounds that such expansion would completely change the ideals, methods, and character of the school. I do not think it is stretching the truth to say that Dewey sensed the need for smallness within large organizations and in this sense foreshadowed aspects of Schumacher's thinking. In any case, Dewey's model for schools that would have the marks of learning-work communities clearly offered an alternative to the Snedden-Prosser job-efficiency model.

This early interchange on the relations between education and industry exposes long-standing value tensions in American life over questions about the quality of life and the meaning of democratic values in relation to our economic system—tensions between the twin needs for rational efficiency and wholeness of persons. But, although we continue to be divided on these questions, clearly we have given priority to applying impersonal rationalization to increase profits, production, and consumption. The choice, however, is not between rationality and hedonistic narcissism, as Bell seems to hold. Rejection of rationality is suicidal, and merely turning inward is irresponsible escapism. The present challenge is to rethink the concept of "rational efficiency" in terms of present conditions. Snedden's version of Social Darwinist rationality, which articulated the main articles of American economic faith, is becoming dysfunctional. The ecological, social, and psychic costs are too heavy.

We are sharpening our awareness of critical new factors in our experience: an awareness that we live on a planet with limited resources and national interdependence; an awareness that a more highly educated populace has new aspirations about life satisfactions and will not tolerate the trivialization of jobs that has long preoccupied scientific management; an awareness that urgent needs for sanity and personal growth move people to reject atomization and manipulation and to seek a more integrated contact with their whole selves.

The new conditions call for a rationality that breaks away from the mechanistic traditions and priorities of scientific management. They call for a rationality committed to helping us establish symbiotic relations with nature, and committed to the redesign of institutions in the interests of survival and sanity—or committed, in Schumacher's words, to the realization of goals of "permanence, health, and beauty."

Where economic institutions are concerned, even on grounds of productivity and profit, the new conditions seem to call for moves in the direction of "industrial democracy"—the kind of moves John Dewey, the philosopher of democracy, called for more than a half century ago. Even those who pay attention only to quantitative results must observe that the Scandinavian countries, which have pioneered experiments of this kind and have reduced economic inequality, are overtaking or have surpassed us in economic growth.

Einar Thorsrud, a leading proponent of industrial redesign in Norway, has said that the term *industrial democracy* has frightening connotations to American ears. But he also predicts serious experiments in this direction within this decade and adds, "America needs this kind of democracy and knows it."[13] It will require, he reminds us, that managers and union leaders become increasingly more progressive and idealistic, possessed of "an interest in the fun and action of experimentation," a frame of mind that he adds means not being afraid to be called crazy.

Thorsrud's optimism is premature. Initial moves have been made by major corporations, but only 1 percent of the work force is involved in efforts that might generously be called *industrial democracy*. We can expect considerable tension, anxiety, and resistance when the principal assumptions and structures created during this century are called into question. Since these tensions seem inescapable, what relation should higher education have to industry as we move into such contentious and exciting times?

Higher education will, of course, continue to provide the conceptual, research, and training skills essential for the functioning of a complex technological society. But if, as Schumacher holds, we are already in an era that requires a fundamental reordering of our values and priorities and a redesign of institutions,

---

[13]In P. Dickson, *The Future of the Work Place* (New York: Weybright and Folley, 1975), p. 134. For a description of countermoves toward trivialization of work, see H. Braverman, *Labor and Monopoly Capital: The Degradation of Work in the Twentieth Century* (New York: Monthly Review Press, 1974).

the primary responsibility of higher education will be to help provide insight into our condition and to participate in experiments that move us in the direction of "wholeness." This means that the suspicions many business and industry leaders already have of higher education will grow. But these leaders will also need to collaborate with university personnel to make the difficult changes required for survival and productivity. Of course, in return for all the "wisdom" that may come from the campuses, universities will require large measures of toleration for the foolishness they also are capable of producing.

2

Values, the Dilemmas of Our Time, and Education

Howard R. Bowen

Instruction—both in and out of the classroom—should be directed toward the growth of the whole person through the cultivation not only of the intellect and practical competence but also of the affective dispositions, including the moral, religious, emotional, social, and esthetic aspects of the personality.[1] No theme runs more consistently through the literature of educational philosophy from the time of the ancient Greeks to the present. Plato quotes Socrates as saying, "And we shall begin by educating the

[1]This chapter originally appeared as "Complexity and Values," in H. R. Bowen (Ed.), *Freedom and Control in a Democratic Society* (New York: American Council of Life Insurance, 1976), pp. 49-62.

mind and character, shall we not?"[2] In our time, Nevitt Sanford wrote, "Our goal is to expand both the intellect and the area of motive and feeling and to bring the two together in a larger whole."[3] Kenneth Keniston expressed it this way: "The critical component of education attempts to expose students to multiple and conflicting perspectives on themselves and their society in order to test and challenge their previously unexamined assumptions. It strives to create conditions that stimulate students' intellectual, moral, and emotional growth, so that they may ground their skills in a more mature, humane framework of values."[4] Faure said, "The physical, intellectual, emotional, and ethical integration of the individual into a complete man is a broad definition of the fundamental aim for education."[5] And many authorities refer to the close interaction between the affective side of human personality and academic learning.

However, a note of caution was recently sounded by the Carnegie Commission on Higher Education on the ground that colleges and universities should concentrate on what they do best, namely academic learning, and not get too heavily involved in what the commission called "totalism." However, even the commission softened its stand by declaring that "the college years are an important development period, and cognitive and affective activities are closely related to each other."[6] And it added, "The college, however, does provide an important environment" for nonintellective personal development. It must be said that many faculty members who are deeply involved in their disciplines are inclined to shrug off responsibilities in the moral and affective domains. But an overwhelming proportion of educational philosophers and educators in their philosophical moments believe that

[2] Plato, *The Republic* (D. Lee, Trans.), 2nd ed. (Middlesex, England: Penguin, 1974), p. 130.

[3] N. Sanford, *Where Colleges Fail: A Study of the Student as a Person* (San Francisco: Jossey-Bass, 1967), p. 76.

[4] K. Keniston and M. Gerzon, "Human and Social Benefits," in L. Wilson and O. Mills (Eds.), *Universal Higher Education* (Washington, D.C.: American Council on Education, 1972), p. 53.

[5] E. Faure and others, *Learning To Be: The World of Education Today and Tomorrow* (Paris: UNESCO, 1972).

[6] Carnegie Commission on Higher Education, *The Purposes and Performance of Higher Education in the United States* (New York: McGraw-Hill, 1973), pp. 13-19.

the scope of higher education extends beyond the intellective domain. Perhaps the prevailing view was summed up by Alexander Heard: "Our first concern is the human intellect, but our ultimate concern is the human being. . . . Involved are the development of standards of value, a sense of civic responsibility, the capacity for religious reconciliation, skills, understanding, a sense of purpose, and all the rest required to be a well-integrated person."[7]

So much for the introduction to my theme. I now must take you on a digression about the fundamental nature of a free society based on the principles of capitalism in the economy and democracy in the government, and then I will return to the role of higher education.

As we were reminded during the bicentennial year, America is very much a product of the eighteenth century. The drafting of the Declaration of Independence in America and the publication of Adam Smith's *The Wealth of Nations* in Britain occurred in the same year, 1776. This coincidence was not accidental. These two documents—and later the Constitution of the United States—all derived from the same intellectual tradition. The guiding principle was individual liberty, which meant minimal intervention by government in the affairs of the people. The idea was to create a society in which government was essentially limited to the protection of life and property, the provision of certain elementary public services (such as roads, schools, monetary system, and post office), and the laying down of the basic rules—especially about the acquisition of property and the freedom of persons.

From the standpoint of the economy, the ruling philosophy was laissez-faire, as expressed by Adam Smith. Laissez-faire meant that people would be free to choose their vocations, to invest their capital, to decide on their rate of saving, and to spend their incomes as they wished without governmental interference. Adam Smith argued that under these conditions of freedom the motive of self-interest and the check of competition would result in the best use of resources and a maximum of welfare. He said that although people intended only their own gain they would be led by the invisible hand of God to promote the welfare of society. Then

_____

[7]A. Heard, "The Modern Culture of Higher Education: Many Missions and Nothing Sacred," *The Wilson Lecture* (Nashville: Board of Higher Education, United Methodist Church, 1973).

he said, in one of his most famous passages, "The statesman who should attempt to direct private people in what manner they ought to employ their capitals would not only load himself with a most unnecessary attention, but assume an authority which could safely be trusted, not only to no single person, but to no council or senate whatever, and which would nowhere be so dangerous as in the hands of a man who had folly and presumption enough to fancy himself fit to exercise it."[8]

From the standpoint of government, the eighteenth-century philosophy was that it should be curbed by checks and balances in such a way that both arbitrary power and headlong change would be restrained. In practice, this meant that every interest group of any size could press its case. Government then became a kind of marketplace or arena where the competing interests would be balanced off against one another and action would occur only when coalitions could be formed that would command a simple majority (or, in the case of constitutional change, a larger majority).

At both levels—the economy and the government—the underlying theory was that out of the rivalry of competing interests would spontaneously emerge an equilibrium representing the best resolution of the contending forces.

In the case of the economy, an elegant theory susceptible to mathematical analysis was developed that purported to prove that market equilibrium would maximize social welfare. The elegance of this theory was due to the fact that economic values are expressible in money and therefore can be quantified.

For government, there are no ready-made measures of welfare, and so the theory was less elegant or perhaps less persuasive than the economic theory; yet there was an underlying faith in the theory of a beneficent equilibrium. This faith was based on the concepts of group initiative and countervailing power. It was assumed that when any group saw a chance to gain advantage or to rectify a grievance, it would organize (perhaps through coalitions) and press its claim through the political process. In doing so, it would run into competition with other groups. Thus, a kind of equilibrium would emerge such that the benefits of society would

---

[8] A. Smith, *An Inquiry into the Nature and Causes of the Wealth of Nations* (E. Cannan, Ed.) (New York: Modern Library, 1937), Book IV, Chap. II.

be reasonably apportioned among the various claimants. The same theory as applied to the balance of power among nations was less elegant and less persuasive than the theory of countervailing power within nations. Yet, given the state of world order, it was accepted as the only available option, and safety was believed to reside in equilibrium and to be threatened whenever the balance was upset.

These three theories of equilibrium were all designed to maximize the freedom of individuals, groups, or nations and to resolve competing claims in a market or an arena where they could be balanced against each other. The process was conceived to be spontaneous and automatic. The motive power came from the self-interest of individuals or groups and from the restraint from competition.

In these three equilibrium theories, society functions through mechanisms analogous to computers. Data are fed into the computers by individuals or groups, and the computers "solve" the problem by working out the equilibrium conditions. In the case of the economy, the market serves as the computer, the market being a neutral mechanism that allocates the resources and distributes the income *according to the values* the participants bring to the process. In the case of government, the political system is a neutral arena, also like a computer, which allocates social benefits *according to the values* fed into the computer by the participants. (In international relations, the process is comparable, although I shall not pursue the international aspects further.) In both cases, the government's role is that of neutral proprietor of a computer.

The system is automatic and spontaneous; miraculously, as if by the invisible hand of God, it produces an equilibrium that yields maximum social welfare. The system requires no specific goals, no forethought or planning, no underlying philosophy, no morality, and no sense of community or common purpose. It calls on each individual or group to identify his or their own interests without regard for the general welfare and to press actively for these interests. It requires the government only to police the basic rules of the game and to see that the computers—the market and the political process—are running smoothly. The job of the politician, as part of the political process, is to be acutely sensitive to what the interest groups want, to be a broker among them in forming coalitions, and to facilitate the achievement of equilibrium. He need not have policies; he need only keep his finger on the public pulse, a task that has been automated by the invention of public opinion polls. No wonder statesmanship is such a scarce commodity!

What I have presented is of course an oversimplified caricature of reality. Yet, it describes the underlying theory of the social system not only in the United States but in most countries having capitalism combined with political democracy. This system is simple because it is spontaneous and automatic. The load of conscious decision making it thrusts on the government is small.

Historically, the trouble with the economic system of laissez-faire was that it left a lot of serious problems unsolved. There was no built-in immunity from monopoly, and the allocation of resources and the distribution of income were therefore distorted from the competitive equilibrium. The system had no built-in protection against inequality of access based on race, sex, religion, national origin, and so on. It provided inadequate protection of the health, safety, and dignity of workers and was not sufficiently attentive to the potential human satisfactions from work. It produced wide disparities in the distribution of income, and it had no adequate system for taking care of family units without employable members. The system by itself could not deliver stability of employment and prices. Finally, it was subject to a massive case of what logicians call the *fallacy of composition*. When everyone pursued his own individual interest, the result in the aggregate was not maximum social welfare but overpopulation, urban congestion, crime, waste of natural resources, pollution, widespread personal alienation, and general malaise.

As if these problems were not enough, another emerged that was even more fundamental, namely, the dubious "quality" of many of the values the people presented to the economy as they registered their demands on it. The function of the economy was to respond to whatever values were brought to it, not to screen the values it served or to elevate them. Rather, it was expected to be morally and ethically neutral and to produce whatever anyone was willing to pay for. The key phrase was "consumer sovereignty." It was up to the family, the church, the school, the mass media, and general cultural norms to shape the values for which the economy would cater. The system was dependent on the strength of these institutions. But the outcome—despite the efforts of family, church, school, and so on—was a predominantly materialistic and acquisitive set of values. The chief goal of individuals came to be that of maximizing the values that could be obtained with money. And that objective was translated into the predominant societal goal, growth of gross national product. Moreover, as it turned out, the economy did not remain neutral in the realm of values but developed its own powerful apparatus of communication in the form of selling and advertising. This apparatus, by constantly advocating materialistic values, may have overwhelmed the moral influence of family, church, and school. Indeed, some argue that advertising and selling subverted the very principle of consumer sovereignty and that the economy shaped the values of consumers rather than responding to their values as derived from outside the economy. These issues about the effects of advertising and selling are controversial, but there can be no doubt that the actual values to which the economy was expected to respond were predominantly materialistic.

I have referred to the economy as a computer. One of the standard remarks about computers is that the printout is only as good as the data fed in. The colloquialism is "garbage in—garbage out." The same thing is true of an economy. Its output is only as good as the values fed into it. One of the most telling criticisms of our economy—vividly illustrated in our television commercials, printed advertising, and in the ways of life we see about us—is that our wonderful computer has directed our limited resources to the production of a great deal of garbage.

The agency at hand to cope with the economic problems was the government. By resort to the political process, it was argued, every group with a proposal or a grievance could press its claims and counterclaims. Through the competition of all the claimants, an equilibrium would be reached embodying the "public interest."

As the government was loaded with increasing responsibility for policy making and administrative decision making, social affairs became more complex. Today, this complexity produces the frustrating sense of indecisiveness, stalemate, and unsatisfactory compromise that we all experience. But the political system suffers from other infinitely more disabling maladies.

First, influence in the political process is distributed unequally for reasons relating to the distribution of wealth, education, information, connections, personal persuasiveness, and access to the media.

Second, a political system that responds primarily to the values of various interest groups and seeks an equilibrium among competing forces is likely to be short-sighted. The time horizons of interest groups are likely to be fairly short relative to the historical continuity of societies.

Third, a political and economic system that responds mainly to the self-seeking of individuals or interest groups and plays them off against each other rewards aggressive and selfish behavior on the part of its citizens and gives weak encouragement to cooperative behavior rooted in a sense of community and directed toward the broad public interest. The people are thus conditioned to regard society as an arena for self-seeking rather than as a collectivity of humanity toward which individuals have responsibilities to give and to serve. The maximization of private income becomes the object of both the economy and the polity, and the ultimate good of the society is growth of gross national product which is merely the sum of the incomes of individuals.

Fourth, a political system conceived as a computer that responds to the demands of interest groups, whatever they may be, is likely to be a victim of the "garbage in—garbage out" syndrome. For example, the political process in the United States responds to a large variety of groups such as the National Rifle Association, Sierra Club, Home Builders Council, AFL-CIO, National Manufacturers Association, American Council on Education, the electric utilities, the American Indians, the Farm Bureau, the military, and thousands of others. The values that these groups bring to the process determine what will come out of it. On the whole, they are materialistic values very similar to the ones that actuate the economic system. The question that the computer is solving is "Who gets how much of what?" The import of this question has been aptly explained by Ralph Ketcham, the distinguished editor of the Franklin and Madison papers, who said:

Obviously, the framer [of this question] considers government a device for deciding how to parcel out gratification among clashing individuals and groups. That there is no agreed upon or

*even debatable concept of a good society is, of course, assumed—
just grasping and conniving. There is but one justification for the
existence of the state under such a "political theory": if it ceased
to exist, division of the spoils would be more troublesome and
turbulent. The founding fathers, of course, would have understood
that to decide "who gets how much of what" was one function of
government, but they would also have been appalled at any impli-
cation that the state had no other purpose. Their climate of opinion insisted that many other questions be asked, and that men and
societies seek answers to them out of the moral and social heritage
of the classical, Christian, and Augustan world views.[9]*

Adam Smith, who was a social philosopher, and the founding fathers of the United States, many of whom were schooled in
social philosophy, understood well that a society of freedom,
which would be essentially spontaneous and automatic, would be
only as good as the values fed into it. They took for granted the
values supplied by classical, Christian, and Augustan world views.
To form these values, they relied on the several educational institutions of society, especially the family, the church, the school,
and the college. The outcomes depended on the strength of these
institutions, and the founding fathers had great faith in an educated citizenry.

We sense that the source of our difficulty is that the values
that actuate the political system are not consistent with our better
natures, not in accord with the authentic values embodied in
teachings of wise men of all ages, and not conducive to the long-
range public interest. We sense that there is no way in a free-enter-
prise economy and a democratic polity to achieve a good society
merely by seeking materialistic values through "grasping and conniving." Moreover, we sense that the rivalry among competing
claims often results in stalemated inaction or in compromises satisfactory to no one or in short-sighted expediency. And so in our
frustration we cry out for charismatic leadership to show us the
way, and we are frustrated when all we get is politicians who carry
out their accustomed function of mediator among conflicting
interest groups and who are ready to serve any coalition that will
produce a majority. Then, in our disillusionment with democratic

[9]R. Ketcham, *From Independence to Interdependence* (Princeton,
N.J.: Aspen Institute for Humanistic Studies, 1976), pp. 11-12.

political leadership, we flirt with various totalitarian systems in which the problems would be turned over to an anointed elite such as an aristocracy, a communist party, or a fascist party. We suppose that in totalitarian countries there is order, discipline, rational planning, decisive decision making, Puritan values, and economic and social progress. The current growth of communist movements in western Europe and the increasing interest in intellectual Marxism in the United States are evidences of the seductiveness of the totalitarian solution. When we cannot quite bring ourselves to accept the totalitarian way out, because we know that in practice it invariably involves a loss of freedom for the individual citizen, we then wistfully search for some compromise that will preserve the freedom we cherish, will promote the elevated values we long for, and will produce the order and decisiveness that would relieve us of the sense of intolerable stalemate.

It has been said that Marx tried to reform society by changing social institutions and that Jesus tried to reform society by changing the hearts of men. More specifically, the choices before us are to change the structure of our government or to alter the values of our people. These two approaches are not mutually exclusive; rather, they are interdependent, because people do not change their government without a change in their values and because they do not change themselves without its having an effect on their government.

I shall not dwell at length on institutional change. I see no reason to rule out change in our governmental structure. It is not hard to imagine several reforms that might improve the capacity of government to deal with problems in a longer time perspective and with considerations of the consolidated public interest as distinct from separate and conflicting private interests. One example would be to invent ways of insulating governmental decision makers from the hurly-burly of competing self-interest while preserving their ultimate accountability to the people. Another more modest example would be to adopt economic planning along the lines suggested by Senators Javits and Humphrey and others. Still another example would be the reform of urban local government by unifying metropolitan areas and consolidating the confused proliferation of separate authorities that make up the government of all our cities.

I must admit, however, to skepticism about a nation's

being able to change itself in any fundamental way merely by tinkering with its governmental structure. Moreover, most proposals for change in governmental structure run contrary to strong sentiments toward populism and "participatory democracy."

I also have little faith in an anointed aristocracy or party to provide better values than will flow directly from the people—although Plato's idea of the philosopher king is a seductive concept. Once the totalitarian model is rejected, we are faced with the solution of Jesus and of virtually all the other great religious teachers, which is to change the hearts of men—that is, to change the values they try to seek through the economy and the government. If the values fed into the economic and political computers are worthy values, the market economy and the political system will respond to them. The computers are far from perfect, but they are remarkably responsive to the will of the people as they spend their money, vote, and exercise political persuasion. The basic objective, I think, is to change the values of the people.

The chief instruments available for the purpose are our various educational institutions. These are chiefly the media of mass communications, the workplace, the family, the church, the school, and the college or university. Of these, the media and the workplace have been almost totally co-opted by the economy and are busy reinforcing the prevailing materialistic values. The family also has been partially subverted by the economy and is certainly a weaker source of basic, nonmaterial values than it once was. Indeed, in large segments of the population, the family has become a negative rather than a positive influence on the development of the life goals and behavior patterns of children. The school has fallen on uncertain times. The influence of the church has also waned, although there are signs of renewed religious interest—especially in the spectacular growth of fundamentalist approaches to religion and in the popularity of Oriental religious thought and practice. A religious revival in this country is by no means impossible, but it is far from assured.

This leaves the colleges and universities. They too are partial captives of the prevailing values of society. They are expected to be supportive of this value system, and their chief function is thought by many to be preparing specialized "manpower" that will fit into particular slots in the work force. However, the academic community has an ancient tradition of liberal learning. The specific purposes of this kind of learning are to free the mind, to encourage inquiry, to consider the great moral and social issues, to promote a philosophical cast of mind, to cultivate the arts, literature and other sources of humane values, and to foster understanding of the world of science and politics. Liberal education today is on the defensive. Each year it occupies a relatively smaller part of the higher educational enterprise because the growth in student enrollments has been occurring mainly in the more vocationally oriented state colleges and universities and community colleges rather than in the traditional institutions dedicated primarily to liberal learning. However, in virtually all colleges and universities, public and private, the liberal tradition survives, and there is a continuing effort to combine liberal learning with vocational preparation. Moreover, despite efforts of the public and their representatives to bring higher education under the control of the "system," the traditional separation of university and state has survived, the freedom of the academy has been maintained, and the liberal tradition persists. The university also continues to have substantial influence over primary and secondary education, because it trains the teachers, writes the books, and conducts the research and development for the lower schools.

If the media and the workplace have been co-opted by the system, if the family, the church, and the school are weak, then higher education may be the point of maximum leverage for changing the values that actuate the system. I would argue that a major thrust in the direction of liberal learning for both young people and adults is the place to start reorienting the values that propel our economy and our government. This would require not only increasing enrollments in genuinely liberal programs but also increasing emphasis on liberal learning in connection with vocational programs.

The place of the university is particularly strategic, because it educates virtually all the people who are destined for leadership in our society in the professions, business, and politics. Its main duty should be to make sure that the leaders of our country have a sound liberal learning not only when they are young but intermittently throughout their lives.

The university, because of its comparative freedom and strength, may be the most strategic place to begin value improvement, but it is not the place to stop. Liberal education in subjects such as history, geography, literature occurs in the lower schools and needs strengthening there. Educational television, which has made enormous strides, needs support for reaching larger audiences and perhaps greater freedom in dealing with controversial issues. The church and the new religious movements have much to offer and need encouragement. Perhaps most important of all, we should make an all-out effort in the area of early childhood education and in providing appropriate educational and work experience for the millions of teen-age youth whose lives are being sacrificed by the lack of both meaningful education and meaningful work.

It is only as we improve our people that we can hope to improve our society. I have no illusions about the perfectibility of human beings or about the possibility that they will through education all come to share noble values. I do believe, however, in the improvability of people and society. Indeed, I regard the recent increasing concern in our society about problems such as poverty, pollution, racial injustice, urban blight, and so on to be a product of our widespread education. It is no accident that many of these problems were first rediscovered on our campuses or that students were among the first to agitate about them. As we sensitize people, through education, to the inconsistencies between basic values acknowledged by the great thinkers of all ages and the realities of American society, they will use the economic and political computers to produce new and different answers. The computers will respond.

My theme is that the problems of capitalism and democracy can be solved, not by opting for totalitarianism and only marginally by modifying the structure of government, but primarily by elevating and enriching the values that actuate the system. This can be done only through education broadly defined—especially liberal education. And the leadership in this educational task must be assumed primarily by the universities. And for this task they must be able to avoid domination by the same values that have subverted the economic and political processes. They must be free to cultivate uninhibited and inquiring minds, humane values, and understanding of social and moral issues. They must not serve merely as purveyors of lifelong meal tickets, or socializers, or pillars of the establishment. Rather they must try to change the values of people—not by indoctrination but by the enlargement of horizons that flow from true liberal education.

My theme is, of course, trite. It is that in education lies the main hope for the good society. It is a theme that has been advanced with special force by Thomas Jefferson and John Dewey. It was epitomized by H. G. Wells when he said, "Human history becomes more and more a race between education and catastrophe."[10] It is also, in a sense, a modern version of Plato's concept of the philosopher king—except that in twenty-first-century democracy, every man and woman will be a king or queen. A government of the people, by the people, for the people is only as good *as* the people.

---

[10]H. G. Wells, *Outline of History*, Chap. 15.

3

Ironies and
Paradoxes

Thomas F. Green

Three main points come to mind on the relationship between education and work. The first is that attempts to maximize the utility of education, especially its utility for work, are subject to the constraints of the *hedonistic paradox*. The second is that any attempt to ease the transition from education to work by making educational programs interdisciplinary is subject to *the fallacy of the misplaced question*. The third is the claim that, in our attempt to understand the relation of education to work, the work we should be discussing is not the work defined by jobs but *the way jobs are related or unrelated to the possibilities of human work*.

The *hedonistic paradox* is the idea that the elusiveness of happiness is guaranteed by our single-minded search for it. Happiness will fall within our grasp only if getting it is no preoccupation of ours. The proposition is not that we shall find happiness if we do not seek it but rather that if we do seek it, it will escape us. This is an extremely ancient bit of wisdom, and one reason it has endured is that it is confirmed by our experience. It commands belief because it is true.

One must be cautious, however, about appealing to "truth." Given the current climate of educational debate, appeals to "truth," as opposed to the polling of opinion—especially in matters of good and evil—are extremely rare. They often strike our consciousness as an intrusion, even as an embarrassment. If, then, we accept the proposition that the hedonistic paradox is confirmed by our experience, we may be obliged also to accept the view that experienced people may know things unlikely to be known by the young—precisely because the young are inexperienced. For some, such a conclusion is embarrassment enough. But there is more. If there is truth expressed by the hedonistic paradox, it is the kind of truth that will neither be confirmed or disconfirmed by any social science method that we know or by any we are likely to develop. Truth, even in matters of good and evil, is always more than mere opinion. Indeed, the truth in such matters is likely to be hardly anyone's opinion. The paradox is not disconfirmed by the fact that people reject it. It is commonplace that some, even many, will reject the truth. We can be certain that the wise are few even while we are uncertain in proclaiming who they are. Appeals to truth are, of course, appeals to philosophy, and the embarrassment they evoke is the embarrassment of an unphilosophic, untutored, and unreflective temperament.

At one level, the value of the hedonistic paradox is no greater than the value of most pulpit wisdom and advice for living. But at another level, a deeper level, it informs us. It provides a start toward understanding the nature of human happiness, what kind of good it is, and what relation it has to other goods. The fact is, however, that when we grasp this deeper meaning, we shall find that there is no singular wisdom expressed in the hedonistic paradox. Happiness is not the only human good that we would do well to seek by seeking other goods instead. The hedonistic paradox belongs to an extended family of ironies. Whether it has economic and political formulations, I cannot say, but I am quite certain that it has educational versions. And among them is the claim that in seeking to maximize the utility of education, especially its utility for work, we shall reduce its utility, and its value will escape us. I am not proposing in this formulation that education should have no utility. I mean to suggest only that its utility, like happiness, is the kind of good that we chase away by chasing after.

Dewey managed to state the relevant point in a memorable formulation. Education, he said, is the reconstruction of experience. Like all other fundamental statements of unusual brevity, this one deserves extended commentary. The essentials, however, may be captured in a single illustration. I borrow the example from my colleague Emily Haynes, who has used it in classes she teaches.

Let us imagine ourselves—the two of us—watching a regatta. I can enjoy the beauty of the scene, the sails against the sky, the blue of the water, and the silent movement of the boats as they struggle for position at the start. Seen in that way, the regatta is a fluid composition of unconscious art. I can tell that the boats are moving all in the same overall direction but do not understand the apparently random departures from their course that stem, in truth, from the logic of their tacking.

You, on the other hand, knowing much more about the problems and solutions of sailing, can appreciate the unexpected tack that places one boat in the best position at the start, the clever positioning of each to capture the last ounce of assistance from the wind, the practiced coordination of commander and crew, the foresight and luck that is needed to gain every advantage for a lesser craft against superior ones, and the inventiveness of strategy and tactics.

In one sense, the two of us see the same thing, namely a regatta. But in another sense, we do not see the same thing at all. The difference between us is the difference between two contrasting orders of experience. There is no difference in the events. Dewey's proverb that education is the reconstruction of experience is exemplified in the difference between you and me at a regatta. You are an educated viewer. I am not. Your experience is different from mine, and the difference is the difference education makes. That difference, by the way, is the same as the difference between hearing the hedonistic paradox pronounced as an ordinary piece of advice and hearing it as commentary on the nature of a monumental human good.

Suppose I ask now, "Was your education useful?" I hope you see that the very asking of the question is a mistake. It doesn't belong. The proper response would be to simply point to the regatta. The question constitutes a grand irrelevance and can only emanate from some kind of gross misunderstanding of what education, especially higher education, is all about. Any answer will do as an answer to the question, which is to say that no answer is any good. One can say "Yes, it was useful," and one can say "No, it was not useful." Both answers may be defended, and both will miss the point. I am reminded of those rare occasions in teaching when a student grasps a point that makes a fundamental difference in self-understanding or competence. Were someone to come on the scene at such a time asking, "Is teaching worth the effort?" the right response would be to order them away. To say, "Yes, it's worth the effort" or "No, it isn't" would be to concede a kind of seriousness to the question that by itself it lacks. It is a nonquestion. It does not touch what matters. Asking it betrays a failure to understand what is taking place.

One might argue that a knowledge of fluid mechanics, weather, strength of materials, and other aspects of sailing is essential to one's education as a viewer of regattas. But even though these areas of knowledge are useful in becoming an educated viewer of regattas, utility is not why anyone learns them. Nor is their lack of utility any excuse for not learning them. The point is rather that they enter into the reconstruction of experience, the enlargement of vision, the cultivated capacity to reach beneath the most gross and overt events to see meaning and design.

I do not deny that such studies have utility nor even that they can enter into one's education because of their utility. I wish to point out, rather, that their *educational* value is a particular *kind* of utility. If we are to understand the educational value of any activity, it is not utility in general that counts, but only a particular kind of utility. The educational value of any activity is the kind of utility that matters, and it is also precisely that kind that is likely to be ignored when we overtly and single-mindedly seek to make education useful in some other ways.

We seldom teach with a consciousness of what is educational and how it contributes or does not contribute to the reconstruction of experience. And we are even less likely to do so if we are continually concerned about the utility of what we teach for the world of work. Such a misplaced concern simply forces us to formulate those empty, tortuous, and involuted rationalizations for the utility of such things as history, philosophy, literature, and accounting. For teachers of such studies, the proper response to a demand for greater utility in what they teach would be to turn to better teaching and to reject the question altogether. It is, after all, a question that rests on a thorough misunderstanding of what education is all about.

This argument is not an attack on the value, importance, or dignity of vocational education. It is a plea that we become more conscious of what it means to say that something is educational. We cannot justify the educational value of any education on grounds of its utility for the world of work. I remind you of two truisms. The first is that truisms, whatever their faults, have the considerable virtue of being true. And the second is that, whatever else higher education should be about, it should at the least be about education. We may reason by extension that vocational education should also be educational. In seeking to maximize the utility of education, especially its utility for work, we shall reduce its utility, and its value will escape us. This is the educational rendering of that hoary truth, the hedonistic paradox.

My second point is that any attempt to improve the relationship between education and work by making educational programs interdisciplinary is subject to the fallacy of the misplaced question. Arguments that support interdisciplinary education grow out of a conviction that educational activities should, as far as possible, reflect life itself. Since the problems and ordinary affairs of life are not presented to us in neat disciplinary divisions, the argument goes, neither should education, especially higher education. It should be interdisciplinary.

This is a view with which I sympathize. Nonetheless, it is fraught with difficulty. The root meaning of *discipline* is found in the concepts of rule, order, and regularity. The disciplines of life are those standards and regularities that give it structure and form, such things as getting to work on time and meeting deadlines. When they are embodied in habit, they are barely noticeable. They are like style in a work of art—something present but not paraded. A monk submits to a discipline "of the order," which is to say that his life is arranged by an established sequence in which things are done and by standards as to how they shall be done. There are disciplines of prayer, of piety, and of work, all lending shape to his life. Liturgy is perhaps the paradigmatic discipline. It consists of an established outline, form, or sequence in which symbols are ordered, meaning is voiced, and a certain practice is conducted. And there we have an important point. "Discipline" is always connected to "practice." Whenever we speak of a discipline, we should ask, "What is the practice of which the discipline provides the form and structure?"

What, then, is the practice of the academic disciplines? It is the practice of *theoretical* reason, the practice of inquiry. It is the exercise of reason in response to a particular kind of human interest, namely the interest in knowing. Yet most of life is the practice of *practical* reason, which is the exercise of reason in response to a different human interest—the interest in choosing and acting. Theoretical reason asks, "What can I know?" Practical reason asks, "What should I do?" The apparent breach between the academic disciplines and the disciplines of life arises not because the academic disciplines lack utility for practical affairs but because there is an inherent difference between theoretical and practical reason, between the disciplines of knowing and the disciplines of deciding.

If we agree that the academic disciplines, taken singly or in series, do not sufficiently inform us of the practices of life, then we are inclined to suppose that the remedy lies in something interdisciplinary. But this move is a delusion; the argument is fallacious. Although it is true that life is not arranged for us according to divisions of the academic disciplines, neither is it arranged in interdisciplinary ways. The important point is that organizing the activities of education along interdisciplinary or multidisciplinary lines makes sense only within that precinct of life where the disciplines of knowledge make sense. It does nothing to draw the disciplines of knowing and the disciplines of life into closer association. Their separation arises not from the insular life of the academic disciplines, but from the basic division between the disciplines of knowing and the disciplines of deciding.

The point is not only logical but phenomenological. In the serious affairs of ordinary life, there is such a thing as focusing our consciousness on the problem, the question, or the issue to be acted on. There is also such a thing as focusing our consciousness on the conduct of the mind in thinking about one or another aspect of the problem. For example, when we ask, "How can we provide better housing for a community?" or "How can I compensate for my failures to my friends?" we touch on questions of history, psychology, ethics, and economics, but we are not doing history, psychology, or any of the rest. Our attention is on the problem, not on the disciplines.

The problems of life are neither disciplinary nor interdisciplinary. Nonetheless, if we are habituated to the disciplines of knowing—and not to one alone—then when our consciousness is focused on the practical problems and questions of life, those disciplines will be displayed in the quality of our reflection. They provide the structure of reflection in ordinary life, just as the "discipline of the order" would provide the structure of daily life for the monk even if he were outside the monastery. It is in this sense that the disciplines of thought are reflected in ordinary life. They are present even though their presence is not paraded.

We shall find no short cut to this end by making education interdisciplinary any more than we shall find a short cut by making the curriculum an endless succession of problems. Perhaps there is an intractable breach between the disciplines of knowing and the disciplines of life itself. If so, then what we may need is not the effort to bridge it but the wisdom to accept it. In any case, there seems to be little wisdom in trying to invest education with a utility that it does not have and cannot incorporate. Why can't we learn to leave its utility alone and let it be, like prayer, something to be treasured?

The last of my observations is that if we are to understand the relation between education and work we need to mark *a sharp distinction between work and job*. There is an enormous difference between the person who understands his career as a succession of jobs and a person who understands the succession of jobs he has held as all contributing to the accomplishment of some work. Only the latter can be said to have a career in any strict sense of the term. The fact is that there is no conceptual possibility of defining the concept of "career" in terms of jobs held without also tying the possession of a career either to the pursuit of upward social mobility or to acquiescence in the absence of upward mobility. That is an invidious conception of careers. If the concept of career is understood, however, in the light of having a work to perform, such considerations are irrelevant. Whether a particular job or succession of jobs advance one's career is determined in total independence of job status or rank. This is no small difference.

This distinction between work and jobs is essential for understanding the problems of modern work life. The central question is always whether it is possible to find work through roles validated within the employment structure. We cannot even ask such a question if we do not distinguish these two concepts. What is often referred to as *alienation from work* is seldom that. It is, rather, alienation from the job structure of modern society. Such alienation is often the expression of discontent with the possibilities of finding a work to do through the constricted avenues of remunerative employment. When we can bring ourselves to make the distinction between work and jobs, we can see how little evidence there is that we suffer from the liabilities of a work ethic or that people are alienated from work.

Resolving the tension between work and job requires not only the sensitive observance of the distinction between them but also a more receptive world. When the social world stands related to men as the natural world did in the classical period, then the problem of finding a work is either beyond solution altogether or rendered nearly impossible. Work is basically the way that people seek to redeem their lives from futility. It therefore requires the kind of world in which hope is possible, which is to say, the kind of world that yields to human effort. A world in which these conditions are unsatisfied is a world filled with labor, but without work—a world perhaps with "free time" but without leisure.

It is instructive to recall that beneath the Greek experience, where these ideas had their origin, was a deep awareness of how men differed both from the gods and from nature. Unlike the gods, men are mortal. And although as animals they are a part of nature, as men they are not. As animals, they are tied to the inexorable and endless cycles of nature. They must wrest life itself from the elements and submit to the necessities imposed on them by the passage of the seasons, planting and harvesting only to plant again. And in this submission to the laws of nature, they leave nothing durable to remind their descendants that they had lived, toiled, aged, and died. The entire ancient Greek experience can be understood as a struggle to surmount the limits of mortality and the laws of nature. The very idea that a hero is one who lives and dies at the peak of his powers and in the midst of some great deed testifies to the drive to make some lasting mark on the world, to make the world yield. Mythology too is filled with stories of the endless cycle of the seasons and the precariousness of human existence. To influence the passage of the seasons was folly, but to transcend the necessities they impose by engaging in action—that was the path of heroes, the path, as Homer put it, of men who, like Achilles, are the speakers of words and the doers of deeds. It was the path out of the futility of labor into the meaning of memorable works and acts.

For 400 years, it has been the dream of Western man not to escape from these necessities but to surmount them through science and technology. We need no longer be merely submissive in the face of nature. We can understand the forces of nature and use them to advance our own intentions. Yet this hope too may prove to be little more substantial than a dream. We now live in a world of institutions, organizations, regulations, rational planning and ever-expanding bureaucracies. We used to speak of the republic in its literal sense as the *res publica,* the "affair of the public." Now we concern ourselves with "public administration." It seems sentimental to speak of "the public" at all nowadays, except as a set of individuals who in the aggregate have opinions. We used to speak of history as the acts of men; we now concern ourselves with the historical process and the play of forces. All of these changes in the metaphors of thought suggest that we have managed to subsume the social world under the category of nature.

It is not apparent that the world we have created is any more yielding to the efforts of men than was the natural world of the ancients. Our impotence in the face of the modern social world is as devastating to the basic human need to escape futility as was the natural world to ancient man. In view of this, it makes compassionate sense to say that more people need to find a work to perform as well as a job to do. Yet that is the problem. If work is a human necessity, then what will be the quality of life in a world that cannot contain work? Human beings being what human beings are, I doubt that our world will be filled with heroes.

The problem that we must learn to deal with is the conflict between the ways we have thought of work and jobs and the ways that we shall have to think of them in the future. Work really is a human necessity. It is necessary even for leisure; for leisure, in the classic sense, exists when work discloses a self that is satisfying. Such a conception of leisure has no relation to free time whatever. The key to it is competence, and the place where competence is

displayed is work. The demonstration of competence is the experience of worth; for being competent is being good *at* something,
for something, and *to* someone. Part of the solution, then, lies in
discovering how to assure the presence of an element of craft *in*
jobs when jobs are purely instrumental; how to assure that action
is possible in a world infused with processes unyielding to human
effort; and how to create a myriad of publics within which self-
disclosure can take place in ways that confirm one's dignity and
worth. In a world such as that, there will be education and there
will be human work. But the relevance of education to work will
not be its utility for jobs. It will be what it has always been—valuable in letting the disciplines of knowing have their play and their
effect on the quality of reflection in the disciplines of life.

4

Work, Education, and Leisure

Mortimer J. Adler

We are going to consider first the distinction between work and leisure; second, the relation of education to both work and leisure; and, finally, the relation of all three—education, work, and leisure—to the living of a good human life.

We begin with the distinction between *work* and *leisure*. Both of those words name activities: working and leisuring. The word *leisure* should never be used as an adjective, modifying time. We should never say *leisure time* when what we mean is *free time*. Nor should the word *leisure* ever be used as a synonym for another form of activity: play, recreation, or amusement. Like play, leisuring is one of the ways men do and should fill their free time—time not consumed by compulsory activities, by activities necessary for life itself or for obtaining a livelihood.

But, unlike play and like work, leisuring is a serious activity that results in products of value to the individual and to society.

The Greek word for *leisure* was *schole*—the word from which we derive *school*. Its basic meaning was learning or human growth.

There are four questions to be answered in distinguishing different forms or categories of human activity. First, is the activity compulsory or optional? It is compulsory, if necessary for staying live, for living, if not for living well. Second, if optional, is it morally desirable? Morally obligatory? Not just for living, but for living well? Third, what purpose does it serve? What goods or values does it achieve for ourselves, for others, or for society? Finally, how is the activity related to the result it achieves and to the agent producing the result? Is the result immanent or transitive, or both? Is the result intrinsic or inherent to the activity, or is it a consequence of the activity?

Before we ask these questions about working and leisuring, let me apply them to two other forms or categories of activity to make the analysis clear—sleeping and playing. I would like to use the term *sleep* to cover all forms of biologically necessary activity, not just slumbering, but eating and cleansing and exercising, as well as slumbering.

Sleep in this sense is compulsory, necessary for life itself. The good result it achieves is bodily health and vigor. That result is a consequence of the activity, not inherent in it, and it is almost wholly immanent. It is a good that remains in the agent, not something external to him. Play, on the other hand, which covers all forms of recreation and amusement, is optional, not compulsory, not necessary for life itself. It may be regarded as desirable for a good life, but only within certain limits, not unlimitedly. And it is not morally obligatory. The good result it achieves is pleasure, and that result is inherent in the activity itself, not a consequence of it. In fact, playing is the only form of activity that has a good result that is inherent in the activity itself and also immanent in the agent or actor, not transitive.

Still considering sleep and play, we can observe a few additional points that will be helpful to us when we come to consider working and leisuring. A particular activity may belong to both categories. For example, eating or drinking merely for the pleasure inherent in the process may be compared with eating or drinking solely for the sustenance derived therefrom. When eating or drinking, which in its primary or pure form belongs to the category of biologically necessary activity, is thus transformed into another category, we should note this transformation by calling it "playful eating or drinking." Similarly, swimming for the sake of one's health, under doctor's orders, may be compared with swimming for the sake of the pleasure inherent in the process. Here we have swimming as play versus therapeutic swimming—swimming in the category of sleep, serving the purpose of health.

A given activity, in addition, may of course fall under both of these distinct categories at the same time. It may be an admixture of both, in varying proportions.

One further characteristic of the two forms or categories of activity we have been considering is this: Although both achieve good results, those results are entirely immanent—a good that benefits the agent or actor, his health, his enjoyment of pleasure. In sharp contrast, the two forms of activity to which we now turn, working and leisuring, usually result in extrinsic commodities: marketable goods or services. As we shall see, the results they produce may be both transitive and immanent—a product external to the agent and a result remaining in the agent.

In the light of these preliminary clarifications, let us now examine working and leisuring. It is of the utmost importance to note two distinct considerations that affect our understanding of how work and leisure are related. One is whether the activity engaged in involves extrinsic compensation needed by the individual because it is necessary for him to earn a living—to obtain the means of subsistence. Unlike play, which is always optional, work is compulsory. But unlike sleep, which is compulsory for all, work is compulsory only for those who do not have independent incomes and so must earn their livelihood.

The other consideration concerns the character of the activity itself as it affects the person doing it. If the activity engaged in for subsistence benefits the worker, improving him in one respect or another, then it has the aspect of leisure. If, however, the activity does not benefit the individual and, far from improving him, may cause his deterioration, then it has the aspect of drudgery.

Work for subsistence may consist in pure drudgery or may be entirely leisure work, or it may involve admixtures of both aspects in varying degrees. In other words, there is a spectrum of work for subsistence, with pure drudgery at one extreme and pure leisure work at the other and with admixtures of both components in between.

This leads us to still one further consideration with regard to work and leisure. One and the same activity may be performed solely for the benefit it confers on the person doing it, for extrinsic compensation, or for its self-rewarding quality. When, for example, composing music, doing scientific research, or teaching is done as a creative activity and without any extrinsic compensation, let us call that activity a *leisure pursuit*. But when that kind of activity is engaged in not only for the inherent reward or benefit it confers on the agent but also for the extrinsic compensation that it earns, let us call it *leisure work*.

Thus we see that the leisuring may enter human life in three ways:

1. As an uncompensated leisure pursuit.
2. As pure leisure work, to which some compensation is also attached.
3. As an aspect of work for subsistence in which some element of drudgery is also involved.

Work that earns an extrinsic compensation does so by producing marketable commodities—goods or services. These may take the form of economic goods and services—the various forms of wealth. Or they may consist of the goods of civilization—contributions to knowledge, artistic productions, political or religious activities, and so on.

Since work is by definition an extrinsically compensated activity, work always produces a transitive result, a marketable commodity, regardless of whether the immanent result of the work (its effect on the worker) makes it pure drudgery, pure leisure work, or some admixture of the two.

In contrast, leisure pursuits, which are not work, have an immanent result only—the beneficial effect on the person engaging in them, the improvement of his mind or his character.

The quality of the activity may be exactly the same whether it is a self-rewarding, uncompensated leisure pursuit or whether it is extrinsically compensated leisure work. The reason for calling the same activity a *leisure pursuit,* on the one hand, and *leisure work,* on the other, is that in the one case the activity is engaged in solely for its immanent result, the moral or intellectual growth or improvement of the individual, whereas in the other case there is an additional purpose, the earning of a livelihood.

The confusion of play and leisure (or playing and leisuring) occurs because some leisuring, in the form of leisure pursuits, is, like play, purely optional—something we do in the time that is not occupied by sleep and work. When the activity that is a leisure pursuit for some is leisure work for others, it is not likely to be confused with play.

Before I attempt to summarize the spectrum of work from pure drudgery at one extreme to pure, but compensated, leisuring at the other, let me ask you to consider two questions. What is the character of those activities in which no one would willingly engage unless he could not earn a living in any other way? I think the answer is that such activity is drudgery, sheer toil—activity that carries no intrinsic reward for the person engaging in it, because it is mechanical, repetitive, stultifying, totally noncreative.

On the other hand, what is the character of the activities in which everyone should engage if he did not have to do a stroke of work to earn a living and if he recognized that he was morally obligated to occupy his free time with optional activities other than purely playful ones? Imagine a man whose whole time is free after eight hours of sleep, eight hours of biological activity, with sixteen hours of free time. Can he play for sixteen hours a day? If not and if he does not have to earn a living, what does he do with that time? The answer must be, it seems to me, the pursuits of leisure—all of them creative rather than mechanical and repetitive activities, all of them resulting in some form of learning, personal growth, or self-improvement.

Among those who have to earn a livelihood by work, the most fortunate individuals are those who can do so by pure leisure work, the kind of activity that would be a leisure pursuit if it were uncompensated, if no compensation were needed. Not quite so fortunate but nevertheless happily circumstanced are those who can earn a living by work that has a large component of leisure in it and very little drudgery. The least fortunate are those who earn their living either by work that has a large component of drudgery in it, or is nothing but drudgery, and results in their deterioration rather than in their self-improvement.

Let me now recapitulate all these points by describing the spectrum of work, from drudgery at one extreme to pure leisure work at the other.

At one extreme are those tasks or jobs that no one would ever engage in for a moment except to earn a living and in which one engages under the dire necessity of having no other alternative way of getting the means of subsistence, except by theft or charity. These are all mechanical, repetitive activities, involving no mental or creative input, and so they are stultifying to the person engaged in them, detrimental to the mind and body of the worker. These are all tasks that one hopes might be completely done by machines and not by men—and by automated machines, largely unattended by men. Karl Marx in the *Communist Manifesto* was completely right in describing such work as activity that improves or enhances the materials worked on (the raw materials turned into salable products), but which at the same time degrades or deteriorates, both in body and mind, the condition of the worker.

At the opposite extreme are those tasks or undertakings for which a person may be in fact compensated, but in which a person would engage even if he did not have to do anything at all in order to earn a living. They are such activities as: all forms of artistic work; all forms of scientific research or philosophical thought; all forms of political or religious activity (engagement in the work of the state or of the church, or of society generally); and all forms of truly professional activity, such as teaching, healing, nursing, and engineering. What characterizes all these activities is that:

• Engaging in them is self-rewarding in the sense that the individual learns or grows—improves as a human being—by doing them.
• They are all creative, involving intellectual inputs that are not routine or repetitive. They are the very opposite of mechanical activities.
• They are essentially work rather than play because they may be done for compensation and because they may be done without any intrinsic pleasure in doing them; they may be tiring or fatiguing, as tiring or fatiguing as other forms of work.
• Like all other forms of work, they may be productive of goods valuable to others and even marketable, as well as of goods that enhance the person and life of the individual who engages in such work.

In between the extremes of work that is pure drudgery and that therefore should be eliminated from human life and work that is compensated leisuring are many degrees and modes of admixtures.

Many tasks or jobs that men engage in for compensation

because they have to earn a living involve admixtures of repetitive chores (drudgery) and creative input (leisuring). Obviously, the larger the creative input and the fewer the chores, the better the work is for the human being doing it, regardless of the amount of money that is compensation for doing it. Some persons wisely choose lower emoluments because they want a job that is intrinsically more rewarding.

One further observation should be added concerning the spectrum of subsistence work from pure drudgery at one extreme to compensated leisuring at the other. It is sometimes unfortunately the case that persons engage in activities that have the character of leisuring but do so for the wrong reason—just for the extrinsic compensation involved. For example, the teacher who does not learn anything in the course of teaching, and teaches only to earn a living, has transformed leisuring into drudgery. The same thing holds for all the creative arts and the learned professions. One can think of lawyers or physicians, even of writers and musicians, who turn leisuring into nothing but compensated drudgery.

The opposite transformations seldom, if ever, occur. An activity that is nothing but drudgery (because it is mechanical, repetitive, and so on) rarely gets turned into something like leisuring. Higher or better activities can be debased and deformed, but the lowest forms of activity can seldom, if ever, be elevated.

The moral ideal that emerges from this analysis can be simply stated. It concerns the role of compensated leisure work and uncompensated leisure pursuits in the accomplishment of a good human life. For those who need to work in order to earn a living, that work should, so far as possible, involve some degree of compensated leisuring and should never be pure drudgery. And in relation to the individual's talents and capacities, the subsistence work he engages in is better for him as a human being in proportion as it involves fewer chores or less drudgery and more creative leisuring. For all, whether they need to work for a living or not, and especially for those who earn their living by work that does not involve a large component of leisuring, a larger proportion of the individual's free time should be spent in leisure pursuits or activities than in the various forms of play or recreation.

While play and leisuring—the two main fillers of free time— are neither biologically nor economically necessary, they are both morally desirable. I would go further and say that, from the point of view of the human potential, leisuring is morally obligatory.

One cannot discharge one's obligation to make a good human life for one's self without engaging in the pursuits of leisure.

The educational significance of this understanding of the spectrum of work and of leisure pursuits beyond any need for extrinsic compensation, in relation to the good life, can be simply summarized. In 1817, Thomas Jefferson recommended to the legislature of Virginia that all children be given three years of free public schooling, after which those destined for labor should be separated from those destined for leisure learning, the former to be sent to the shops and the farms and the latter to colleges of education. Today, everyone who not only is committed to but also understands the democratic ideal should agree that all children are destined for leisure, whether or not they have to work in order to earn a living.

Hence the controlling objective of formal and informal education in a democratic society—education before school, in school, after school, on the job, and off the job—can be stated as follows: Prepare and school the young—liberally, not vocationally—so they can earn a living by doing work that has as large a component of leisuring in it as they are capable of by their talents and native endowments. School them in such a way that they can use as much of their free time as possible for the pursuits of leisure. And provide all citizens, during the years in which they are engaged in subsistence work and after they have retired from it, with continuing formal and informal facilities for learning and self-education, since learning is the very essence of leisuring.

Let me add to this one final comment. The ideal of the educated man at the end of the twentieth century differs sharply from the aristocratic ideal of the past, which more or less prevailed from the time of the ancient Greeks to the end of the nineteenth century. That aristocratic ideal is no longer viable or applicable in our industrial democracy, where universal citizenship is accompanied by universal schooling and where everyone, not just the fortunate few, is entitled to think of the ideal of becoming an educated human being as a condition that he or she can attain. The old aristocratic ideal was stated in terms of intellectual content—things known, skills possessed—and, as so stated, was open only to the few. We must replace that ideal with one more appropriate to our kind of society and our commitment to the education of all or at least to helping all to become educated.

Let me restate the ideal. An educated person is one who can

and does work creatively and who uses what free time he or she has for the pursuits of leisure, each according to his or her native talents and capacities. The ideal, as thus restated, is, in my judgment, a viable one in our society, one that is applicable to all, except the few in asylums of one kind or another. It is an objective that the educational and economic institutions of a democratic society should aim at and should be able to serve effectively.

5

Good Work

E. F. Schumacher

To understand the meaning of "good work" and "education for good work," we must first face such age-old questions as "What is man?" "Where does he come from?" and "What is the purpose of his life?" Today such questions are called "prescientific" and there is no attempt to answer them. If they are indeed "prescientific," this can only mean that science is not of essential importance for the conduct of human life. Good answers to such "prescientific" questions are of infinitely greater importance.

Some time ago I visited Leningrad and did some sightseeing in that beautiful city. At one point, I consulted a map to find out where I was. I could see several enormous churches, yet there was no sign of them on my map. An interpreter came to help me and said, "We don't show churches on our maps." I pointed to some other churches, which were clearly indicated. "These are museums," he replied. "We don't show living churches on our maps."

It then occurred to me that this was not the first time I had been given a map that failed to show many of the things I could see right in front of my eyes. All through my so-called education at schools and universities I had been given maps of life and of knowledge that bore few traces of many of the things I considered of the greatest possible importance to the conduct of my life. For many years my perplexity was complete, and no interpreter came along to help me. It remained complete until I ceased to suspect the sanity of my perceptions and began instead to suspect the soundness of the maps.

Our ancestors did ask and did answer questions like "What is man?" and "What is the purpose of human life on earth?" But the maps I was given—and nothing seems to have changed since then—advised me that virtually all our ancestors, until quite recently, were rather pathetic illusionists who conducted their lives on the basis of irrational beliefs and absurd superstitions. Even illustrious scientists such as Johann Kepler and Isaac Newton spent most of their time and energy on theological studies of "nonexisting" things. None of it was to be taken seriously today, except of course as a museum piece.

I was taught all this and many similar things at school, although not so plainly and frankly. After all, ancestors had to be treated with respect: They could not help their backwardness; they tried hard and sometimes even got quite near the truth in a haphazard sort of way. Their preoccupation with questions of meaning and purpose, with religious and metaphysical questions, was just one of many signs of their underdevelopment. There is, of course, a degree of interest in religion today, which legitimizes some of the beliefs of earlier times. It is still permissible, on suitable occasions, to refer to God the Creator, although every educated person knows that there is no real God, certainly not one capable of creating anything, and that the things around us came into existence by a process of mindless evolution—that is, by chance and natural selection.

Modern education insists that only such things as can be proved to exist should be taught. "If in doubt, leave it out." The question of what constitutes proof is, however, a very subtle and difficult one. Would it not be wiser to invert the principle and say, "If in doubt, show it prominently"? After all, matters that are beyond doubt are, in a sense, dead; they do not constitute a challenge to the living. If I limited myself to knowledge that I can consider true beyond doubt, I minimize the risk of error, but I also maximize the risk of missing out on what may be the most important and most rewarding things in life. Thomas Aquinas, following Aristotle, taught that "the slenderest knowledge that may be obtained of the highest things is more desirable than the most certain knowledge obtained of lesser things."[1]

Western civilization, like all great civilizations, was built on this scale of values. But since Descartes it has turned the scale upside down and declares that the pursuit of knowledge of the highest things is a waste of time and "prescientific," and that nothing is worth knowing unless it can be known with certainty. "Those who seek the direct road to truth," said Descartes, "should not bother with any object of which they cannot have a certainty equal to the demonstrations of arithmetic and geometry."[2] That is, we should study only those objects "to the sure and indubitable knowledge of which our mental powers seem to be adequate."[3] The Cartesian revolution has led Western civilization into a total rejection of "the slenderest knowledge that may be obtained of the highest things" and a total fixation on scientific knowledge of the lower things. As a result, questions like "What should I do with my life?" cannot really be answered any more. To ask them is considered a lapse into prescientific modes of thinking, something long abandoned by well-educated modern people.

What, then, is the meaning of "education" or of "good work" when nothing counts except that which can be precisely stated, measured, counted, or weighed? Neither mathematics nor geometry, neither physics nor chemistry can entertain qualitative motives like "good" or "bad," "higher" or "lower." These disciplines can entertain only *quantitative* notions of "more" or "less." It is easy to distinguish between "less education" and "more education," and between "less work" and "more work," but how can we make a *qualitative* evaluation of education or of work? This, we are told, would be purely subjective; it could not be *proved*; it would be anybody's guess, since it cannot be measured and made objective.

The Cartesian revolution has removed the vertical dimension from our map of knowledge. Only the horizontal dimensions are left. Science provides excellent guidance through this flatland. It

[1] Thomas Aquinas, *Summa Theologica* I, 1, 5 ad 1.
[2] R. Descartes, *Rules for the Direction of the Mind*, Rule II.
[3] Descartes, Rule II.

can do everything except lead us out of the dark wood of a meaningless, purposeless, "accidental" existence. Modern science answers the question "What is man?" with such inspiring phrases as "a cosmic accident," or "a rather unsuccessful product of mindless evolution or natural selection," or "a naked ape." It is not surprising that it has no answer to the question of what this absurd, accidental product of mindless forces is supposed to do with itself—that is to say, what it should do with its *mind*.

In these circumstances, what could be the purpose of education? In Western civilization, as in all other great civilizations, the purpose used to be to lead people out of the dark wood of meaninglessness, purposelessness, drift, and indulgence up a mountain where the truth that makes you free can be gained. This was the traditional wisdom of all people in all parts of the world. We modern people, who reject traditional wisdom and deny the existence of the vertical dimension of the spirit, also, like our forefathers, desire nothing more than somehow to be able to rise above the humdrum state of our present life. We hope to do so by growing rich, moving around at ever-increasing speed, traveling to the moon and into space, but whatever we do in these respects, we cannot rise above our own humdrum, petty, egotistical selves. Education may help us to become richer quicker and to travel further faster, but everything remains as meaningless as before. As long as we remain entrapped in the metaphysics represented by the Cartesian revolution, education can be nothing but a training that enables people to establish themselves more comfortably—the body, not the soul—in the dark wood of meaningless existence.

In other words, as long as we arrogantly persist in dismissing traditional wisdom as "prescientific," and therefore not to be taken seriously, fit only for the museum, there is no basis for any form of education other than "training for worldly success." Education for good work is quite impossible. For how could we possibly distinguish good work from bad work if human life on Earth has no meaning, no purpose? The word *good* presupposes an aim—good for what? Good for making money? Good for promotion? Good for fame or power? These things can also be attained through work that, from another point of view, would be considered very bad work. Without traditional wisdom, no answer can be found.

Traditional wisdom derives all its answers from a knowledge

of the tasks and purposes of human life on earth. The human being's first task is to learn from society and tradition and to find its temporary happiness by following directions from outside. The second task is to interiorize this knowledge, sift it, sort it out, keep the good, and jettison the bad. This process may be called *individuation,* or becoming self-directed. The third task, which cannot be tackled until the first two tasks are accomplished, is dying to oneself, to one's likes and dislikes, to all one's egocentric preoccupations. For this task, a person needs the very best help he can find. To the extent that he succeeds, he ceases to be directed from outside, and he also ceases to be self-directed. He has gained freedom or, one might say, he is God-directed. If he is a Christian, that is precisely what he would hope to be able to say.

If these are the tasks that face each human being, we can say that "good" is what helps me and others along on this journey of liberation. I am called on to "love my neighbor as myself," but I cannot love him at all, except sensually or sentimentally, unless I love myself enough to embark on the good work of personal development. I cannot love and help my neighbor as long as I have to say, with St. Paul: "My own behavior baffles me. For I find myself not doing what I really want to do but doing what I really loathe."[4] In order to become capable of doing good work for my neighbor as well as for myself, I am called upon to love God—that is, strenuously and patiently to keep my mind stretching towards the highest things, to levels of being above my own. Only there is goodness to be found. This is the answer given by traditional wisdom, that is to say, by the metaphysics that has given rise to all the great civilizations of humanity. From this wisdom, we can derive all the guidance we need.

What are a human being's greatest needs? In our spiritual lines, we are primarily and inescapably concerned with values. In our social lives, we are primarily and inescapably concerned with people and also with other sentient creatures. As individuals, our greatest need is self-development.

Accordingly, as anyone can confirm from experience, there are three things healthy people most need to do, and education ought to prepare them for these: first, to act as spiritual beings—that is to say, to act in accordance with their moral impulses;

[4]Rom. 7:14.

second, to act as neighbors—that is to say, to render service to their fellows; and third, to act as persons, as autonomous centers of power and responsibility—that is to say, to be creatively engaged, using and developing the gifts that have been laid into them. These are the human being's three fundamental needs, and in their fulfillment lies happiness. In their unfulfillment lies frustration and unhappiness.

In a subtle way, which ought to be studied, modern society has made it increasingly difficult or even impossible for most of the people, most of the time, to meet these needs. And education, including higher education, seems to know little about them. Strange to say, most people do not even know what their needs are. For reasons well known to traditional wisdom, human beings are insufficiently "programmed." Even when fully grown, they do not move and act with the surefootedness of animals. They hesitate, doubt, change their minds, run hither and thither, uncertain not simply of how to get what they want, but uncertain, above all, of what they want.

If education is unable to teach them what they want, is it of any use? Questions like "What shall I do with my life?" or "What must I do to be saved?" relate to ends, not merely to means. To such questions, it does not help to say, "Tell me precisely what you want, and I shall teach you how to get it." The whole point is that I do not know what I want. Maybe all I want is to be happy. But the answer, "Tell me what you need for happiness, and I shall then be able to advise you what to do," again, will not do, because I do not know what I need for happiness. Perhaps someone says, "For happiness you need the truth that makes you free." But can the educator tell me what *is* the truth that makes us free? Can he tell me where to find it, guide me to it, or at least point out the direction in which I have to proceed? Maybe I feel that good work is what I am really longing for. Who can tell me what good work is and when work is good?

Traditional wisdom teaches that the function of work is at least threefold: to give workers a chance to utilize and develop their faculties; to enable them to overcome their inborn egocentricity by joining with other people in a common task; and to bring forth the goods and services needed by all of us for a decent existence. Now, I think all this needs to be *taught*.

Until quite recently, I heard it said everywhere that the real task of education was not education for work, but education for leisure. Maybe this extraordinary idea has now been abandoned. Fancy telling young and eager souls, "Now, what I really want you to envisage is how to kill time when you have nothing useful to do." As our ancestors have known (and as it has been expressed by Thomas Aquinas), there can be no joy of life without joy of work. This is a statement worth pondering. Laziness, they also knew, is sadness of the soul. This, too, is worth pondering. A nineteenth-century thinker said something to this effect: "Watch out—if you get too many useful machines, you will get too many useless people."[5] Another statement worth pondering.

The question is raised: "How do we prepare young people for the future world of work?" And the first answer, I think, must be: we should prepare them to be able to distinguish between good work and bad work and encourage them not to accept the latter. That is to say, they should be encouraged to reject meaningless, boring, stultifying or nerve-racking work where man (or woman) is made the servant of a machine or a system. They should be taught that work is the joy of life and is needed for our development but that meaningless work is an abomination.

A sensitive British worker wrote: "It is probably wrong to expect factories to be other than they are. After all, they are built to house machines, not men. Inside a factory, it soon becomes obvious that steel brought to life by electricity takes precedence over flesh and blood. The onus is on the machines to such an extent that they appear to assume the human attributes of those who work them. Machines have become as much like people as people have become like machines. They pulsate with life, while man becomes a robot. There is a premonition of man losing control, an awareness of doom."[6] This worker has been conditioned not even to expect good work. He has been conditioned to believe that man is nothing but a somewhat complex physiochemical system, nothing but a product of mindless evolution. So he may suffer when machines become like men and men become like machines, but he cannot really be surprised nor expect anything else.

It is interesting to note that the modern world of work takes a lot of care that the worker's body should not accidentally

[5] Attributed to Karl Marx, source unknown.
[6] R. Fraser (Ed.), *Work* (New York: Penguin, 1968), pp. 17-18.

or otherwise be damaged. If it is damaged, the worker can claim compensation. But what of his soul and his spirit? If his work damages them, by reducing him to a robot, that is just too bad. Materialistic metaphysics, or the metaphysics of the doctrine of mindless evolution, does not attribute reality to anything but the physical body. Why then bother about the safety or health of such nebulous, unreal things as soul or spirit? Anyone who says the worker needs work for the development of his soul sounds like a fanciful dreamer.

In depriving work of any higher purpose, we reduce it to the level of "unpleasant necessity." At this level there is no use talking about good work, unless we mean *less* work. What is the point of making something perfect, when it is easier and cheaper to make something imperfect? Ananda Coomaraswamy used to say, "Industry without art is brutality," because it damages the soul and spirit of the worker. He could say this because his metaphysics is very different from that of the modern world. He also said, "It is not as if the artist were a special kind of man; every man is a special kind of artist."[7] This is the metaphysics of good work.

How, then, could there be education for good work? First of all, we should have to alter the metaphysical basis from which we proceed. If we continue to teach that the human being is nothing but the outcome of a mindless, meaningless, and purposeless process of evolution, a process of selection for survival—that is to say, the outcome of nothing but utilitarianism—we can come only to a utilitarian idea of work, an idea that work is nothing but a more or less unpleasant necessity, and the less there is of it, the better. Our ancestors knew about good work, but we cannot learn from them if we continue to regard them with friendly contempt, or if we continue to treat traditional wisdom as a tissue of superstitious poetry, or if we continue to take materialistic scientism as the one and only measure of progress. The best scientists know that science deals only with small, isolated systems, showing how they work, and provides no basis whatever for comprehensive metaphysical doctrines such as the doctrine of mindless evolution. But we nevertheless still teach the young that the modern theory of evolution is a part of science and that it leaves no room for

---

[7]A. K. Coomaraswamy, *Christian and Oriental Philosophy of Art* (New York: Dover, 1956), pp. 92, 112.

divine guidance or design. We thus wantonly create a conflict between science and religion that causes untold confusion.

Education for good work could then proceed to a systematic study of traditional wisdom, where answers are to be found to questions about the purpose and meaning of life. It would emerge that there is indeed a goal to be reached and that there are many paths to the goal. The goal can be called "perfection"—"Be ye therefore perfect as your father in heaven is perfect"—or "the kingdom," "salvation," "nirvana," "liberation," or "enlightenment." And the path to the goal is good work. "Work out your salvation with diligence." "He who has been given much, of him much will be demanded." In short, life is a kind of school, and in this school nothing counts but good work—work that ennobles the product as it ennobles the producer.

In the process of doing good work, the ego of the worker disappears. As he frees himself from his ego, the divine element in him becomes active. None of this makes sense if we proceed from the basic presuppositions of materialistic scientism. How can the product of mindless evolution—whose abilities are only those selected by blind nature for their utilitarian value in the universal struggle for survival—free itself from its ego, the center of its will to survive? What a nonsensical proposition!

The world of work created by modern metaphysics is a dreary place. Can higher education prepare people for it? How do you prepare people for a kind of serfdom? What human qualities are required for becoming efficient servants of machines, systems, or bureaucracies? The world of work of today is the product of a hundred years of "deskilling"—why take the trouble to let people acquire the skills of craftsmanship when all that is wanted is the patience of machine minder? The only skills worth acquiring are those which the system demands, and they are worthless outside the system. They have no survival value outside the system and therefore do not even confer the spirit of self-reliance. What does a machine minder do when, let us say, an energy shortage stops the machine? Or a computer programmer, without a computer?

Maybe higher education could be designed to lead to a world of work that is different from the one we have today. But this cannot be as long as higher education clings to the metaphysics of materialistic scientism and the doctrine of mindless evolution. Figs cannot grow on thistles. Good work cannot grow out of such metaphysics. To try to make it grow on such a basis can do nothing but increase the prevailing confusion. The most urgent need of our time is the need for a metaphysical reconstruction, a supreme effort to bring clarity and cohesion into our deepest convictions with regard to such questions as "What is man?" "Where does he come from?" and "What is the purpose of his life?"

6

The Current State of Recurrent Education

Stanley D. Nollen

The concept of recurrent education emerged into consciousness at the beginning of the 1970s. It started in Sweden and was quickly picked up, studied, and supported by the Organization for Economic Cooperation and Development, the International Labor Organization, and UNESCO.[1] It is also an increas-

This paper was written with the assistance of working papers commissioned especially for this purpose. I wish to acknowledge the Spencer Foundation for supporting this effort. I am indebted to Werner Sengenberger, Sture Strömqvist, Douglas Smith, and Norman Kurland for their inputs. I am also indebted to Mark Blaug and Gösta Rehn for early encouragement. All errors of fact or opinion remain my responsibility.

[1]See Center for Educational Research and Innovation, *Equal Educational Opportunity* (Paris: 1971). J. Bengtsson, *The Swedish View of Recurrent Education* (Paris: Organization for Economic Cooperation and Development, 1972). UNESCO, *Learning To Be: The World of Education Today and Tomorrow* (Paris: UNESCO, 1972). In addition, Organization for Economic Cooperation and Development published studies of recurrent education in

ingly fashionable topic in the U.S., where the term *lifelong learning* is used.[2] Although a diverse variety of programs may be included under the umbrella of recurrent education, its defining characteristics are that it is formally organized and undertaken in alternation with work after the initial youth schooling period. It is further restricted in this study to adults in the labor force and to cases in which there is employer support or involvement. The education may be vocational or not, full time or part time, undertaken inhouse or outside, and provided by educational institutions, labor unions, or employers themselves. On-the-job training and apprenticeship programs that occur during work or on the work site are different and not usually thought of as recurrent education; nor is adult education of the evening or weekend continuing-education variety.

Many public policy claims have been made for recurrent education—efficiency claims, such as increased productivity, and equity claims, such as providing a second chance to disadvantaged people. Study and planning on the design and implementation of recurrent education continues, highlighted in the U.S. by the 1976 enactment of the Lifetime Learning Act.[3] But is recurrent education actually taking place? Are workers undertaking education in alternation with work and in cooperation with employers, aside from evening adult education? At present, only a small proportion are doing it. But times are changing. There are some profound new developments occurring in the work sector in Europe and the

several countries in 1972. More recent work includes five OECD publications: *Alternation Between Work and Education* (forthcoming), *Developments in Recurrent Education* (forthcoming), *Developments in Educational Leave of Absence* (1976), *Education and Working Life in Modern Society* (1975), and *Recurrent Education: Trends and Issues* (1975). The International Labor Organization has sponsored work here also. See V. Stoikov, *The Economics of Recurrent Education and Training* (Geneva: ILO, 1975).

[2] See S. J. Mushkin (Ed.), *Recurrent Education* (Washington: U.S. National Institute of Education, 1974). D. W. Vermilye (Ed.), *Lifelong Learners—A New Clientele for Higher Education: Current Issues in Higher Education 1974* (San Francisco: Jossey-Bass, 1974).

[3] See U.S. Congress, Senate Subcommittee on Education of the Committee on Labor and Public Welfare, *Hearings on the Lifetime Learning Act* (Washington: U.S. Government Printing Office, 1976). This act establishes an Office of Lifetime Learning within the Office of Education and authorizes evaluation of existing lifetime learning activities and research designed to encourage new activities. A notable ongoing study is the Study of Adult Education in the New York State Department of Education.

United States which are creating a new demand for recurrent education. There are now some real world examples of new linkages between education and work.

Theoretically, if recurrent education for adult workers is going to happen, there must be an ample supply of educational services, a demand for these services, and a price that buyers (workers, employers, or labor unions) can afford to pay. In general, the supply of educational services from institutions of education ought to be adequate since there is if anything a surplus of spaces and faculty in the education system in the United States. The demand for recurrent education, on the other hand, appears to be deficient. Few workers take advantage of tuition refund programs or educational leaves of absence, and less-educated workers seldom participate in adult continuing education.[4] But of course the demand for education depends on the economic and social returns on the investment of time and money required. In the case of recurrent education, these returns will depend on the employment outcomes which are tied to the completion of the education. But no such tie is usually present, at least for production workers. Consequently, demand is weak and recurrent education infrequent.

The idea that recurrent education is most likely to be undertaken when both workers and employers have a stake in it is illustrated by developments in West Germany.[5] One of the most notable developments has been the increasing participation of German workers in management. Soon after World War II, workers in the coal and steel industries and later in other industries began to participate in management through membership on the supervisory board or *Aufsichtsrat* (roughly comparable to a U.S. board of directors) and a works council or *Betriebsrat*—an in-plant decision-making body on the allocation, training, and pricing of labor. Thus workers who become board members or works councillors are confronted with new tasks and new requirements for compe-

[4]See H. A. Levine, "Labor-Management Policies on Educational Opportunity," in Mushkin, *Recurrent Education*. S. D. Nollen, "Paid Educational Leave in the U.S.," in Organization for Economic Cooperation and Development, *Alternation Between Work and Education* (Paris: OECD, forthcoming).
[5]This sector is based in large part on a working paper by Werner Sengenberger of the Institut für Sozialwissenschaftliche Forschung in Munich.

tency. As a result, labor unions and legislators have called for more
training opportunities, and in 1972, works councillors received the
right to three weeks of management training and labor education
at full compensation for all training costs and loss of earnings.
Consequently there has been a substantial increase in education
for adult workers at both union and nonunion schools.

A second major change in the work sector in Germany is the
growing tendency of companies to meet their employment needs
by upgrading the work force inside the company by using an internal labor market, rather than relying on the external labor market.
Internal labor markets were developed in part because of the increased job and product specialization associated with advanced
technology and the expanding size of firms. Because the desired
skills are more specific—demanded by fewer employers and acquired by fewer workers—traditional external labor markets are
less suitable. There is more demand for training inside the firm.
Many of these skills are firm-specific, being more usable and productive in the firm where they are acquired than in any other firm.
In addition, the attachment of workers to the firm in these cases is
more likely to be of long duration. Thus it is in the interest of
firms to provide this training.[6] Internal labor markets also resulted
from the shortage of skilled labor in the 1960s. As external recruitment became increasingly expensive due to high search costs
and the low quality of supply, and as market wages rose, firms
turned to their incumbent work force. They installed training
facilities on their premises and expanded their educational activities to upgrade the skills of their workers.

Skilled labor shortages also meant that more low-skill workers, often foreigners, were hired from external labor markets. Although firms did not train these workers, expecting their tenure to
be short, they did redesign jobs and provide supervisory training to
nonmanagerial personnel, such as skilled craftsmen, so that the
low-skill workers could be better utilized. Public support for this
training was substantially increased in 1969. By 1973, nearly two
thirds of the people who received public support for this kind of

---

[6]The human capital theory that underlies these propositions and predicts the outcomes is found in G. S. Becker, *Human Capital*, 2nd ed. (New
York: National Bureau of Economic Research, 1975). The theory applies
both to on-the-job training and off-the-job recurrent education.

training were skilled workers trained to become supervisors, technicians, or engineers.

Internal labor markets in Germany have stimulated education for workers provided by employers in yet another way. When there are internal labor markets, more administrative decisions have to be made inside the firm rather than given from an outside market. This includes decisions about wage rates, job structures, worker assignments, and training itself. Thus there is an increased need for rationales for these decisions as well as loyalty and commitment of the workers to the firm. In the 1970s, especially during the recent recession, education to meet these needs grew rapidly. This education, which is partly ideological in nature, helps workers share the firm's goals and values and thus mitigates potential labor unrest when technological change or economic conditions reduce employment.

The combined effect of internal labor markets, job specialization, and skill shortages on education for adult workers in West Germany is statistically impressive. In 1973, outlays by employers and employee associations for adult education and training were 2.12 billion Deutschmarks (about $800 million), or roughly 1 percent of their total wage costs. This exceeded the federal outlay (from the Bundesanstalt für Arbeit) of 1.47 billion Deutschmarks ($560 million). (By way of comparison, this federal training outlay just exceeded the federal cost of unemployment benefits.) Only three years earlier, in 1970, the federal expenditure on adult training was just 600 million Deutschmarks. Most of the training expenditure is for skill updating or upgrading and for retraining in different skills. The figures include compensation for earnings lost during the period of education (two thirds of the total) as well as direct costs. About 40 percent of all firms with more than 50 employees had adult education programs by 1974. Nearly all large firms (more than 1,000 employees) had such programs in 1974, whereas only half provided training in 1960. A major German car maker spent three times more on adult training than on apprenticeship in 1972, whereas in 1960 the ratio was 9 to 1 in reverse. A provision for paid leaves of absence from work for educational purposes was written in 194 collective bargaining agreements covering 4 to 5 percent of the total labor force by 1974. In addition, some states of the West German Federal Republic have legislated paid educational leave. For example, in the state of Hamburg every employed person is entitled to twelve working days of paid educational leave every two years.

Although some education undertaken by adult workers is not directly related to work sector changes, such as basic education done under paid leave, much of it clearly is, as indicated by the profile of adult learners. The typical adult worker who receives training is likely to be employed in an industry of large firms or capital-intensive firms or by a public agency; he is likely to be male, age twenty-five to thirty-five, and to have quite good professional or vocational qualifications; and he is likely to be a member of a stable, well-integrated segment of the firm's work force—in other words, a worker whose future employment at the firm is expected to last long enough to yield favorable returns to educational investments.

A somewhat more ideological rationale has supported the growth of recurrent education in Sweden.[7] Beginning in the late 1960s, experiments with industrial democracy began there in both the private and public sectors. Currently all firms employing fifty or more workers must give trade unions a seat among management on the board. A new 1977 law on co-determination requires employers to inform workers and unions about planned changes in such matters as the terms and conditions of employment, modes of production, and financial policy, and to negotiate with them on these matters even though retaining the right to make the final decision. Such movements toward worker participation are responses to union and worker pressure and to the need to make employment more attractive for young people.

Just what this increased worker participation in management means in terms of education for workers cannot yet be clearly documented, but labor unions estimate that each year 10,000 to 15,000 of their members will need some education due to the 1977 law, after a larger start-up demand. In general there is a growing demand for education among workers, according to survey research findings. This demand depends mainly on the perceived value of education as a means to exercise the new rights of industrial democracy, to keep up with technological changes, and to improve one's position in the labor market.

---

[7]This section is based largely on a working paper by Sture Strömqvist of the Ministry of Education in Stockholm.

Skill obsolescence and the need for basic education have also resulted in education for adult workers. New employment legislation in 1976 is directed in part toward adults whose basic education is defective and whose vocational skills, acquired through lengthy past experience, have been rendered obsolete by technological developments. For these people there are courses in preparation for new jobs and basic education in preparation for later vocational training.

The chronically high level of unemployment in Sweden—especially among young workers—has been another stimulus for recurrent education. A subsidy scheme was implemented in 1976 in which the central government makes a grant out of general tax revenues to an employer to support the release of workers to undertake education, in return for which the employer hires replacements who are twenty-five years old or younger. In addition, training grants are made to employers so that workers who are not needed during slack demand can receive education as well as income instead of being laid off. Training in these programs is geared to the needs of the firm. The new government, elected in September 1976, has tripled the training grant for these purposes to 25 kroner ($6) per hour. These two programs are too new to have yielded any aggregate empirical data. However, in the case of a steel works in western Sweden, when workers were trained instead of laid off under the grant scheme, the demand for education increased by some 30 percent among other workers at the plant. Thus, a spillover effect from specific training programs to education undertaken by adults in general may be predicted.

Paid educational leaves of absence for workers have long been a part of some collective bargaining agreements in Sweden, but in 1975, the Act on the Right to Educational Leave established the right in principle of all employees to take educational leaves of absence after six months of service. The only constraints are the employer's right to postpone a requested leave up to six months, and the level of government financial support which determines the maximum number of leaves available. In 1977, financial support was made available for the first time to workers for short-term, part-time study at the rate of 22 kr. ($5.25) per hour (57,000 places available) and for long-term, full-time study at the rate of 110 to 150 kr. ($26-$36) per day (10,000 places). The Act also includes a 100 kr. ($24) per day board allowance for full-time, short-term courses (19,000 places). All places are filled, with applications for the longer full-time benefits exceeding the number of places by 2 to 1. Taking all the paid leave programs together, just over 2 percent of the labor force can be accommodated each year. The source of support is a payroll tax of .25 percent, which is expected to generate $100 million in the 1977-78 fiscal year. One policy of the program is to discriminate in favor of less-educated workers. Early data show that 70 percent of all full-time benefits are going to workers with 9 years or less of schooling.

Responding to the increased interest adults are showing in education, Swedish universities have, since 1969, permitted the substitution of working experience for upper secondary school completion as a qualification for university admission. Called "extended admission," this policy applies to persons age twenty-five or older and requires four years of work experience plus some basic education received previously from municipal adult education or people's high schools. Partly due to extended admission, Swedish higher education now has more older students, fewer degree programs, more short-cycle technical and vocational courses, courses with a reduced pace of study, and procedures that make it easier to alternate between work and education. A further example of university-labor linkage is a joint project between the University of Lund and a regional trade union, in which the university adapts course content and teaching to trade union needs while the union supports research relevant to union interests.

Another pattern of recurrent education, combining elements of both West German and Swedish practice, is exemplified by Great Britain.[8] Increases in recurrent education for adult workers in recent years in Britain appear to be associated with work sector developments such as skill obsolescence and lagging productivity, high unemployment (especially among young people), shifts in the occupational distribution, and changing labor-management relations. Overall, an estimated two million workers out of a labor force of twenty-four million received training of some kind in 1971, but how much of this training qualifies as recurrent education is not clear. But the government's concern to make education more responsive to work sector changes is illustrated by the pas-

[8]This section is based in large part on a working paper by Douglas Smith of St. Catherine's College, Oxford.

sage of the Employment and Training Act in 1973, under which government training activities were reorganized and located in manpower agencies.

A chief mechanism by which recurrent education for adult workers is delivered is the levy-grant system used by the Industrial Training Boards (ITB). Under authority of the Industrial Training Act of 1964, there are twenty-four ITBs, one for each industry, covering 63 percent of the labor force. They levy a payroll tax on employers, who in return receive a grant from their ITB if certain standards of training are attained. About £200 million ($480 million) in grants were paid in 1973, including a government funding supplement of £44 million.

The total number of workers trained and the type of training they received are not known. Available data show that the Foundry ITB trained 62,200 workers in 1971, the Road Transport ITB increased off-the-job training 242 percent from 1966 to 1970, and the Engineering ITB experienced a 50 percent increase in numbers from 1966 to 1969, but a 20 percent decline to 1971. The quality and distribution of training appears to have improved, but employers are reported to be reluctant to release workers from their jobs for training. Much of the ITB training is short term, most of it is geared to the employer's needs, and some of it is on the worker's own time. There has been conflict because employers desire firm-specific training and ITBs want industry-relevant training.

An additional training service conducted within firms is the Training Within Industry Program (TWI). Short courses are provided by the government in topics such as supervision, clerical and operator instruction, export documentation, job relations, and job safety. In 1975, 23,000 workers were trained in this program.

Medium- to long-term off-the-job recurrent education for workers is provided in the Training Opportunities Scheme (TOPS), a government program begun in 1973. Adults take courses lasting from six months to a year at 32 skill centers. They learn occupational skills that meet their needs and are important to the national economy. Workers whose skills have become obsolete due to industrial change are among the participants. All expenses are paid, including a living allowance. Unemployed workers and those who are willing to give up their jobs may also undertake full-time training under TOPS, with paid allowances, in the Colleges of Further Education (CFE).[9] About £170 million ($340 million) was spent on TOPS training in 1976.

Growth in government-supported recurrent education for workers has been large. Between 1973 and 1976 the number of courses offered in TWI and TOPS programs nearly doubled. The number of workers trained under TOPS increased from 15,000 in 1971 to 90,000 in 1976. In the past decade employers have tended to train older workers more readily than younger workers. This is shown by the increase in the release of workers over age twenty-one to take courses of study during working hours and a decline in release of people age eighteen or under.

A major development in worker participation in management in Britain occurred with the publication in January 1977 of the Bullock report, which proposed worker representatives on the boards of private sector firms. If adopted (over substantial employer opposition), the new policy would involve 5,000 to 10,000 worker representatives. Although training needs were only briefly addressed in the report, they are likely to emerge if workers participate on boards. Relatively few worker representatives are now trained for a management role. Currently about 5 percent of shop stewards receive training of a week or more and 33 percent receive a day or less of instruction in industrial relations, while in 80 percent of all enterprises no stewards were trained in 1970. Although these figures do not seem impressive, they represent an increase over 1960 levels. Future trends may be suggested by the Harland and Wolff shipyard, where industrial democracy proposals include a resource center which will employ a training coordinator to identify training needs of worker representatives. The center will be supported by the firm, which will also provide the training.

Occupational safety and health concerns have also resulted in new demands for training. Regulations were proposed in 1976 to permit worker safety representatives to receive paid leave from their jobs for purposes of education in occupational health and safety. These regulations were put into effect in March 1977 despite employer resistance.

A variety of alternative work patterns—flexible hours, compressed work weeks (involving about 100,000 workers each), and

[9]From M. Blaug, "Recurrent Education—The Latest Mania of the Education Lobby," *Higher Education* (in press).

part-time employment—are practiced in Britain, but no direct effect on education undertaken by workers has yet been observed. This may be due in part to the limited opportunities for full-time workers on flexible hours to bank or borrow working time (usually one day a month) and thus free a large enough block of time for educational pursuits.

In general, adult education—only parts of which qualify as recurrent education—has been expanding in Britain. Although direct linkages to changes in the work sector are difficult to establish, certainly some of this expansion is due to such changes. Whether the purpose is to help skilled workers become shop stewards or to help women re-enter the labor force, and whether the method is a weekend at the Trade Unions Congress College or Open University television courses, there is as much concern to make adult education responsive to work sector changes in Britain as there is in West Germany and Sweden.

Compared to developments in these European countries, what is happening in recurrent education for adult workers in the United States?[10] Overall, very little full-scale recurrent education is evident in this country. Among the major labor contracts in 1974, there were few which included provisions for paid educational leaves of absence. Only 4 percent included *unpaid* educational leave. About 9 percent of private industrial firms authorized some workers to take sabbaticals of a month or longer in 1975, but almost none of these leaves were available to all workers in the firm. However, there is a substantial amount of company-provided off-the-job education during working hours. About 3 million workers participate, or 4 percent of all industrial workers; three quarters of industrial firms provide such education. This education is not the type that involves alternation between work and education in which the worker's job is left for any length of time, but it is one form of education for adult workers.

---

[10]The following is based in part on a working paper by Norman Kurland of the New York State Department of Education in Albany, and on the author's "Paid Educational Leave of Absence in the U.S.," unpublished. Data sources in the latter include a study by Seymour Lusterman of the Conference Board in New York on education and training in industry (to be published by the Conference Board) and U.S. Bureau of Labor Statistics, "Characteristics of Major Collective Bargaining Agreements, July 1, 1974," Bulletin 1888 (Washington, D.C.: U.S. Government Printing Office, 1975).

As in Europe, there are work-sector changes that bear on the demand for education by adult workers and employers. One of the major new concerns in the U.S. work sector is with the quality of work life. That concern coincides with labor market conditions of overeducation relative to job requirements. Together they have stimulated a handful of industrial training experiments that contain an element of recurrent education. The Quality of Work Life Program at General Motors, now incorporated into the company's labor agreement with the United Auto Workers, was designed to get workers more involved in such matters as goal setting, problem solving, and job design. One project under this program is a 40-hour training program in problem-solving for supervisors and hourly workers. A spillover effect of increased interest by workers in broadening their knowledge beyond narrow job training has been reported. In this program, the intention of management is not only to improve the general operation of the business, but also to assist workers in finding satisfaction in their work (conceived more broadly than "job") in the face of limited advancement opportunities.

Another noteworthy quality-of-work-life program is the Work Improvement Program of Harman International and the United Auto Workers at a manufacturing plant in Bolivar, Tennessee. One of the features of this program is an alternative work schedule—the task system—in which a day's work is done and "idle time" is earned after the production tasks are completed, even if the tasks took less than eight hours. A result was the use of that idle time for education. A Harman School now provides course work in vocational, management, and cultural pursuits in the plant and outside, and in cooperation with local education authorities. This experience indicates that when workers are given greater control over their work lives, their interest in learning and personnel development is stimulated. There are a few other demonstration projects of this sort.

A shortage of labor together with strong union pressure produced an isolated example of paid educational leaves of absence for hospital and health-care workers in New York City beginning in 1969. Both the private sector (League of Voluntary Hospitals and National Union of Hospital and Health Care Workers) and public sector (New York Health and Hospitals Corporation and American Federation of State, County and Municipal Employees) are included. Between 1969 and 1976, about 1,200 unskilled and semi-skilled workers took part in full-time, formal postsecondary education. Periods of study ranged from 5 months to 2 years, and participants received 85 percent of their salaries while away from work plus all tuition expenses. They earned further credentials and have been promoted to a variety of medical specialities which were in short supply. The educational leaves, which cost $5 million in 1975, were financed either by a one-percent gross payroll tax or a $25-per-head tax imposed on employers. Other workers receive support for remedial education during nonworking hours. However, as the labor shortage has vanished, these programs have recently been cut back severely because of the employer's inability to finance them.

On a much smaller scale, educational leaves of absence without loss of earnings continues for hospital and health employees of the Kaiser Permanent Medical Care Plan in California. This program is part of the collective bargaining agreement with the Service Employees International Union, and allows five days per year of paid leave.

Management initiatives have produced unusual education programs for adult workers in at least two cases. At the Kimberly-Clark Corporation, a belief in the value of education has resulted in payments to employees for either job-related or cultural education. Thirty percent of eligible employees participate in the program, and four fifths of the education is job-related. Much of this education takes place on evenings or weekends but some is done on company time. There are also provisions for year-long paid leaves of absence. In the U.S. Postal Service, a training institute was established in 1970 with the objective of increasing the productivity of postal service workers. In-house but off-the-job courses (some offered for college credit) are taken by about 68,000 blue- and white-collar workers annually at a cost of roughly $14 million in 1975. Courses run from one to twenty-six weeks.

Some education for adult workers is stimulated by technological change. In one case, workers at a small upstate New York firm asked for engineering and accounting education in order to bid against an outside supplier in a "make-or-buy" decision. In other examples, where job content is redefined because of technological changes, recurrent education is needed to help train "gray-collar" workers—quasi-professionals who have to understand and work with the new technology. Programs along these lines have been undertaken by the Graphic Arts International Union and the Jamestown (N.Y.) Labor-Management Committee.

A social movement which bears very directly on the work sector and causes education to be offered to workers by their employers is the press toward equal employment opportunities for minorities and women. This has caused many firms to institute educational activities to upgrade women and minority employees as well as to help managers understand the attitudes and practices underlying equal opportunity.

Despite some similarities, recurrent education for adult workers in the United States is fundamentally different from the European versions. Even the work-sector changes which motivate it are different. The concept of industrial democracy—formal participation of workers in management—is a major concern in West Germany, Sweden, and Britain. In the United States, this concept is at best a latent force. Internal labor markets have developed in West Germany, and educational obsolescence and high unemployment figure prominently in Sweden and Britain, whereas these factors are of lesser importance in the United States. On the other hand, American concerns about the quality of work life and about overeducation for jobs are largely absent in European countries.

The amount of recurrent education taking place in the United States appears to be much less than in Europe—particularly if one uses the restrictive definition of recurrent education. There is little or no alternation between work and education. American workers do not leave their jobs for mid-career retraining. And there is no national or state employment or education policy directed to the implementation of recurrent education as there is in Europe.

But measured in a more inclusive way, the amount of employer-supported education adult workers in the United States receive off-the-job is considerable. American recurrent education is different. It is microalternation, or perhaps integration, with work. It tends to be an individual matter and to be in-service. The boundaries between formal off-the-job education and informal on-the-job training have become blurred. European experiences are instructive for the United States because they are so different. Some of them may not be applicable, but others may be harbingers. The next task is to decide which is which.

7

Education
in Industry

Seymour Lusterman

Employee education by business has burgeoned in the past few decades. This growth is largely the result of a corresponding increase in the number and complexity of work skills that can best be taught where and when they are applied. It has brought into being what has been called a "shadow educational system," but what I think is more properly viewed as a segment of the educational system. Those most aware of employee education have been lamenting the paucity of information about its aims, character, and programs. Incomplete information, they feel, has frustrated understanding of better ways to integrate such activities with other parts of the educational system.

Such considerations led the Conference Board, about two years ago, to undertake a study of corporate education that prompted the Carnegie Corporation of New York and the Rockefeller Brothers Fund to provide generous funding for it. I planned and directed this research and recently completed a detailed report of findings that will be published by the Conference Board this year.

The study embraced something less than its potential universe. Outside the armed forces, about ninety-three million Americans are presently at work or looking for work. When we subtract from this civilian labor force those who work on farms, those who work for federal, state, or local governments, and those who are self-employed or unemployed, we are left with about sixty-three million people. These are the managers, professionals, technicians, clerks, and other salaried and hourly workers who make up the payrolls of private business and industry. Of these sixty-three million, half are employed by a relatively small number of firms—about 7,500—each of which has at least 500 employees. The other half work for the vastly greater number of firms with fewer than 500 employees. It was to the upper half, the roughly 7,500 firms and their thirty-two million employees, that the Conference Board's study was directed—principally because it is rarely feasible for firms with fewer than 500 employees to conduct or sponsor formal, in-house education and training. Among the companies that do sponsor such training, many do not maintain central records about the numbers of employees that participate or the dollars spent on them. Thus, our projected figures incorporate a large number of company estimates and must be viewed as rough approximations. All of the study's projections were based on reports by 610 firms.

We found that during the single recession year of 1975 the nation's 7,500 largest private employers spent over $2 billion on employee education—as much as the annual total in recent years of all contributions and grants to all U.S. colleges and universities from all sources. At least one out of eight of the thirty-two million employees of these firms took part in some formal, off-the-job education or training under company sponsorship.

While incidentally supportive of the job and career aspirations of participating employees, most employer-sponsored education stems from business needs. One of these needs is to qualify new employees, particularly those joining the firm in entry-level jobs, to perform their duties. Programs to train such new employees account for a sizeable share of the education-training efforts of some firms, and even dominate in a few. But it is programs for present employees, programs intended to prepare them for new responsibilities, to improve their present performance, and to maintain their competency in the face of changing knowledge, products, and technology that usually take the major portion of a company's employee-development resources.

Employee education and training under employer auspices may occur during or after work hours; it may take place at the company or at outside institutions. Thus, employee education may occur in four circumstances: after-hours external, during-hours external, after-hours internal, and during-hours internal. After-hours external education is virtually a synonym for tuition-aid programs under which employees are reimbursed for all or part of the costs of courses that they themselves elect to take but that, typically, must be related to their jobs or careers. Such programs were almost universal among companies with 500 or more employees. We estimate that in 1975 these firms spent about $225 million in reimbursements or direct outlays for courses taken by over one million employees. Yet, in terms of expenditures, such tuition-aid programs do not amount to a great deal in the total scheme of employee education. They represent only one corporate dollar out of every ten in direct outlays. External study *during* working hours is, if anything, a slightly smaller component. This kind of study, which is pursued mainly by managers and professionals and which takes place at colleges and universities, in trade groups and professional societies, and in organizations such as the American Management Association and the Conference Board accounts for a second dollar of every ten.

Eight dollars out of ten, therefore, or about $1.6 billion in all, are spent for internal company courses. This money pays for the salaries of full-time education and training personnel, for travel and living expenses of staff and students, and for the purchase and rental of services and materials. This figure does not include the vastly greater but more elusive cost of wages and salaries paid to employees while they are learning. Nor does it include rent and overhead, which are sizeable items in the budgets of traditional educational institutions. Seven out of ten companies incur direct costs in connection with formal, in-house education. In all they employ about 45,000 persons on a full-time basis as instructors, program developers, administrators, and evaluators.

We were unable to apportion the expenditures for internal

courses between during-hours and after-hours programs, but all indications are that the lion's share is incurred for the during-hours segment. According to our projections, about 700,000 employees participated in internal courses after hours, but 3.7 million, more than five times as many, did so during hours. About one third of the latter group studied some aspect of management, supervision, or interpersonal relations; most of the rest studied technical or professional subjects or skills.

Larger firms tend to spend more per employee than smaller ones. Firms in our study with 5,000 or more employees spent about twice as much per employee as those with fewer than 1,000. Company size also influences how expenditures are apportioned among the four possible study situations. For example, smaller firms compensate for their lesser ability to support in-house training by making greater use of outside resources. Larger firms, which are more likely to have in-house staff and programs, actually spend fewer dollars per employee on outside resources than smaller firms.

Among firms of similar size, the prevalence and scope of education and training activities vary widely from industry to industry. This is due to differences in the ability of companies to absorb or pass on education and training costs; differences in management judgments about the benefits of education programs relative to their costs; differences in the degree to which employee populations are clustered or dispersed; differences in the availability and quality of outside educational resources; differences in the availability of already qualified people in the labor market; and, most important, differences in the configurations of skills and knowledge firms require and the rates at which these requirements change.

In addition to being aimed at workers and supported by employers, the corporate education system has three other characteristics that set it apart from more traditional education systems. The first characterisic is the unusually high motivation of its participants. All are adults in learning circumstances where they clearly perceive the rewards of success and penalties of failure. These rewards and penalties involve present and future earnings as well as prestige, self-esteem, and the realization of career goals. Because of the motivation and learning readiness of the learners, it is possible, as two industry educators recently put it, "to accept an educational philosophy which implies that responsibility for failure does not lie with the students ... but with the instructional staff and teaching materials."[1] It is also possible to make extensive use of programmed materials and self-instructional technologies.

A second characteristic of corporate education is that the workplace is the setting for both learning and doing. This means, for one thing, that the formal courses and other off-the-job instruction that one out of eight employees were involved in during 1975 are only the more visible and measurable parts of a far greater whole. Most employee learning takes place on the job—through private instruction and coaching by supervisors and peers and through observation, problem solving, and even trial and error. A good deal of this on-the-job training is planned. Employees may be taken through discrete and formal learning steps; many firms have courses to teach supervisors how to train; specialized training personnel and supportive materials may be used. Moreover, work experience may be integrated with classroom instruction in planned and often individualized and serialized sequences of theory and practice, formal learning and problem solving. It is by no means easy to distinguish work from learning in the corporate sphere.

The third characteristic of corporate education is its pragmatic orientation. It is an instrument for achieving business profit as well as individual growth and vitality, and it is accountable to a private and relatively narrow constituency. This role is part of a larger human-resource system that includes such activities as recruitment, selection, and placement; pay and other forms of compensation; and manpower planning. Through this system, companies seek to assure themselves of the present and future availability of competent employees. Corporate education is concerned with achieving limited and specific ends in the most economic and efficient way. Since paid time off the job is generally the most expensive aspect of employee education, efforts are made to keep courses as short as possible and to make maximum use of self-study materials, which can be used during off-duty hours. The length of company courses tends to be determined by no criterion other than what is needed to convey particular skills

[1] L. M. Branscomb and P. C. Gilmore, "Education in Private Industry," *Daedalus*, 1975, *104* (Winter): 229.

or knowledge to specific employees or groups. Courses or modules of just a few hours are common. ("Off-the-job instruction is given in small doses, as needed," one training official said.) Course content, related as it is to company problems, products, and processes, focuses on the particular rather than on the abstract, on the utilitarian rather than on the theoretical. Appropriately, much of this material is taught by operating specialists and managers rather than by professional educators.

Corporate education embraces not only instructors, education and training departments, classrooms, and even schools and a few residential learning centers, but countless other people and elements as well. The assessment of needs is almost always a responsibility of managers, who are helped and guided by trainers, manpower planners, and other human resource specialists. The processes of developing formal programs and administering them involve a variety of in-house professionals and technicians, particularly as teachers, and outside consultants as well. And providing the system with the evaluative data and judgments it requires for guidance requires the expertise of both managers and educational specialists.

Of course, how much employee education a company will undertake depends on necessity and cost efficiency. Much of the subject matter of in-house courses has to do with unique products and processes, with knowledge that exists only in the company or skills that can be mastered only in the context of actual operations. But the company official who said to me that "if we find it outside, we don't do it ourselves" was, perhaps, less than candid. The truth seems to be that, as company needs grow, the cost-efficiency scale begins to tip toward "making" rather than "buying." And where firms have had to put personnel, facilities, and programs in place to teach company skills—or even to orient new employees to company rules, policies, benefits, and safety procedures—the incremental costs of further programs have often been lower than the costs of acquiring them outside.

Management's judgments about the value of in-house programs also take into consideration benefits that cannot readily be quantified. Internal programs, for example, offer greater opportunity than external ones to shape the content, length, and methods of instruction to the needs of particular employees. Such programs also facilitate the integration of training with performance

appraisal and human resource planning systems. Company specialists may be the best available instructors. Courses may be scheduled for operational convenience or for such pedagogic purposes as
the phasing of classroom learning with on-the-job experience.
Internal programs also afford companies more opportunity to
establish controls and standards for employee performance in the
learning situation. They make it easier to find out how well learning is applied to the job and to make necessary course corrections.
They reduce or eliminate the need to share with outsiders confi-
dential company plans or other proprietary matters. And many
executives believe they tend to engender employee loyalties and
reduce turnover.

Few corporate executives believe that any appreciable portion of their company's programs include subjects or skills that, in
the language of the Conference Board's questionnaire, are "really
the responsibility of the schools to provide." Typically, these
spokesmen regard all or most of the education and training activities of their companies as legitimate and necessary business functions.

Most of them, nonetheless, are critical of the performance
of the nation's schools and colleges in preparing people for work.
They deplore particularly deficiencies among younger employees
in language and communications skills and mathematics. This is no
longer news, I know. What may be worth stressing, however, is
that the complaints of business executives about institutions have
to do much less with technical or professional preparation than
with general competencies—with the ability, even of those highly
schooled, to organize and present information and ideas, to relate
to other people sensitively and effectively, to plan and make decisions, and to connect theory with practice. Many would argue
that, although these deficiencies are seldom sufficient reason for
any of the company's educational activities, they do affect the
scope and character of such activities and, more important, detract
from the efficient performance of work tasks.

It is at least arguable that the special circumstances of corporate education and training—particularly its relatively uncompli-
cated goals—have made it easier for company people than for
others to go to the heart of certain educational matters because
they are less bound by traditional institutional constraints on
innovation. In any event, a large number of human resource execu-

tives in industry believe schools and colleges might profit by their example.

As instances of approaches and methods that merit wider application, these executives point to their growing emphasis on active student involvement in learning processes, ranging from simulation exercises to end-of-course critiques; on their efforts to tailor methods, course length, and curriculum to individual needs; and on their increased use of programmed materials and advanced instructional technologies. They place the greatest stress, however, on the importance of thinking through and specifying the desired outcomes of particular learning programs with respect to changes in the knowledge, behaviors, attitudes, or sensibilities of the learner. They emphasize the importance of making reasonable efforts to appraise results and make appropriate modifications, and they insist that this process is no less essential for music theory or American history than for business management.

Whether one views corporate education as merely a "shadow education system" or as an integral part of the education establishment, it cannot be ignored. As it continues to grow, it will raise some important questions for all who are concerned with education. We ought to begin asking—and answering—some of these questions now. For example, how legitimate are the complaints of business executives about the schools? How well founded are their claims to special methodological skills? Does the deep and growing involvement in education of interests concerned principally with profit pose new issues for society? What is the economic value to the individual of employment in companies with extensive education or training programs, and what are the implications for social equity of intercompany and interindustry differences in this regard? How important is it that communications be improved between industry and education and between the professionals and managers in both sectors, and how can such improvement be achieved? Can corporate education and training resources be put to wider or different uses than they are now, and should they be? Finally, will future growth be greater in the corporate sector than elsewhere and, if so, with what consequences to particular institutions and to education generally?

8

Work as a
Learning Experience

Ted Mills

Since the turn of the century, it has become a commonplace in industrial societies, and especially our own, to view work as essentially a function of economic performance. When we say "He works" or "She works," we tend either consciously or unconsciously to mean he or she is away from home performing some kind of human effort in return for some kind of economic reward, such as a wage or salary. And that wage or salary, in turn, is usually based on the economic return resulting from the work, calculated in units of product or service. Conversely, when we say people are "not working," or "out of work," we usually mean they are not occupied in a way that brings them income. A man may grunt and sweat all day weeding the garden or rebuilding the garage, but if he isn't being paid for his effort, he is not, in the prevailing view of things, working.

Nothing better illustrates the essentially absurd view of

work in our industrial society than our redundant term *working mother*. To most of us, a working mother is not a woman who puts forth the hard physical effort involved in keeping a house: cooking, marketing, cleaning, scrubbing, sewing, ironing, washing, chauffeuring, mending, and the often greater effort of psychologically coping with the random wants and needs of children and husbands. Such a woman is not working. She becomes a *working* mother only when she *also* goes off somewhere to engage in additional activities *for a salary*. Only when she performs an *economic* effort is she working. Working, we believe, is an exclusively economic act.

To most of us, largely without pondering the matter, "working" means employment for income. From this we have arrived, through a perverted twist of logic, at the conclusion that the main *purpose* of human work is economic gain. We talk at length about the "health of the economy," implying a belief that our purpose as a society is also economic. And of course the economic value systems we apply to ourselves we apply to other nations. We regard *their* economic strength (or lack of it) as an essential indicator of their social dynamism. As a nation we have risen to international prominence since the turn of the century, but in the process it appears that our aspirations for the American *economy*—economic growth, the acquisition of wealth, the accretion of profits and shopping malls—have become equivalent to the basic aspirations of American *society*.

It follows logically, like a check on payday, that we view the noun *work*—the human effort itself—as a *unit of economic performance*. Our businessmen and labor leaders, in curious unanimity, see human effort as a commodity, like magnesium or pig iron, in the productive mix of our economic might. "Management science" and its tributary subreligions of mechanism suggest that the worker is not an important concern of efficient management. What counts is the economic effort expended.

We seem to have forgotten that exclusively economic notions about human work and working have not always been the prevailing view of mankind. The output-paycheck-commodity definition of human work is actually a rather new idea, as history tells time. In fact, although many of us may be shocked at the suggestion, that definition may have already had its day in the sun and be on the verge of giving way to quite a different set of notions about human effort, as we shall examine. At the very least, it seems reasonable to suspect that the stringently economic view of human purpose may be just a passing moment in the long, long run of the human comedy.

If one attaches importance to language, one of the most telling clues to the temporal nature of the output-paycheck-commodity notion can be found in the dictionary. My dogeared 1942 edition of *Webster's New International Dictionary* patently refuses even to consider any economic notions about work. *Not once,* in eleven definitions of the noun *work* or in seven transitive and fourteen intransitive definitions of the verb *to work,* do Mr. Webster's conscientious lexicographers suggest considering work as a commodity for sale, or working as an economic act. Steadfastly, throughout the column and a half devoted to the term, they cling to the theme (with variations) that work is an "effort to accomplish something." This is a definition I feel quite sure unemployed mothers as well as physicists could live with comfortably. The dictionary's definition of the verb is particularly intriguing. The preferred definition is to "exert oneself for a purpose." But *Webster's* stubbornly refuses even to suggest that the purpose for exerting oneself might be economic.

The doubt-raising clues multiply as one examines notions about work in other cultures, and in other times and places. In *Le Mont St. Michel and Chartres,* Henry Adams notes that the thousands of artisans who for two centuries constructed these two monuments worked not for gold but for adoration of the Virgin Mary.[1] Claude Levi-Strauss and Margaret Mead, among others, have described pre- and nonindustrial cultures in which the value of human work is measured and compensated in terms of contribution to the community, with taboos and fetishes to formalize such measurement.[2] And in a now-classic chapter on "Buddhist Economics," E. F. Schumacher observes that from a Buddhist point of view, the prevalent output-paycheck-commodity Western view of work is "standing the truth on its head, by considering goods more important than people and consumption more impor-

---

[1]H. Adams, *Le Mont St. Michel and Chartres* (Boston: Houghton Mifflin, 1913).
[2]Claude Levi-Strauss, *L'Homme Nu* (Paris: Editions Plan, 1971), pp. 411-478.

tant than human creativity." He defines the Buddhist point of
view as conceiving the purpose of work to be threefold: "to give
man a chance to utilize and develop his faculties; to enable him to
overcome his ego-centeredness by joining with other people in a
common task; and (lastly) to bring forth goods and services
needed for a becoming existence." The Buddhist, he says, excori-
ating most industrial-age values in eighteen words, "sees the
essence of civilization not in a multiplication of wants but in the
purification of human character."[3] St. Augustine and John Calvin
—and countless millions of their contemporaries—similarly saw
human work as purification, as human striving for the glory of
God, and as a way of seeking a state of God's grace on earth.

Here are notions about work—using strange parts of our language like truth, God, purification, creativity, essence, grace,
becoming—wholly foreign to work cultures in most of twentieth-
century America; none would be a likely candidate for a contemporary stockholder's report. Out of other cultures in human history come clues to wholly different values attached to human
work, and diametrically opposed concepts of work's *purpose.*

Such evidence from dictionaries and from other cultures in
human history, however, could be judged by the pragmatic as
irrelevant today. But there is contemporary evidence that pure
economic purpose is not a primary goal for human effort even
now. The American Center for Quality of Work Life in Washington, for example, is currently involved in nine major organization-
wide work-improvement projects around the country. In each,
workers and managers functioning together in labor-management
committees at many levels have identified ways to improve life at
work and work performance for the benefit of all. In a 1976 project that began deep in the Oregon woods, 24 union workers and
managers were asked to describe at the outset what they hoped
work-reorganization would accomplish, in order of priority. Each
wrote out a list. From those lists, a fourteen-item list was developed that cited their aspirations in order of average ranking. Here
is what came out:

1. Improved working relationship between labor and management.

---

[3] E. F. Schumacher, *Small Is Beautiful: Economics as if People Mattered* (New York: Harper & Row, 1973).

2. Improved communications.
3. Improved working conditions.
4. Combined labor and management efforts to accomplish company goals.
5. Improved safety at work.
6. More satisfaction for people.
7. Creation of trust and a breaking down of prejudicial barriers.
8. Improved work environment.
9. Provision of new ways for every worker to solve day-to-day problems.
10. Improved jobs.
11. Improved quality of product.
12. Resolution of minor bitches.
13. Improved profit for the company.
14. Less supervision.

True, number thirteen on their list was an economic notion, and a sound one; improving the profit of their company increased the security of their jobs. But startlingly absent from all thirteen other points cited by those twenty-four employees and managers were any other purely economic goals. Startlingly present was a human—as distinct from economic—sense of their work's purpose. The goals important to them—better communication, trust, safety, problem solving, reduced supervision—were goals that concern people, not accountants. In fact, an accountant would have the devil's own time placing a dollar value on the human improvements those men sought for themselves in their place of work. (Accountants will, however, be able to measure the *impact* of such human goals on purely economic factors such as increased productivity.)

In another work restructuring project the Center was associated with, the workers and supervisors at an auto parts plant in Tennessee began to find that by cooperating they could do an amount of work that previously took eight hours in considerably less time. Intrigued with their achievement, they invented the term *earned idle time* to describe it. But instead of seeking extra pay, management and workers together decided to create an in-plant school for their earned idle time, a school to improve not their work-related skills but their human skills in languages, music appreciation, cooking, and the like. With almost uncanny accuracy, and presumably with no such thought in mind, they were applying Schumacher's Buddhist view of human work. For they found that by overcoming "self-centeredness by joining with others in a common task" while bringing forth goods "needed for a becoming existence," they gave themselves a "chance to utilize and develop their human faculties"[4]—all in a rural town in Tennessee in the 1970s without a Buddhist in sight.

Here's still another clue. The voice is that of a single, deliberately out-of-work Vietnam veteran. The tone is one of seeking: "I could walk out of here tomorrow morning and get a job doing something. You can always get a job. People who are concerned about income are basing their self-worth on what they own as opposed to what they are. I would rather be able to say that my self-image is based on what I'm worth as a person, not worth in dollars. Anybody can have dollars. If I wanted to have dollars, I could just go out and deal dope and I'd have more money than the president of GM. . . . People are bored with their jobs, with their lives. . . . So by not working, I'm not bored."[5] Some of us might consider an attitude like this a little crazy. But this young veteran —and a growing number of his age-peers—just might suggest that the shoe belongs on the other foot.

Some have suggested that a massive value shift in our society began at the height of the Vietnam war in the late 1960s, when the worldwide revolt of youth in industrial societies against the "system" exploded. Others, perhaps more accurately, might refer to the Arab oil embargo of 1973 as a symbolic date when the first major fissures in American certainty about economic gain as the purpose of society appeared. Still others have pointed to the explosion of "industrial democracy" in Europe in the early 1970s as the telltale sign of a gathering new era. In any event, by 1977 that value shift had many labels. Alvin Toffler called it "future shock."[6] Sociologist Daniel Bell, writing the epitaph for the industrial age, called the arriving one "the postindustrial age."[7] The brilliant industrial anatomist Peter Drucker saw us in the midst of an "age of discontinuity," a halfway house to what he called "a learning society."[8]

[4]Schumacher, *Small Is Beautiful.*
[5]B. Benderly, "Not Working," *Potomac Magazine,* February 6, 1977.
[6]A. Toffler, *Future Shock* (New York: Random House, 1973).
[7]D. Bell, *The Coming of Post-Industrial Society* (New York: Basic Books, 1973).
[8]P. Drucker, *The Age of Discontinuity* (New York: Harper & Row, 1969).

In 1977, Henry Ford II, reputed neither as sage nor out-spoken foe of economic purpose, told the *New York Times* that we as a nation were entering a period of "capitalism on trial," that "the days of high, wide and handsome economic growth are over, and that isn't all bad, since we've been outliving our means for twenty years."[9]

During his presidential campaign, Jimmy Carter reiterated poet Bob Dylan's observation that "we're not busy dying" but "busy being born." On election day, he announced that the focus of his administration would be "human aspirations" throughout the world, and to the consternation of Moscow, he demonstrated that focus in a letter to Russian Nobel prizewinner Andrei Sakharov. Were these the first official sounds of the new age? Few believed it, except perhaps the man who was making them.

Webster and Schumacher, a handful of Oregonians and Tennesseans, Toffler, Bell, and Drucker, the grandson of Henry Ford, and the new President of the United States, like randomly-selected, small telltale pieces of an unfinished picture puzzle, suggest that perhaps when the puzzle is put together, it may look quite different from what the economics-as-usual crowd anticipates. Compared to the massive weight and momentum of a trillion-dollar gross national product and the giant social commitments to economic purpose it symbolizes, these voices and events seem infinitesimal, tiny trickles of evidence. Yet collectively, they bespeak much more: a growing cause for reasonable doubt about whether the economic purpose that steered us through the first three quarters of this century can be relied on in the fourth.

The operative ethic of the moulting industrial age could perhaps best be summarized by the verb *to have* and all its attendant lesser verbs of gain, played contrapuntally against the values inherent in the verb *to be*.[10] Having is objective, and essentially measured in things; being is subjective and quantitatively unmeasurable. Having is essentially external to basic human experience; being *is* human experience.

The American love affair with having began to gain momentum over two centuries ago and has picked up speed rapidly ever since. In fact, American immersion in the having ethic occurred so

[9]*New York Times,* February 16, 1977, p. 27.
[10]See E. Fromm, *To Have or To Be* (New York: Harper & Row, 1976).

fast that it would take other industrialized societies almost an additional half century to catch up. Most did not reach anything resembling parity until after World War II, when they took the quantum leap into made-in-USA ambitions of consumption and production, which many of them would characterize as the "Americanization" of their cultures. We became what historian Charles Beard would later characterize as the first "business civilization."

It is worth pausing to defend much in the having ethic, for it has much to recommend it. It builds. It acquires. It creates. It is dynamic and moving, not static and immobile. It seeks (in the physical world). It induces vision and acts to implement that vision. The having ethic sees possibilities, and makes them happen, for profit. It gets. And to its practitioners, the search itself is often more exciting than the find.

Yet for all the kinetic vitality in it, since the earliest civilizations, the having ethic has generally been viewed pejoratively by human societies. All societies punish stealing, an act of instant having. The Bible announces as a fact that it is "easier for a camel to go through a needle's eye than for a rich man to enter the Kingdom of God."[11] Freud called it anal and castigated individuals exclusively concerned with having as neurotic, mentally sick persons.[12] Much of the world's literature seeks to reveal the hollowness and emptiness in naked having.

The full, gung-ho pursuit of having should (to be true to itself) brook no deterrent to its ends; it should not pause to be nice. Such being values as generosity, compassion, goodness, integrity, charity, forgiveness, trust, or simple faith in humanity can— and often do—get in the way of efficiency and its resultant profit. Whether consciously or unconsciously, while we are at work we tend to act as if such unprofitable feelings do not or should not exist. We are aided in this specious process by the curious objective-subjective difference between having and being. Although having is instantly quantifiable in dollars, acres, or units, aspects of being are quite unmeasurable: being is a wholly inner-experienced set of unquantifiable feelings such as love or hatred. In the absence of statistical proof that they exist, we often prefer simply to

[11]Matt. 12:24.
[12]Fromm, *To Have or To Be*, p. 84.

assume that the being values are unreal, an imagined domain of the poet, sentimentalist, and do-gooder. We forget we are human. And in so doing—particularly in our educational process, as examined later—we run ourselves into a heap of trouble. For we run into the having-being conflict of self-interests, which Dickens immortalized in his character Scrooge.

A good many of us, particularly in the output-paycheck-commodity world of economic purpose, find ourselves leading a double-standard ethical life. At work, in the having mode, we tend to treat our humanity as if it were extraneous to work. Yet at home most of us seek the being mode, filling our needs for loving and being loved, which we feel empty and unfulfilled without.

Fromm described being as "being active, not in the sense of outward activity, or 'busyness,' but of inner activity and the productive use of our human powers."[13] Being includes those aspects of human activity that are *uniquely* human—all that is instinctive, intuitive, felt, and subjective (measurable only by the individual experiencing it). Having is at best amoral, but being is in the domain of human morality. There is the dignity of human reason in being—it is reflected in our laws—but there is also the wonder of human irrationality and feeling, as is shown in our art and our capacity for loving. The energy of having creates banks, markets, palaces, and territorial empires; the energy of being creates religions, hospitals, cathedrals, and democracies.

Learning is a being experience, and throughout civilized history the school and the church have been the protectors and promulgators of the being ethic. Separately or together, these two institutions have served as both teacher and repository, both warder and fount of human experience and human morality. The cloister, removed in time and space from the having hurly-burly, has been the natural locus of the being ethic.

Until just yesterday, as history tells time, this locus-of-being identity of the school and university obtained in all human civilizations. Even though the privilege of seeking knowledge was largely, until yesterday, reserved to an elite few in each society, the quest itself has always been highly regarded; learning has throughout history been a prize of great status and esteem. One of the basic drives of American society has been its insistence on provid-

[13]Fromm, p. 88.

ing an education for its native and immigrant children, and creating an educated, wise, informed society.

Then, suddenly, in the three decades since World War II, that basic drive erupted into a literal revolution in education in the United States, a phenomenon that is one of the extraordinary social transformations of this century or any other. We entered the period of "mass education."

Quantitatively, that explosion in American education can be measured in an exponentially accelerating student population. Almost overnight, the old elitist stereotype of the student as predominantly white, young, male, and affluent was virtually eliminated. The poor, the nonwhite, the middle-aged, and the elderly were encouraged by our society to educate themselves, and they did, by the millions, and are still doing so. In 1950, only two out of five American youngsters starting their work life were high-school graduates; today, four out of five young Americans, white and nonwhite, enter the workforce with a high-school diploma. In higher education, the growth phenomenon was even more dramatic. It was evident not only in the exponential increase in student populations in public and private universities and the proliferation of new community colleges, but in new faculties, new buildings and facilities, new campuses, new curricula, and new disciplines. No society had ever witnessed such a quantitative leap forward in educational availability as ours did in the three decades following World War II. While traditionalists lament, a vast transformation of education in America—a change in the very meaning, nature, and purpose of learning in an increasingly egalitarian society—has taken place under our noses.

Qualitatively, the transformation of the nature of American education was almost as great, but there was less to be proud of. Almost as suddenly as the quantitative explosion itself—and quite probably because of it—the American learning institution began to lose its locus-of-being character. After half a century of banging on the cloister door (with John Dewey standing guard against the incursion), the having ethic and its attendant economic value systems suddenly moved in and began to spread across the American campus. Our two-hundred-year-old national obsession with economic purpose planted itself firmly into our educational value systems. The notion of "education" as a pragmatic set of skills devoted to the exercise of having began to distort the purpose of learning in the United States—up to and including the Ph.D. The merchant ethic had finally invaded education, American-style. And with it came brigades of new merchantmen faculties and new merchant curricula teaching "how to" relevance. The deformation of our institutions of learning into factories for vocational training in having skills had begun.

Although I have been able to find no useful statistics to prove it, I suspect that an impressive majority of the students in our schools today would claim that learning how to perform better in the economic domain has become the primary and, to many, the sole purpose of their "education." And our new mass-education institutions have responded accordingly. More ominously, the promise of supplying such having skills has become a primary means to attract students to financially precarious institutions. Harried university executives admit that enrollments in the new merchant curricula not only provide basic support for their institutional budgets, but actually significantly support the ever-shrinking faculties and curricula still devoted to the old locus-of-being purposes of education.

It is too early to tell whether the merchant disfigurement of our institutions is a permanent or transitory phenomenon. There are, however, already some intriguing signposts of serious and growing social dysfunctions stemming directly from it. One signpost is the sheer volume of educational output: the new graduates. In union circles, one increasingly hears a growing lament that our economic machine is creating more dumb jobs than there are dumb people to fill them. Already, a surprising number of blue-collar hourly employees are college-educated.

Another signpost is the significant increase in frustrated expectations of young people. I often hear my children's friends complain, as they loll about morosely on unemployment income, that "the system" (which, for some reason, they believe owes them a living) has no acceptable place for their college-honed merchant skills. They grumble, quite correctly, that they wasted years of their young adulthood (and, they rarely add, some $20,000 to $30,000 of their parents' or somebody's money), learning how to be executives, only to find out that industry cannot meet their expectations. The producers of American goods and services have good reason to complain that we are alarmingly "overeducating" our young citizens, but they are using the wrong words. Our students are not overeducated. They are *overtrained* in the merchant ethic and deluded by that overtraining into untenable economic expectations. Actually, educators at every level of our schools are justifiably concerned that America's young people are becoming seriously, perhaps critically, *undereducated.*

Drastically diminished reading and writing skills testify to a whole syndrome of qualitative decay in the American institution of learning: *the growing absence of education in our education.* Some educators blame the undereducation of our youth on television, with its overload of distracting, titillating pap. Some trace the problem to the mass-education revolution, and its powerful downward tug on older academic standards of excellence. Some have blamed the sixties-bred permissiveness of frequently absurd "elective" systems. Some have put the blame on student (and parent) demands for pragmatic, dollar-winning "relevance" in what an education should provide in return for its ever higher costs. But such explanations miss the basic point, or avoid it. The point is that educational *purpose* has changed from the old being values to the new, "relevant" having values. Undereducation is the social fallout of that value change. By turning our institutions of learning in ever larger measure into vocational centers dominated by sheer economic purpose, our educators have, to a considerable degree, foresworn the age-old purpose of learning: the search for being. And without understanding why, our undereducated young are saying no thanks through a multitude of rebellious behaviors. To accuse our schools of selling out to the merchant ethic may be too strong, but the tendency and trend are there.

There is another signpost of evident social dysfunction that may bode well for all of us, including our ethically troubled learning institutions. Paradoxically, this indicator is in the economic system itself. It is a changing concept of work in industrial society and of the purpose of work out there in havingland. During the late 1960s, the producers of things and services began to find their workers (a growing number of them the grumbling young products of the "relevant" new education) increasingly turned off at work. There are many reasons why,[14] but almost all of them are *noneconomic.* Almost all are "being" reasons: attitudes, feelings,

[14]See T. Mills, "Human Resources: Why the New Concern?" *Harvard Business Review,* March-April 1975, pp. 120-134.

angers, frustrations, expectations. And almost all have a negative impact on economic performance.

The past few years, a growing number of troubled producers in the economy, particularly in the most conspicuously well-managed public and private-sector organizations, have begun to discover that far more careful attention to the being ethic at work has measurable payoffs in industrial effectiveness. To the astonishment of many having-ethic traditionalists in business, some notions about work sounding strangely like Schumacher's have crept into labor and industrial relations, *and worked.*

In March 1977, George Morris, vice president of industrial relations for General Motors, said in a speech to the Society of Automotive Engineers: "When we began applying organizational development principles about seven years ago, our focus was on improving organizational effectiveness. We saw improvement in the work climate as naturally flowing from these efforts. I think now we have reversed those objectives. Our primary objective is improving the quality of work life. We feel that by concentrating on the quality of work life, and wisely managing the systems that lead to greater job satisfaction and feelings of self-worth, improvements in the effectiveness of the organization will follow."

In Europe, a similar kind of societal movement has been taking place. Operating under many aliases, this movement is perhaps best known by the term *industrial democracy.* Unlike the U.S. effort, the European movement was political; its output was not speeches to the Society of Automotive Engineers about wholly voluntary union-management agreements, but laws—legislative mandates seeking to join the having ethic and the being ethic in European industry into a new kind of "democratic" industrial ethic. The result, a blend of economic efficiency (having) and social equity (being) was remarkably like the employee-manager goal articulated by General Motors.

In the economic language of supply and demand, increasingly our educational-turned-vocational institutions are supplying more and more of what people at work (and the work organizations they work for) need less and less, or can get better and more effectively in on-job training in their place of work. Put conversely—and perhaps more accurately—what our high school and college graduates will be needing more and more at work is exactly what they have been getting less and less of at school at every level: a taste of human wisdom, an understanding of inner, human needs, the meaning of self-worth. If this double-direction trend continues, as seems likely, we will be tragically undereducating the coming generation of Americans in the very stuff of learning that generation will—and has already begun to—demand from the work experience.

If educators do not perceive or heed the signals coming loud and clear from the society, there is a distinct possibility that the workplace will slowly become the locus-of-being repository of postindustrial society, and working will become the learning experience of that society. In this scenario, our long-standing veneration for "education" will dwindle to nothing, and many of the mercantile colossi we still call "learning" institutions will become extinct. In deserved financial ruin, American education might then shrink towards excellence again, restoring its old locus-of-being purpose.

Far-fetched? Perhaps—and perhaps not. "Work as a learning experience" is already a reality in workplaces across the United States. GM's Morris called it "quality of work life," which he equated with learning to provide "feelings of self-worth" to employees. An example of this trend in action is the fourteen points identified by those twenty-four woodworkers and supervisors in Oregon (who call their activity a "quality-of-work-life" effort). Recalling just a few is enough to prove the being focus of work as a learning experience:

1. Improved working relationship between management and labor. (*Or learning how to work with, not for one another in a cooperative win-win sense of purpose.*)
2. Improved communications. (*Or learning new ways, methods, systems to keep everyone informed of what is happening and why.*)
3. Improved working conditions. (*Or seeking and learning ways to improve the quality of human experience physically and emotionally while at work.*)
4. Combining labor and management efforts to accomplish company goals. (*Or learning by all what those goals are, and how each individual and all together can help achieve them.*)

And so on, through all fourteen. This is learning not of the output-paycheck-commodity brand at all, in which the worker learns his task and no more, but learning how to satisfy *human* needs and aspirations *along with* economic needs and aspirations. It is learning in which the teachers are one's peers, the classroom is the workplace, and there is no written text—experiential learning, being learning, human (not humanoid) learning.

The term *quality of working life* has been rapidly gaining acceptance by both management and union communities in the United States and Europe to describe this learning phenomenon. As a term it is awkward, but its use of two words—*quality* and *life*—identify its being focus. As its practitioners perceive it, the term *quality of work life* could be defined as faith in the capacities of human nature, faith in human intelligence and the power of pooled and collective experience. It is not belief that these things are complete, but that if given a show, they will grow and generate the knowledge and wisdom needed to guide collective action.

It is at least fitting, in closing these thoughts of having and being, to give credit to the author of the definition of quality of work life above. The author was John Dewey, in his classic *Democracy and Education,* a synergism he devoted his professional life to fighting for.[15] It is also fitting to note that his definition was not of quality of work life at all. The term had not yet been invented in 1928, when he wrote his book. It is Dewey's definition of democracy, that ultimate social expression of the being ethic.

[15]J. Dewey, *Democracy and Education* (New York: Macmillan, 1929).

9

Three Factors of Success

George O. Klemp, Jr.

At thousands of commencement exercises held annually in America, college students receive degrees for attending the required number of courses and are welcomed into the fellowship of educated men and women. Their experience of higher education, it is commonly held, has better prepared them for a career and life. Yet soon after embarking on their new careers and lives, these graduates discover that the knowledge and ability acquired in school are not enough, that something is missing in their preparation that prevents them from translating what they have learned into effective performance. Actual work experience is part of the answer, of course, but neither experience nor knowledge is a guarantee of individual success.

Within the walls of academe, practically everyone has a theory about what ought to be learned in college, but relatively few educators have been able to test their hypotheses in the world outside. As director of research for a behavioral science consulting firm, I have had the opportunity to examine this problem from the perspective of both the employer and the educator. Over the past five years, we have tried to identify the kind of knowledge, skills, abilities, and other characteristics that are tied to effective performance. Our approach, which has been more empirical than theoretical, consists of three steps: first, identify individuals who are successful in a variety of occupations and professional roles; second, find out what they are doing that makes them successful; and third, examine how and why they are doing what they do. Our study has involved people in career areas as diverse as human service work, the military, alcohol abuse counseling, small business, police work, process consulting, sales, the State Department, the civil service, and industry management. Through a combination of direct observation, interviewing, and direct assessment, we have been able to identify a number of important characteristics that effective performers possess. In reporting our findings, my emphasis is not so much on the characteristics that are necessary for acceptable performance as on those characteristics that clearly distinguish the outstanding performer from his or her less effective counterpart. We have also tried to determine what effects postsecondary institutions have had on the development of these characteristics.

Our most consistent—though unexpected—finding is that the amount of knowledge one acquires of a content area is generally unrelated to superior performance in an occupation and is often unrelated even to marginally acceptable performance. Certainly many occupations require a minimum level of knowledge on the part of the individual for the satisfactory discharge of work-related duties, but even more occupations require only that the individual be willing and able to learn new things. Since most of the specific knowledge acquired in the classroom is forgotten in a year or two anyway, there must be something about the learning process itself that accounts for the differences between the effective and ineffective performer. In fact, it is neither the acquisition of knowledge nor the use of knowledge that distinguishes the outstanding performer, but rather the *cognitive skills* that are developed and exercised in the process of acquiring and using knowledge. These cognitive skills constitute the first factor of occupational success.

The cognitive skills most familiar to psychologists and educators are the information-processing skills related to learning, recall, and forgetting. These, however, are not as important to success as cognitive skills that involve the ability to conceptualize. These conceptualizing skills enable individuals to bring order to the informational chaos that constantly surrounds them. Such skills go beyond an ability to analyze, which consists of the identification of parts; they involve an ability to synthesize information from a prior analysis through a process of induction.

One of these cognitive skills that is particularly important to managers is the ability to see thematic consistencies in diverse information and to organize and communicate this perception. New information is thereby created in the sense that a "signal" has been extracted from the "noise." People who are thought to be good at problem solving or are merely described as intuitive are really just good at conceptual thinking. They are able to organize and present complex information thematically and logically.

A related cognitive skill—one that is especially useful whenever people take part in negotiations—is the ability to understand many sides of a controversial issue. Conflicting information results in a kind of cognitive dissonance that some people are better at resolving than others. Those who are able to see things conceptually understand both the underlying issue and the different perspectives on it. This allows them to resolve informational conflicts better than people who are unable to conceptualize in this way. The less conceptual individuals typically resolve dissonance by denying the validity of other points of view and are ill equipped to mediate disputes. These people, who may appear dogmatic and unreceptive, are simply unable to understand what their positions have in common with the positions of others.

Finally, a cognitive skill often taken for granted is the ability to learn from experience. Found in the most effective process consultants and workers in human services, this is the ability to translate observations from work experience into a theory that can be used to generate behavioral alternatives. The information that is conceptualized looks very different from facts and figures gleaned from memoranda, articles, or lectures. This skill involves participating in an experience and analyzing one's behavior in the context of the behavior of others People who excel at experiential learning tend not only to be more astute observers of behavior but also to recognize that direct experience is an important primary learning mode. It is indispensable, for example, in work that involves helping and counseling others.

Cognitive skills, because of their association with the attainment of knowledge, have been the primary focus of postsecondary educators. Perhaps because of this emphasis, colleges have left virtually untouched another area of process skills that may be characterized as *interpersonal skills.* These skills are the second factor linked with success in the world of work. When interpersonal skills have been consciously introduced into the curriculum, they have usually appeared as communication skills. The word *communication,* however, is so broad in its connotative meanings as to encompass all observable behavior, and so narrow in its practical meaning as to include only speaking and writing skills. Fluency and precision in verbal communication is important, of course, but often it is the nonverbal component of communication, both in sending and receiving information, that has the greater impact.

We have found that the interpersonal skills most closely related to effective performance on the job are related to the communication process. For lack of a better word, I shall refer to one of these skills as *accurate empathy.* This is a vague term on the surface, yet it means specific things for the effective performer. It means that when someone says, "I am depressed," the listener does not simply conclude that the person is indeed depressed. Nor does accurate empathy mean the actual sharing of feelings, a state more appropriately described as sympathy. Instead, accurate empathy may be defined as both the *diagnosis* of a human concern (based on what a person says and how he or she behaves) and as the appropriate *response* to the needs of the person. Contrary to popular belief, there is nothing magical about being empathic; one simply interprets and acts on cues that are constantly given off by others. People who are accomplished at this skill are effective in professions that involve working with individuals in a helping role but are also effective in communicating with fellow workers in any work situation. Accurate empathy helps clients and coworkers understand what is being said or done in a way that makes them feel that they are themselves understood.

One reason that accurate empathy is related to occupational success is that the client or coworker is apt to feel stronger and better able to cope as a result of the interaction. This interpersonal skill promotes feelings of efficacy in another person. There are three aspects to this skill. One is a positive regard for others, the belief that people are capable of doing good things with a bit of support and encouragement. For example, it has been documented in the classroom that positive expectations of students result in better student performance.[1] Workers whose expectations are positive and high are also more likely to behave in ways that encourage and reward the people with whom they come in contact. The second aspect of promoting feelings of efficacy involves giving another person assistance, either solicited or unsolicited, that enables the other person to be effective. The third aspect involves an individual's ability to control impulsive feelings of hostility or anger that, when unleashed on another person, make that other person feel powerless and ineffective. The least successful managers and military officers try to motivate their subordinates by "chewing them out." In the end, such behavior infuses the work climate with a negative, unpredictable and often punitive character.

The cognitive and interpersonal skills of which I have spoken, although demonstrably related to effectiveness in work, do not by themselves guarantee success for the person who possesses them. The mere possession of these skills does not ensure that they will be used and does not determine how they will be used. Throughout our research into what makes some people more effective in their work than others, a third factor was undeniably present—*motivation*. Although *motivation* is a very broad term that encompasses everything that drives an individual, there are particular aspects of motivation related to career performance, aspects that reflect individual needs as well as characteristic ways of thinking about the world.

Careers that offer an individual the possibility of doing something new and original, such as those of the scientist, entrepreneur, or planner, are populated with people who have a high need for efficiency, a need to do something better than it has ever been done before. People motivated in this way set high standards of performance for themselves and work to meet these standards rather than standards set by others. Their rewards lie primarily in

[1] R. R. Rosenthal and L. Jacobsen, *Pygmalion in the Classroom* (New York: Holt, Rinehart and Winston, 1968).

the satisfaction that comes from accomplishing something unique, rather than in the money that may be earned in the process. Among the skills they demonstrate are the ability to take moderate risks to achieve maximum gain for the costs incurred, the ability to set time-phased, realistic goals, and the ability to seek information to use as feedback on their performance. Scientists and engineers need a high level of these skills for even acceptable performance, and certain types of businesspeople can become outstanding performers through their use.

In contrast, people whose careers require them to get other people to do things, are likely to have a high need to influence others. This need for power, which is characteristic of managers, sales people, military leaders, and the like, manifests itself most effectively when the individual does things for the good of the organization rather than for personal gain. People who need this kind of power think in terms of influence through service. Rather than being primarily competitive and assertive, they view their power as a shared resource. Some of the skills demonstrated by people concerned with this kind of power are the ability to learn interpersonal influence networks and use them to do their jobs, the ability to influence others by sharing with them a superordinate goal, and the ability to identify work-group coalitions in terms of their level in the hierarchy and their orientation to the goals of the organization. The most effective military officers, government officials, sales managers and executives possess a greater concern for and demonstrate a more consistent use of this form of power than do their less effective counterparts.

It does not necessarily follow that an orientation toward efficiency or influence will lead to success. Motivation is, after all, a need state—a prerequisite for behavior—and for a variety of reasons people are often unable to translate their dispositions into effective action. Recent research strongly suggests that *cognitive initiative*—the way one defines oneself as an actor in the motive-action sequence—is an important variable. This variable describes a person who habitually thinks in terms of causes and outcomes as opposed to one who sees the self as an ineffective victim of events that have an unknown cause. It has been empirically demonstrated, for instance, that women who think of themselves in terms of cause-action-effect sequences are more successful in careers ten years after college than women who do not think of themselves as the link in the cause-effect chain.[2] Our own analysis of complex managerial jobs and the people in them has shown that a person who takes a *proactive* stance, who initiates action and works to dissolve blocks to progress, will, with few exceptions, have the advantage over a person who is *reactive,* who does not seek new opportunities, but sees the world as a series of insurmountable obstacles. From the evidence available, certain habitual thought patterns, like motivation, may be causally related to effective behavior in work and in life.

Our analyses of successful performers in a variety of occupations have brought us to the conclusion that the cognitive, interpersonal, and motivational factors discussed here are critical to effective performance. But having identified these factors, we must ask whether postsecondary education has a positive effect on their development within the individual. Some of the results are already in, and they are mixed.[3] It appears that the major impact of a college education is on the development of cognitive skills. Differences among students and colleges in this regard are large, but, in general, individuals are better able to think conceptually after the undergraduate experience than before. By contrast, neither interpersonal skills nor motivation appear to be altered by a college education. In light of the observations we have made about the skills that are related to success in the world of work, this finding is disappointing indeed.

Is higher education doomed to be ineffective in furthering the development of critical work and life skills? Or can postsecondary institutions hope to meet the skills requirements of the future? Based on the evidence to date, the cognitive, interpersonal, and motivational attributes of successful performers can all be observed in behavior, and *all of these skills can be taught.* Group interaction and programmed instruction techniques have been useful in teaching interpersonal skills.[4] Curricula have been designed

[2] A. J. Stewart and D. G. Winter, "Self-Definition and Social Definitions in Women," *Journal of Personality,* 1974, *42*: 238-259.

[3] D. G. Winter, D. C. McClelland, and A. J. Stewart, "Competence in College: Evaluating the Liberal University" (Unpublished monograph, Wesleyan University, 1977).

[4] L. P. Bradford, J. R. Gibb, and K. D. Beane (Eds.), *T-Group Theory and Laboratory Method* (New York: Wiley, 1967). R. Carkhuff, *Helping and Human Relations,* 2 vols. (New York: Holt, Rinehart and Winston, 1969).

to develop motivation.[5] Much of the technology involved in realizing these ends has been available for years. Most educators, however, have assumed that these skills would develop as by-products of an education in the liberal arts, and so this technology has seldom been implemented. The weight of recent evidence suggests that this assumption is not valid.

Some colleges, referring to themselves as "competency-based" or "outcome-oriented," have been working hard to change this state of affairs. One of the things they are doing, which other institutions would do well to emulate, is carefully defining the objectives of their curriculum. Rather than specifying learning outcomes in terms of required course loads, they are concentrating on communication, analysis, problem solving, and social interaction and are experimenting with more interactive, experiential modes of instruction than the lecture presentation. Acquisition of knowledge in a particular major content area is still an important part of these programs, but it is no longer an end in itself. These colleges measure their own success by their students' abilities to perform and to participate. Even if these colleges are only partially successful, the expanded concept of a liberal arts education that will result can only benefit the students of the future.

I observed earlier that the more enduring outcomes of higher education are the cognitive processes that develop as a function of the acquisition of knowledge, rather than the knowledge itself. Keeping this in mind, we need to turn away from the traditional view of process in the service of content and look instead to content in the service of process. Cognitive skills, interpersonal skills and motives are processes that enable individuals to apply their knowledge base to new life and work situations. In order for postsecondary education to nurture these processes, our notions of what constitutes a good curriculum will have to undergo radical change. We must be willing to use our findings from the world of work and to accept a new perspective on the purpose of higher education. If we can do this, perhaps we can truly begin to initiate the graduates of the future into the fellowship of educated men and women.

[5]R. DeCharms, *Enhancing Motivation* (New York: Irvington, 1976). D. C. McClelland and D. G. Winter, *Motivating Economic Achievement* (New York: Free Press, 1969).

Education, Work, and FIPSE

Russell Edgerton

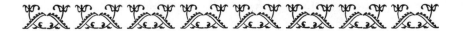

I am going to give a brief overview of what the Fund for the Improvement of Postsecondary Education (FIPSE) has done with $42 million, allocated over four annual grant cycles to 380 separate improvement projects. The majority of these struggled with some facet or other of the many problems and issues involved in relating education and work. I have elected to emphasize three things.

The first is defining where the action is—and is not—in the whole area of education and work. The Fund is (among federal agencies, at least) the most open, comprehensive, and responsive source of funding there is. Our guidelines give the applicant the initiative for defining both the particular problem to be addressed and the approach to be taken. So, while the approximately 2,000 proposals submitted to us each year are not a perfect mirror of the interest in improvement, they do give a good idea of the trends at work and the kind of problems people are chasing.

Second, from the best of these proposals and from our ongoing projects, we learn what effective practices are being developed in response to the persistent problems people are tackling. It is like watching new products coming on line. I do not have space here to describe any single practice in depth, but I will try to identify the kind of practices that are emerging.

I should add that we are chary about endorsing any particular approach out of context. We find that the quality of our projects lies less in the novelty of their approach than in the effectiveness of their implementation. There is no magic, no intrinsic merit, to competency-based education, community-based counseling services, outreach programs to adults, or any other approaches we have supported. The quality lies in the particulars.

Third, I will try to make a few general observations about the entire range of projects attempting to relate education and work.

To do these things, I need to discuss proposals and funded projects. I have organized the discussion into three parts, around the three broad problems people are confronting in relating education and work: (1) providing new avenues for out-of-school adults, routing them back into education and through education to work opportunities; (2) providing new avenues for youth who are typically in school and need to get into contact with work; and (3) helping people who are struggling, not with the problems of access to new opportunities, but with problems of substance and outcomes. What is it that people need to learn in order to perform more effectively in work and other adult roles?

By far, the greatest number of proposals submitted to us about education and work have concerned the plight of the out-of-school adult. The quest of women to change and improve their lives is being felt everywhere, and education is an obvious means. The higher education enterprise knows it is running short on young people to fill the classrooms. The scramble is on, and we have seen the interest build each year.

We have received a considerable number of ideas from colleges and universities seeking to bring about internal reforms and adjustments. Typically, these are ideas for improving supportive services (such as the creation of a women's center), for changing schedules, for breaking down the organizational distinctions between continuing education and regular, day time education, and other measures designed to treat adults more as first-class citizens.

We have received a great number of proposals for moving educational services out beyond the campus into new settings. Just as banks have opened drive-in windows, local branches, and twenty-four-hour checking services, colleges and universities have proposed satellite centers in libraries and other locations, courses on television, and videotapes for showing in homes and other settings, weekend colleges, courses on the morning commuter train, and other schemes designed to provide education on terms more convenient to adults.

And we have received proposals from a variety of noncollegiate institutions—fraternal societies, service organizations, local governments, unions, hospitals—for providing new services to adults.

The most common deficiency in all these proposals is that they do not focus on real human needs. Many are from colleges and universities making their first moves toward what they sense is a new market. An approach is proposed, but it is not derived from being in touch with the feelings and interests of particular adults.

The better proposals, which we have funded, address one or a set of clearly perceived needs. I will mention three particular needs and indicate some effective practices that seem to be emerging from these projects.

We are talking about individuals in transition—mainly women searching for personal and career changes. Many of their educational needs cluster around the difficulty of taking the first steps toward improving their situation: determining what it is they really want to do; understanding their abilities; finding information about available educational and work opportunities; realizing they are not alone, and getting support from people like themselves; talking to someone who not only tells them where to go, but helps to overcome the bureaucratic obstacles that can so easily deter them.

We have supported some thirty to forty projects intended, in one way or another, to help adults get started. Some, such as the Oregon Career Information project, do not rely on counselors as the linkage agents. In this project, an individual could go right to a computer terminal located in a shopping center and question the computer about both employment opportunities throughout the state and educational programs that would prepare one for these employment opportunities. But most of our projects have involved setting up staff to act as "educational brokers."

These staffs operate in various settings. Some are based right in the community and are affiliated with free-standing agencies, such as the Regional Learning Service of Central New York. Some, such as the Regional Educational Consortium for Women in Philadelphia, are sustained by a consortium of colleges. Some are part of centers or new units within a particular college, such as the Women's Opportunity Research Center at Middlesex Community College in Massachusetts or the School for New Learning at DePaul University in Illinois. Finally, the faculty in a number of experimental institutions, such as Empire State College in New York, Minnesota Metropolitan State University in Minnesota, and Vermont Community College, have shifted into facilitative and counseling roles that involve them in educational brokering.

Looking over this whole group of projects, I am impressed, first of all, with what we have learned about the kind of people who can do effective counseling. Many of the new centers we have helped establish have had a hard time settling down and defining the particular blend of counseling and information-providing that is most cost-effective. The free-standing agencies have had a devil of a time tapping into ongoing sources of support. But their lack of structure has also been their greatest strength—for they have been able to identify and recruit an extraordinary number of effective counselors *from the community*. These, by and large, have been individuals who have not had formal training as counselors but rather are engaged, active, caring human beings who want to help others and are willing to learn how to do it. Some broker part-time, others full-time. Few see brokering as a career.

This is significant. Counseling is the Achilles heel in providing effective opportunities for both education and work. Historically, our efforts to institutionalize counseling have led us to a situation in which thousands of uninspired people sit in their offices with their card files wondering why people do not come see them. There are important exceptions, but I have rarely talked to a student or anyone else who has been especially eager to seek out a high school guidance counselor, a college placement officer, or a bureaucrat in the Labor Department's employment office. Unless the service rendered is truly professional, such as psychiatric counseling, might it not be better to abandon the notion of professionalization altogether and go for people who have energy, commitment, and concern for others?

Who are the people who are going to take on the counseling function in a society gradually shifting toward lifelong learning? Our projects suggest that there is an untapped potential in every community. There are thousands of women, for example, whose children are now in school for the entire day and who are no longer satisfied with volunteer work, but who do not want to work full-time. Can we mobilize their talents without requiring them to commit themselves to a career in counseling or to spend time acquiring credentials they do not need?

I am also impressed, in looking at the projects that help adults get started down the right avenue, with the emerging curriculum in career and life planning. At DePaul's School for New Learning, at Vermont Community College, at Northeastern University, at Minnesota Metropolitan State University, at Empire State College, at the College of Community and Public Service, University of Massachusetts—and there are others—our project directors have invented a variety of processes producing significant gains in self-awareness, personal direction, self-confidence, and so forth on the part of the adults who go through them. The "Discovery Workshops" at DePaul's School for New Learning are one good example.

Returning to college for many adults is like driving up to the border of a foreign country. You present who you are, but your papers are not in order. You might have done all the proper things, but the appropriate officials have not put their stamps on your work; or, if they have, their approvals are not about to be recognized by the officials in *this* country.

We have supported a number of projects designed to overcome such barriers. One group focuses on the assessment of individual performance and the development of ways to recognize learning in nonacademic as well as academic settings. DePaul's School for New Learning has developed a framework that individuals can use to translate what they have done into terms that DePaul can assess as worthy of academic credit. The Educational Testing Service has developed a taxonomy of the kind of competencies women tend to acquire when they are engaged in managing households and doing volunteer work. And the Cooperative

Assessment of Experiential Learning (CAEL), of course, has confirmed the validity of many methods for assessing what one learns
in action settings. Many of our projects report that putting individuals through the process of articulating what they have done and
what they know has a marvelous side benefit of heightening their
self-confidence. These activities, now under way, have not yet
come together in a mutually reinforcing "movement." But we can
imagine a future in which we might have *real transcripts* about
people's abilities, rather than academic transcripts that merely list
courses they have taken.

Employers, of course, patrol their borders too, and some of
our projects are working directly on this problem. At Northeastern
University, for example, Norma Fink and Marilyn Weiner, working
in collaboration with ten different employers, have developed "job
competence profiles" that focus on the real competencies women
need to perform in work settings rather than on the traditional
requirements for degrees and previous work experience.

Paralleling these efforts, another set of projects are attempting to assess and recognize for credit, not individuals, but entire
programs being conducted outside the college-university sector.
The American Council on Education and New York State have a
project under way which, at my last count, had sent review
teams to sixty-five different businesses, unions, and government
agencies. These teams had examined and made recommendations
about the credit worth of 875 different courses taught in these
settings. Southern Illinois University is engaged in an effort to
establish academic equivalency for courses taking place under
CETA training. Seven community colleges in Hawaii are establishing academic equivalency for training being conducted on military
bases.

Besides help in getting started and in acquiring the proper
identity papers, adults need truly responsive instructional programs. It is hard to generalize about what a truly responsive
program looks like, since what is required varies according to who
is being served. Let me cite two examples of responsive programs
aimed at adults in working settings.

Parkersburg Community College in West Virginia is located
in an urban setting, surrounded by industry. Most plants work on
shifts, which change from week to week, so the average worker in
the plant finds it difficult, if not impossible, to pursue college

work. To respond to these workers faculty from Parkersburg Community College have started a pilot project at one of the largest plants—Walker Parkersburg, a division of Textron. The faculty travel to the plant. The management gives the workers time off during regular shift hours and pays their tuition. And the instruction offered is individualized—tailored to the interests of the workers themselves.

In Hempsted, New York, the faculty at Hofstra University are undertaking a similar project with the Distributive Workers of America, District 65. The faculty travel to the union headquarters. The union members receive release time to attend the courses. The courses themselves focus on problems in the social sciences in which the union members are interested.

In both these examples, much more is involved than simply offering up some courses that overcome situational barriers of time and place. Both the faculty of the colleges and the managers of the workers have extended themselves to an unusual degree. They have both worked hard to bring about a curriculum that provides enrichment and career mobility for the workers themselves.

One generalization that occurs to me—looking back over all these efforts to provide new avenues for adults—is that there is no such thing as a quality educational program for adults. There are only quality educational programs for *particular* adults, in *particular* circumstances, with *particular* needs and interests. Educators often talk about "adult education" as if all we need to know about the people being served is that they are over twenty-five years of age. If we could talk less about adults as a homogenous category, and more about the enormous variety of different people, needs and interests to be met, we would be in a better posture to provide more effective opportunities to them.

Now I want to turn to the problems faced by young people. The general diagnosis should be familiar. As Jan Rakoff of Lone Mountain College puts it, the young stand at the edge of a "great divide"—on the other side of which are a whole series of requirements and responsibilities we call *adult*. But as years of schooling have increased, as opportunities for work have diminished, and as television and other forms of leisure have come to fill the empty hours, young people have become increasingly cast as consumers and spectators. There seem to be fewer and fewer bridges across the divide. So we have a situation in which thousands of young people are suspended in a great social holding action, playing bit parts, losing confidence in their capacity to find work, and losing trust in the capacity of the market to provide meaningful work. The problem is how to move individuals who are based in formal education along avenues leading to productive engagement with the economy and society at large.

What is striking to me, given the obvious social importance of this problem and the visibility given to it by James Coleman and others, is how *few* proposals the Fund has received that address it. Explanations come to mind. A number of programs were started in the late 1960s, in response to student unrest, before the Fund was in business. So we did not catch the first waves of interest. Other sources of support, such as the cooperative education program and the University for Action program, have been available. And, admittedly, we in the Fund have been quite selective about what we will support—looking for ideas that represent genuine improvements in, rather than simply expansions of, field experience programs.

Yet these explanations are not adequate. There is also the elementary point that colleges and universities are not terribly motivated to figure out how to move students *out* of their classrooms. The need is clear. The potency of experiential learning is evident. But colleges and universities lack the incentives to respond.

Those proposals we have supported address a range of particular problems that must be confronted during the course of establishing an effective program. First, positions—be they labeled *internships, apprenticeships, jobs, action projects,* or whatever—must be identified and developed. Second, the question of subsidies for the young people in these positions must be faced or finessed. Third, the quality ingredients must be built in—such as the counseling and assessment necessary to convert work experiences into reflective learning experiences; and the formal academic curriculum, especially the issue of credits, must often be confronted. I have a few observations about effective ways our projects are addressing some of these problems.

Developing positions for students in work settings requires commitment, energy, and skills not in abundance among college faculties. It is also often not cost-effective for a single institution to take on this task. Two of our projects demonstrate a sensible alternative, which is to have a central agency or consortium do it. In Virginia, a state agency was used by Tom Little as the base of operations. Starting off with a survey of existing positions and then following up with personal contacts, Tom created 168 public-sector internships in just one year. In Illinois, Charles Bayer initiated a similar undertaking, based at the Chicago Urban Corps, and also managed to convince a group of colleges and universities to subsidize the internship positions with work-study funds. Both projects report that faculty resistance to experiential learning programs as part of the curriculum is lessened when the difficult, logistical issues of position development are solved.

I do not have space to describe what quality work-study experiences look like. I do want to say that the ingredients that spell the difference between just a job and a growth-producing experience, between an internship and a genuine opportunity for career exploration, *can* be defined and recognized. Just as a group of professors in a discipline can look at a course syllabus and say, "That's a lousy syllabus," individuals knowledgeable about work experience programs can look at a program design and say, "That's a lousy design." Put more positively, there are in existence some excellent designs—Jan Rakoff's Tunbridge program at Lone Mountain is an example from which others can learn.

Finally, I want to mention a way in which a thoughtful educational investment has converted a jobs program into an experience leading to meaningful careers. In California, the Citizens Policy Center has a new jobs program operating in four counties. For each county, the center has trained a young staff to identify apprenticeship opportunities and place in these positions other young people who qualify for six-month subsidies. With a grant from the Fund, each of these county youth organizations has added a career counselor who works with the apprentices and links them to further educational and work opportunities. These career counselors are also young people selected, like the counselors in many of our adult projects, for their motivation to function as advocates for their peers.

The third broad problem people are confronting in relating education and work is how to relate the substance of the education offered to the requirements for effective performance in work and other roles. Many of the projects I have already described have backed into these issues as a result of trying to open up new avenues to school and work. But a number of other applicants to the Fund have tackled, head on, the complex issues of substance and outcomes.

In particular, as the job market for college graduates worsened in the mid 1970s, colleges have become increasingly concerned about how to respond to this new condition. Some have simply proposed adding placement offices and other such places to which the faculty can send their casualties. But a growing number of institutions have also perceived that the new environment is a challenge to the academic curriculum as well. The question is, what should students be prepared *for*? Or, as many colleges have posed it to the Fund, how can we combine the advantages of a liberal and general education with the necessities of equipping people with the means to secure jobs? I want to comment on two different approaches.

A number of institutions have sought to *combine* liberal arts education with training in practical, job-related skills and knowledge. Sometimes this effort takes place within a single institution. But the more ambitious and interesting ideas have involved new efforts at collaboration among several different kinds of institutions. The objective sought is not simply sharing of resources but new options for students.

Henderson State University in Arkansas, for example, was worried about heavy attrition among its freshman and sophomore students. A study found that these students were leaving primarily because they wanted jobs, or at least job-related training. So Henderson got in touch with five nearby vocational schools and initiated a joint associate degree program in career studies. Faculty at Henderson travel to the vocational schools and teach there. Vocational students, who never before had an option for an Associate of Arts (A.A.) degree (only certificates), now have one, and Henderson students also have a new option for an A.A. rather than only a B.A.

In Los Angeles, Pepperdine University several years ago initiated an A.A. program in two computer fields by hooking up with the Telco Institute, an adjacent proprietary school. And, in the midwest, twelve private colleges have been brought by a consortium, the Associated Colleges of the Midwest, into an arrangement with Rush Medical Hospital wherein students can combine a liberal arts B.A. with two years of medical training. In this last case,

the fact of gaining admission to medical training as a college freshman or sophomore has freed these students from the pressures of
vocationalism. No longer needing to hedge and play safe, they can
enjoy liberal arts courses. The staff at Rush are delighted and
regard this as *better* preparation than trying to acquire at a private
college the kind of training Rush itself provides.

Another group of institutions have said, in fact, that neither
the traditional liberal arts curriculum nor occupational training
adequately prepares students for the contemporary world. What is
needed is a third alternative, or at least a new focus within the
existing curriculum. The focus is on a set of learning outcomes
described by some as "competencies," by others as "liberal skills,"
and by still others as "generic skills." What these approaches all
have in common is an interest in certain fundamental core abilities, such as the ability to analyze problems, to synthesize information, to communicate persuasively, and to deal effectively with
people. The pacesetting institutions in this group are by now
familiar to many AAHE members. They include Alverno College
in Milwaukee, the College of Community and Public Service at the
University of Massachusetts in Boston, the College for Human
Services in New York City, Mars Hill in North Carolina, certain
departments at Florida State University, and others. More recently, the testing agencies have become involved in the effort to
develop new ways of assessing student attainment of the kind of
abilities these colleges have identified. The Fund currently supports the McBer Company in Boston, the Educational Testing
Service, and the American College Testing program in this effort.

Overall, we have approximately forty separate projects and
close to $9 million invested in this fascinating effort. I cannot de-
scribe or even summarize these efforts here, but let me note some
milestones:

> These projects have pointed the conversation about educational
> reform in a positive direction. Prior to the interest in defining
> what the competent graduate should know and be able to do,
> the discussion about reform was dominated by individuals who
> defined what they wanted in terms of what they were
> against—for example, "alternative education" and "nontradi-
> tional education." Now people are talking about the positive
> outcomes we are after.

- They have found an operational language for talking about educational purposes, a language that has become the basis for reevaluating instruction and developing new ways of evaluating student learning.
- A consensus is emerging on what the fundamental, core abilities indeed are, and each of these abilities is being isolated for work in many different settings.
- Studies of the requirements for effective performance in various roles are beginning to verify the importance of these abilities. And the colleges furthest along, such as Alverno, are beginning to get feedback that their graduates are viewed as *more effective performers* than graduates from other institutions.

The implications of all this are just now beginning to inform the reexaminations of liberal and general education going on around the country. As a parting shot, I cannot resist posing some questions. Is there a common set of requirements for effective performance, across many roles in work and other settings? Should there be a common-core curriculum? And is the core a core of knowledge or a set of abilities, like communications skills, or a combination of both?

Finally, I would like to make some general observations pertinent to the entire range of projects attempting to relate education and work. What stands out? What can we say about the larger issues raised in this book? One such issue is the demand for education—a subject about which educators seem to be very uneasy. We have been especially uncertain about the out-of-school adult. A substantial proportion of the adult population *say* they are interested in further education, but the *kind* of education they mean appears to be outdoor gardening, effective parenting, and other highly utilitarian functions. Workers, I am told, are not using the tuition plans and other funds already available to them. The National Manpower Institute is trying to figure out why.

Our projects, I believe, represent strong testimony on one point: Out-of-school adults, when sensitively and intelligently approached with truly responsive programs, *are* interested—*especially women*—when they see a realistic, meaningful opportunity for self-improvement. At Northeastern University, Norma Fink and Marilyn Weiner found in a survey that 74 percent of adult female students took only one or two courses at a time. At that rate, many would take ten years or more to complete a traditional program. So, as an alternative, this duo developed, in collaboration with ten employers, a short-term, job-focused curriculum. They held what they called a "career incentive conference," intended to identify twenty-four women who might be interested in taking the course. Four hundred showed up.

This is not an isolated story. With a Fund grant the National Council of Negro Women began working with Pace College some time ago to develop a two-and-a-half-year A.A. program focused on employed, working women trapped in clerical jobs and interested in moving into sales and management positions. They held a conference in April 1976 to describe the program. Two hundred women had to be turned away for lack of room.

The demand is there, but the qualifier is crucial. People need to be met on *their* terms and often need to be disabused on stereotyped images of what a college education is all about. Once this happens, the word spread very quickly.

A second observation is that the task is always more difficult than initially assumed. Efforts to relate education and work typically require complex collaborations, within and often among institutions. To move work-study off the campus, you must get financial-aid officers and academic administrators talking to each other. To make adults feel more like first-class citizens, arts and sciences faculties must deal with their counterparts in continuing education. And so it goes.

When the action moves across dissimilar types of institutions, the problems are compounded by differences in culture. As one of our projects reported, industry and education, for example, are "unlikely twosomes." People in business see college faculty members as an impractical, vastly arrogant lot, steeped in theory. And the faculty have a stereotype of their own of the businessman as a narrow-minded materialistic type interested only in the kind of training that will maximize profits. Whether we are talking about liberal arts and vocational institutions, colleges and unions, colleges and business, or whatever, stereotypes such as these get in the way and inhibit communication. Breaking them down takes time. When Pepperdine College decided to join forces with Telco, representatives of the two held fifty-eight separate meetings in the first six months in an effort to hammer out the arrangement. Even when the cultural walls are bridged, there is usually someone who feels threatened. So the message we keep hearing is that lead times are long and that commitments at the highest levels and at the working levels are essential.

This brings me to my third general observation. I have noted that the individuals running our most successful projects are in touch with the feelings and needs of the people being served. And I have noted that the tasks to be accomplished often amount to an arduous organizational and political challenge. I am fascinated by the people who have stepped forward to take on these challenges.

A remarkable proportion consists of individuals who are *not* from the academic mainstream. They may have gone to graduate school and have Ph.D.s, but their relevant training seems to have been in prior organizational work in the community—as Peace Corps volunteers, ministers, civil rights activists, dedicated volunteers. This is not true of my third problem area, the work on substance and outcomes, but it certainly is true of those who have taken up the challenge of developing new avenues for adults. Fran Macy, at the Regional Learning Service, has a background in the Peace Corps; his partner, Don Vickers, is from the ministry; and Bob Steiner at the New Jersey Educational Consortium is from the Peace Corps.

Many of our projects that developed to serve the needs of women for self-improvement were begun by women who simply muscled their way into an academic institution and started organizing. Norma Fink and Marilyn Weiner did this. So did Lila Hexner at Middlesex Community College. Project directors at places such as DePaul, Minnesota Metropolitan, Empire State, and Vermont Community College might be characterized as more closely associated with, but not "of," the academic mainstream.

Or look at those involved in creating new avenues for youth. Barbara Gardner developed a whole network of inner-city internships at the University of Southern California without any status whatsoever and finally was given status because of what she had accomplished. Charles Bayer came from the ministry to develop the Chicago Urban Corps, as did Tom Little in Virginia.

These people tend to see their lives not as advancing on the rungs of a particular career, but as a series of adventures. Our project directors who are from the academic mainstream tend to share this enjoyment of adventure and risk. Sometimes, the most important thing to be learned is how to ask the right question. So I will end with this one. How can we attract this kind of individual into educational and work settings and *reward* them for their efforts?

$\mathcal{X}11\mathcal{X}$

Vocations and the Liberal Arts

Arthur W. Chickering

The separation of living from learning and the consequent rupture between work and education is an historical development that has reached fullest expression in a limited number of educational institutions in the United States and Europe.[1] But the studies of adult learning by Kidd, Tough, and others at the Ontario Institute for Studies in Education make clear that even today the distinction does not hold for most persons or most learning.[2]

---

[1] This paper makes substantial use of materials from two forthcoming publications: *Handbook on Curriculum Development*, to be published by the Council for the Advancement of Small Colleges, and *Experience and Learning*, a "white paper" to be published by Educational Change Inc. and *Change* Magazine.

[2] See R. M. Smith (Ed.), *Adult Learning: Issues and Innovations* (Columbus: ERIC Clearinghouse on Career Education, Ohio State University, 1976).

The bulk of this learning does not occur in our formal educational institutions. Perhaps one reason most of the learning goes on elsewhere is the compartmentalization we impose. Of course, we did not create the separation all by ourselves. It really began with the medieval universities.

In his delightful and scholarly chapter on the deep traditions of experiential learning, Cyril Houle reminds us of the craft guilds and apprenticeship systems that provided so much advanced education from the medieval period through the industrial revolution. The original word for "guild" was *universitas,* and parallel to this system there developed a guild of scholars who appropriated the term while developing institutional homes for themselves at Bologna and Paris. These university models, which gradually spread both west and east, basically asked students to master content delivered by books and lectures. Even in professional areas such as medicine, learning occurred according to rules given by learned authorities; systematic observation, dissection, and practice had no place.

While vocational training was provided by the guilds and apprentice relationships and while scholarly training was provided by the universities, the education of the elite was carried by the chivalric traditions. This system was performance oriented—and competency based. Houle shares some of the required proficiencies: "The squire must be able to: 'spring upon a horse while fully armed; to exercise himself in running; to strike for a length of time with the axe or club; to dance and do somersaults entirely armed except for his helmet; to mount on horseback behind one of his comrades, by barely laying his hands on his sleeve; to raise himself betwixt two partition walls to any height, by placing his back against one, and his knees and hands against the other; to mount a ladder, placed against a tower, upon the reverse or under side, solely by the aid of his hands, and without touching the rounds with his feet; to throw the javelin; and to pitch the bar.' " Moreover, these practical skills had their liberal arts component, exemplified by Chaucer's squire in *Canterbury Tales*:

> *He could make songs and poems and recite,*
> *Knew how to joust, to dance, to draw, to write.*
> *He loved so hotly that when dawn grew pale*
> *He'd slept as little as a nightingale.*

Courteous he was, and humble, willing, able;
He carved to serve his father at the table.

Then as now, informal learning activities provided a rich ground against which these more formal systems cut their figures. Libraries, monasteries, museums, churches, and courts provided resources and events. Annual rounds of feasts and festivals carried cultures and taught traditions. Wandering minstrels and storytellers, traveling salesmen and itinerant tradesmen brought news, myths, and words of other lands. The local pub, inn, and village green provided meeting grounds to exchange common wisdom, examine current practice, and share and test new knowledge.

Then the industrial revolution began its work. Factories replaced the craftsmen, unions replaced the guilds, job simplification reduced complex tasks to easily learned skills. Chivalry died. The indivisible link between riches and royalty was broken. Feudalism and monarchy gave way to economic systems and the politics of republicanism and democracy. An educated citizenry with a wide range of professional and vocational skills became increasingly necessary.

With the death of chivalry and the decline of the guilds, only the university survived, with its emphasis on content and authority, its rejection of direct experience and useful applications. In the absence of other alternatives, pressures mounted for a university education that would be practical as well as theoretical, that would meet the needs of new professions in agriculture, engineering, architecture, and forestry. Enter the land-grant colleges in the mid nineteenth century, about the time that the natural sciences were finally given curricular recognition by the classicists who dominated Oxford and Cambridge. With the turn of the century, several major areas of professional preparation began to require apprenticeships and practical applications as integral program elements. Medical schools incorporated not only laboratory studies but also hospital internships, law schools included moot courts and clerkships, normal schools required practice teaching, forestry and agriculture required fieldwork. These institutions also had their required general education or liberal arts core that all students had to fulfill. But these requirements were seldom integrated with students' professional or vocational aspirations or with the training provided in other university courses or settings.

This compartmentalization was reinforced by concurrent development recently noted by James Hall, president of Empire State, when he said, "Another irony is that during the past several decades subjects that once formed the core of general education have been heavily vocationalized; that is, the overstress on the discipline of certain subjects (such as history, philosophy, and linguistics) has led to a high degree of specialization more characteristic of professional training. This emphasis has led to a decline in the relative value of these studies as part of the general education component."[3]

This institutional separation of work and the liberal arts has been accelerating in the academy for many years. Of course, that generalization is not true for all colleges and universities nor for all programs. But the general thrust of development has been in that direction.

Perhaps the major reasons for these developments are to be found in the changing nature of "work" and our attitudes toward it. Of course, when it comes to talking about work, we find ourselves a bit like the patriotic gentleman and the Monroe Doctrine. His friend said, "What's this I hear about you? They say you do not believe in the Monroe Doctrine!" His reply was instant and indignant: "It's a lie. I never said I didn't believe in the Monroe Doctrine. I do believe in it. It's the palladium of our liberties. I would die for the Monroe Doctrine. All I said was that I don't know what it *means.*"

In today's society, it is hard to know what we mean by *work.* The dictionary is little help. The *Oxford* gives nine pages of small type to its various meanings, and even *Webster's New Collegiate* has so many definitions—many of which could apply equally well to vigorous recreation and leisure activities—that clear distinctions between work and a host of other activities are difficult to make.

Ancient man probably had no concept of "work." Primitive societies that still exist frequently have no vocabulary that distinguishes between "work" and "free time." In such societies, a person does what is expected, which includes domestic duties, gather-

---

[3]J. W. Hall, "Thoughts on General Education," *ESC News* (Saratoga Springs: State University of New York Empire State College, December-January, 1976-1977), p. 7.

ing and raising food, performing various rituals and ceremonies, occupying time with conversation, singing, dancing, sleeping, eating, and having sex. Persons felt as constrained to do one as they were to do another. "Work" appears as a category we construct when we try to classify these varied activities. And if we limit the definition to those activities involved in gaining sustenance and producing goods, then in many primitive cultures persons spent much less time in work than we do.

Our Greek and Christian heritages clearly set work apart. For the Socrates of *Xenophon,* work was an expedient, and in Hesiod's *Works and Days* it is a necessity and a curse. The Bible indicates that work became necessary because of a divine curse. When Adam ate that apple, he turned the world into a workhouse and threw away Paradise without toil; the Lord said to him, "Cursed is the ground because of you; in toil you shall eat of it all the days of your life; thorns and thistles it shall bring forth to you; and you shall eat the plants of the field. In the sweat of your face you shall eat bread till you return to the ground, for out of it you were taken; you are dust and to dust you shall return."[4] This view reached full bloom as the Protestant ethic turned work and play into opposites and in some of its more extreme manifestations equated play with sin. Thus the idea—that if an activity is to be called *work,* it must be something painful, unpleasant, that we do not want to do—became embedded in Western culture.

This view would certainly not have been understood by medieval craftsmen nor by craftsmen and artists since then. Now we are moving toward a view that work is not a curse but a blessing. It may even become a privilege. Useful occupations are an antidote to stagnation. Complex and challenging work is less boring than pleasure. Achievement, contribution, and productivity are the cornerstones for self-respect. In the United States, the dominant orientation is moving beyond viewing work as a curse or a privilege to calling it a "right."

Our changing orientation toward work is consistent with the changing nature of the activities called *work,* which have shifted dramatically as we moved from an agrarian, through an industrial, to a technological and "posttechnological" society.

Consider energy as one key indicator. In 1850 people and

[4]Gen. 3:17-20.

animals produced 65 percent of the horsepower, and inanimate sources produced 35 percent; in 1950 98 percent of our energy was supplied by inanimate sources. People used to be major sources of energy; now they manage and consume it in massive amounts. The need for individual labor and muscle power as a means of achieving progress and well-being no longer really exists. What we need now are skills to manage energy. This new type of work makes active participation, social power, and a sense of contribution and worth difficult to achieve, because the effect of each person's work is determined not by the direct output from his or her labor but by the amount of energy he or she controls.

Today the center of the work force is the "service worker" and the "knowledge worker." That shift is vividly documented by Eli Ginsberg: "Almost the entire growth in post-World War II employment has been in the service sector. Among the goods-producing industries, only construction shows any sizeable increase. Agriculture declined by more than half, from some 7.6 to 3.5 million; mining declined by approximately one third, from 995,000 to 672,000; manufacturing—the backbone of the economy—showed only a small absolute increase: approximately a third, from 15.6 to 20 million, which meant that its share of total employment dropped from about 27 percent to 21 percent! In general, the share of the goods-producing industries (agriculture, mining, manufacturing, and construction) in total employment dropped from 45 percent to 33 percent, while the share of services (trade government, education, welfare, transportation, utilities, finance, and others) increased from 55 percent to 67 percent."[5] In output, services increased from 31 percent to 41.5 percent, while goods-producing industries dropped from 69 percent to 58 percent. And the most striking rate of growth within the services area has occurred in the not-for-profit sector, which jumped by half in the years between 1950 and 1960 from about 20 percent to 30 percent.

These shifts have triggered other major changes. One is the rapid growth of female employment. According to Ginsberg, "Between 1950 and 1974 the civilian employment of males sixteen years and over increased from 41.6 to 52.5 million, or by

[5] E. Ginsberg, "The Pluralistic Economy of the U.S.," *Scientific American*, 1976, *235* (6): 25-29.

approximately 26 percent. During the same period, the number of female workers employed increased from 17.3 to 33.4 million, or by 93 percent, three and a half times as much."[6]

Part-time employment also jumped. The services were more able to offer less-than-full-time employment, which both the employers and many women preferred. This rapid expansion of service employment also created many part-time or intermittent jobs for young persons whose main activity was pursuing education. After World War II, the rapid expansion in postsecondary education was supported by the enlarged earning opportunities for students in a broad array of service industries.

Another striking consequence is that only 55 percent fit the stereotype of the conventional worker employed full-time for the full year from young adulthood until retirement; of all people who work during the course of a year, almost 45 percent are employed less than full time for the full year. Even if the calculation shifts from the number of workers to total work, about 30 percent of all work is performed by part-time employees.

A major concomitant of the expansion of the services sector has been increased demand for professionals in education, health, management, science, engineering, and many other fields. The foundation of an advanced service economy is trained and well-educated persons, because the key to effective service is quality, not quantity. Achieving high-quality service is more complicated than producing high-quality goods. Given human complexity and orneriness, it is difficult to develop solutions and formulae that work for large numbers. A television set is a complex instrument, but producing high-quality sets in large numbers is much easier than producing high-quality programming. Designing high-powered automobiles, fast trains, and supersonic airplanes requires high-level technological skills and scientific knowledge, but we are far from designing environments and related transportation systems that effectively serve human needs. In fact, in some cases we are losing ground. Motor trucks average six miles an hour in New York City traffic today, as against eleven miles an hour for horse-drawn trucks in 1910. And, given the escalating ratio of divorces to happy, solid marriages, it looks as though putting a chicken in every pot is easier than having a congenial family dinner.

[6] Ginsberg, "The Pluralistic Economy of the U.S."

These enormous changes in the world of work have consequences that penetrate every aspect of higher education. Many already have been felt. The shift to part-time employment and the need for continued professional up-dating of skill and knowledge already have been reflected in the rapid rise of part-time students and in the numbers of adults seeking college and university work. We are challenged to provide more effective integration of earning and learning and to see that vocational and professional training are integrated with studies in liberal arts and general education.

In the past, the pressures for increased knowledge and competence have been met by extending the years of schooling—first beyond elementary school to high school, then beyond high school to college—so that now almost 50 percent of our high school graduates pursue some form of higher education. This response has assumed the separation of schooling and work; it has assumed that in a given number of years an institution can cram into a person's skull most of what he or she needs for the rest of life. Even if those assumptions made sense a hundred years ago, they are now absurd. None of us knows the knowledge and competence a person will need fifteen or twenty years from now. We do know that much of that knowledge does not yet exist. We know also that learning occurs most effectively when it connects with the immediate concerns of the learner, with important experiences and responsibilities, and that learning is lost fast if it is not built through action and use. The fundamental requirements of the posttechnological and service society mean that past and current arrangements that viewed (and view) education as preparation for life will no longer serve. We need to develop alternatives that make education part of life, that capitalize on the educational experiences available through daily living, and that make use of learnings that can be gained from ongoing responsibilities. I do not think these challenges threaten either professional and vocational training, or liberal and general education. On the contrary, I believe that the relationship is fundamentally synergistic and that we can make it work that way.

Consider the following course description:

Race Relations in the United States *has as its major objective, helping students obtain knowledge of and insight into the history of race relations in the United States during the past 100 years and to acquire concrete impressions of the current situation.*

*The class will read the following books: Malcolm X, Auto-
biography; Synnestvedt, Sig, White Response to Black Emancipa-
tion; Rudwick, Eliot M., Race Riot in East St. Louis; Hersey,
John, Algiers Motel Incident; Carter, Dan T., Scottsboro: A Trage-
dy of the American South.*

*For each of these books, students will prepare a written cri-
tique not more than four pages in length—which includes a single-
page synopsis of the book and one to three pages of assessment,
evaluation, analysis, judgment, and reaction.*

*On the basis of these readings, each student will prepare a
list of five or six basic questions on white-black relations in the
United States. These questions should be designed to get at some
basic assumptions about race and the white or black attitudes
which may be involved or implicit in these assumptions.*

*Each student will select ten persons, five white and five
black, and pose these questions to each individually in an interview session.*

*Then each student will write a short paper which discusses
the results of this small collection of impressions. (Note that this
assignment is not conceived to be anything more than the collection of a limited set of current impressions which relate to the
readings noted above.)*

*Each student will play the game "Blacks and Whites" for at
least an hour with a small group of people, including some blacks
and some whites. Cross-assign race roles in advance of starting
play, that is, have some blacks play white roles and vice versa.
Write a one-to-three-page summary of the results of the game.*

*The methods and criteria for evaluation will be as follows:
Knowledge of the books read will be judged on the quality and
accuracy of the written critiques. A one-page summary should
compress the book, retaining the essential facts and conclusions of
the author. They should emerge as a brief but comprehensive outline of the book. The critique should address such questions as:
Did the author handle his evidence accurately and fairly? Did he
omit important evidence which might have changed his conclusions? What types of evidence did he stress? On a comparative
basis, did the author present as convincing a case as the other authors read for this course or other authors which the student may
have read at some other time?*

*Judgment on the student's knowledge of the books and
their implications will also be drawn from the nature and quality
of the interviews themselves. The questions should demonstrate
that the student is aware of such considerations as: differing perceptions and assumptions of blacks and whites in the United*

States; particularly friction-laden experiences of the past; particularly sensitive issues in the present; overall perceptions of progress toward greater and more equal justice or lack of progress toward these goals.

Use of the game "Blacks and Whites" is deliberately designed as a subjective experience without concern for a specific set of outcomes. This experience should be sought at the end of the course and might be most fruitful if conceived as a rudimentary means of testing some of the assumptions and perceptions dealt with in the books and revealed in the interviews.[7]

Would individual interviews or class meetings with persons actually working to create more equal and just conditions for minority groups—in courts, housing, education, and employment—have strengthened the learnings from this liberal arts study? Would such contacts and some discussion of the difficulties of change in these key areas give students a chance to see how studies that provide historical and cultural perspectives contribute understandings directly pertinent to potential career alternatives? Would some consideration of the kinds of knowledge and competence required for the varied jobs and information about typical career trajectories have helped them see how the ability to communicate effectively, to think critically, to understand themselves and others, and to take initiative and function independently are necessary qualifications? Would the need for additional information concerning race relations, interpersonal dynamics, group processes, political, economic, and social forces become more apparent? I think so.

Take another. The following course, called "Bio-Research in Environmental Studies," illustrates an approach familiar to many science teachers. The major objectives were "to help students gain experience and knowledge in bioassay techniques and methods as applied to environmental problems," and "to increase the ability to plan research projects, evaluate results, and write final reports."

Each student will design, carry out, and report on a research project. The exact nature of the project will be worked out in con-

---

[7]This course description and the two that follow are from F. Clark, *Contract Learning Casebook* (Saratoga Springs: ERIC Center for Individualized Education, State University of New York Empire State College, 1976).

sultation with the instructor, but it will involve a study of the environmental toxicity of a particular chemical, using fish as subjects. The following activities will be included:

1. Background reading and study in biology, biology of the fish, ecology, biology of water pollution, and bioassay techniques and methods (see attached bibliography); further readings will be identified as each project becomes focused and the student will keep notes on all readings, which will become part of the bibliography for his final report.

2. A visit to the Environmental Protection Agency Bioassay Lab to learn more about specific techniques and methods. Each student will prepare a report on this visit.

3. Planning and writing a formal research project proposal, including background for the problem, objectives, and methods.

4. Carrying out the project and collecting data, using the college laboratory facilities. Each student will keep an accurate lab notebook.

5. Evaluate and interpret the data and write a research report.

Each student's progress and performance will be based on discussions with the instructor during class sessions, on the work done in the laboratory, and on the written research proposal and research report. The following criteria will apply:

1. Evidence of adequate background knowledge to develop a proposal.

2. Evidence of ability to formulate a reasonable and scientifically sound research project, and ability to present this project in a clear, well-organized, and appropriate format in the research proposal.

3. Ability to apply bioassay techniques and methods in the laboratory.

4. Ability to interpret data and results, draw valid conclusions from the results, and ability to present these results and conclusions in a clear, well-organized, and appropriate format in the research report.

Bibliography

Johnson, W. H., and others. *Biology.* (4th ed.) New York: Holt, Rinehart and Winston, 1972.

Odum, E. P. *Fundamentals of Ecology.* (3rd ed.) Philadelphia: W. B. Saunders, 1971.

U.S. Department of the Interior. *Biology of Water Pollution.* Washington, D.C.: U.S. Department of the Interior, 1967.

Wilber, C. G. *The Biological Aspects of Water Pollution.* Spring-
     field, Ill.: C. C Thomas, 1971.
Cairns, J., Jr., and Dickson, K. L. (Eds.). *Biological Methods for the
     Assessment of Water Quality.* American Society for Testing
     and Materials, 1973.
U.S. Environmental Protection Agency. *Biological Field and Labo-
     ratory Methods for Measuring and Quality of Surface Waters
     and Effluents.* Cincinnati, Ohio: U.S. Environmental Protec-
     tion Agency.

Could this course include the political and practical issues involved in selecting sites for collection and analysis and in decisions concerning the disposition and use of reports once results are in? Both these elements are matters of consequence in planning research projects and in preparing reports, and they can be significant for the application of research techniques to environmental problems.

Would one or two references concerning social consequences of water pollution, specific instances of sickness or disease, examples of degraded lakes or rivers, with cases drawn from Japan, Europe, India, or Latin America, be useful? Would they make more vivid and powerful the potential value of the students' learning and the work it makes possible?

Would the achievement of course objectives be enhanced by beginning with visits to major polluters and polluted waters, by observing the effects of different toxicity levels and different pollutants? Would using water samples from observed sources with known pollutants have increased motivation and added useful side effects?

Would it be possible to make more substantial cooperative arrangements with the EPA and its Bioassay Lab? Could student research contribute to the work of the Bioassay Lab? Could students work in close enough relationship with Bioassay Lab staff and administrators to encounter the practical problems and policy issues involved in carrying out such work and discover the added training required to pursue it?

Such activities could not only enhance the professional/ vocational relevance of this course but could also increase consciousness of and knowledge about a major social problem. Whether or not students pursued more advanced studies or sought employment in this critical area, they would be better positioned for responsible citizenship.

Let us consider one more course that is broadly professional in its orientation.

Early Childhood Education [is] aimed to help students achieve the following objectives:

1. To understand the needs of educationally and socially deprived children, the kind of curricular enrichment called for, and the kinds of testing procedures which may be useful.

2. To gain knowledge of the establishment, administration, operation, curriculum, and education practices of a daycare center.

3. To study innovative alternatives which might be applied to improve the quality of daycare programs.

To work toward these objectives:

1. Each student will participate for a minimum of two full mornings a week as a teacher's aide in one of the community daycare centers. The students will work with children who require individual attention in language enrichment, reading readiness, social skills, and motivation.

2. The student will participate with the staff in planning sessions and will study literature on curriculum design and program planning generally applicable to daycare centers and pertinent to the particular center at hand. Lesson plans will be created in the areas of language development and learning readiness, submitted to the director, and carried out as part of the curriculum, if feasible, and approved by the director.

3. Once each month the student will spend a full day at the center to become aware of the problems in planning and carrying out a full day's program.

4. Each student will research innovative programs that might be applicable to daycare centers and whenever possible, will visit other centers using innovative programs. This research will include study of television programs such as Sesame Street, Electric Company, *and cartoon programs as a source of useful ideas.*

5. Each student will keep a weekly log of activities at the center, meetings, and readings. Basic readings pertinent to general objectives of the course and to particular issues students may encounter are available from the attached bibliography.

6. Each student will submit a final paper analyzing the center operation and outlining any innovations or recommendations which may seem appropriate. The analyses and recommendations offered will be supported not only by the student's own observations but by references to pertinent principles, theories, or research findings given in the literature.

Student performance will be evaluated as follows:

1. The student's weekly log will be reviewed periodically and will serve as a framework for ongoing evaluation. The consistency of effort, the level of responsibility, and the integrity of reporting will be taken into account at the point of final evaluation.

2. Both the director and the instructor will evaluate the student's analytic paper and recommendations for improving center operation. They will look for the degree to which the student identifies critical problem areas and is able to apply pertinent information from the literature to recommendations for change.

A substantial bibliography accompanied this description, with readings concerning the development of preschool children, teaching disadvantaged children, approaches to beginning reading, television production for children, and experimental approaches to preschool programs. But there is nothing in the readings or discussions that asks students to examine underlying assumptions about how "educational and social deprivation" is defined, nothing that leads them to wonder about the inevitability of current patterns of child rearing and current educational priorities. Suppose students were asked to examine films and print that describe child rearing and "early childhood education" in Africa, Israel, Latin America, the Far East. Or were asked to put the practices of the 1970s in historical perspective for this country, looking at the ungraded and one-room schools of the 1870s, the activities and responsibilities of preschool children 150 years ago. Would students have a better perspective on the strengths and weaknesses of daycare centers and on the reasons for their emergence? Might they see their own future work as teachers somewhat differently? Would the range of improvements that occurred to them expand and the range of possibilities for their own learning do the same? I suspect so.

My point in these examples is simply this. It does not require any great creative leaps of imagination to think of ways to connect liberal arts or general education courses with pertinent social problems and related employment. Neither does it require any great leap to identify novels, plays, poems, and films pertinent to many jobs and working contexts. There are concepts from the social, behavioral, and natural sciences that underlie effective performance in the world of work as well as effective citizenship. Furthermore, many professional training activities themselves and the internships, field experiences, or apprentice relationships associated with them can contribute directly to key liberal arts objectives. Pursuing a vocation, a calling, and pursuing a liberal education do not have to be incompatible or in conflict. They can be mutually reinforcing.

The time has come to move beyond the limited role set by the medieval universities. Our main disposition has been to create increasingly small and watertight compartments, dividing and redividing disciplines and major areas of knowledge. True, we have recently seen interdisciplinary, area, and ethnic studies emerge, forerunners overtaking our increasing specialization. But we need to open the doors wider, connecting those studies as well as the rest with the vocational and social responsibilities students will carry and to which such learning can contribute so strongly.

We should not underestimate the importance of integrating professional and vocational preparation and liberal studies. If it is true that *love* and *work* are the basic ingredients for a meaningful existence, then that is what we are attempting. The liberal arts can expand the capacity to love life, to experience it more richly, to continually increase one's range of satisfying activities. Effective professional and vocational studies that not only prepare us for productive work but also help us grow in scope and capacity offer the other essential. But one in the absence of the other leaves us crippled, hopping along with one leg, negotiating tough terrain with difficulty, feeling less than we ought to be, and getting less from our living than we know we should.

Most of us share the orientation of Robert Frost's tramp, who said:

> *But yield who will to their separation,*
> *My object in living is to unite*
> *My avocation and my vocation*
> *As my two eyes make one in sight.*
>
> *Only where love and need are one,*
> *And the work is play for mortal stakes,*
> *Is the deed ever really done*
> *For Heaven and the future's sakes.*[8]

[8] R. Frost, "Two Tramps in Mudtime," *Complete Poems* (London: Jonathan Cape, 1951).

Few of us achieve that unity, but most of us strive for it. It has to be recreated continually as the life cycle and its vicissitudes toss us to and fro. A college that helps us learn how will make a major contribution indeed.

12

Reassessing General Education

Burton J. Bledstein

For years, American educators have debated the advantages of a liberal education versus a professional one, a general education versus a specialized one. The human awareness derived from general education, we have heard, makes people with active minds free. General education develops a synthesized, integrated, connected view of things, thereby helping people perceive, judge, and choose alternatives to custom and tradition. It focuses their attention on a common historical legacy and on their relationship to the goods and evils of complex human purposes and actions. It facilitates rational discourse under criticism and increases the confidence of individuals in their capacity for both intellectual and moral discrimination.

Words, words, words, William James once complained, are the professor's chief failing, and there has been no lack of professorial words about humanistic learning. But a few more words must be added to the already considerable confusion, because general education may be facing a showdown. In the shadows surrounding the current debate lie deep-seated apprehensions about the very core of higher education and the declining respect for its worth in American society.

Those who support the idea of general education offer several arguments in its behalf. First, they maintain, all students need the basic knowledge and life skills general education can provide. Entering students are often ill prepared for academic studies, and many show uneven skills even after graduation. The abilities to read, write, analyze a problem, communicate information, and present reasoned arguments for a point of view are so basic to adult life that a core of required courses is needed to ensure that college graduates will develop them. Educators must agree on a ground level of competence, or public confidence in the enterprise will be shaken even more than at present. In a democracy, ideological reasons favor the pursuit of general education. Our shared humanity, our spiritual equality bequeaths to Americans a common heritage of expectations. By means of education, individuals can transcend their diverse backgrounds, their private ambitions, and their petty vengeances and can agree to public standards of performance. It is an article of faith in a democracy that the educated opinion supported by reasons and evidence must be worth more than the uneducated opinion advanced by verbal abuse, slogans, and threats. What educated people share is a common familiarity with the major spheres of learning that comprise the basics of civilization.

Second, the American marketplace of the future favors general education. Because a service-oriented economy is less likely to employ students who prepare too narrowly, it makes sense to emphasize basic academic skills that enable the individual to adapt to changing circumstances. Career education defeats its own end if it produces journalists who cannot write about a broad range of subjects, business majors who cannot analyze the abstractions of political and economic systems, and public accountants who cannot communicate with clients in clear English. The general educator is concerned with teaching useful mental skills, the kind that make it possible for an individual to deal effectively with the unanticipated problems of any career or to pursue interests that may not be vocational at all. In other words, the college graduates, to enliven their sense of human worth and to continue to learn, take on goals, and work with others, must possess liberal arts which empower them to make "interesting" lives in their occupations and their social existence.

There are indications that many of today's students would be willing to sacrifice money and material possessions for freedom over their time and personal satisfaction in a continuing accomplishment, which may or may not be vocational. This trend requires educators to ask some hard, and perhaps painful, questions. Do we devote enough time to teaching? How much of the research coming out of universities is justifiable as a "contribution" to knowledge? Do too many unproductive people in universities benefit from the research ideal? Is American higher education overmanaged? Is too large a percentage of the higher-education budget going for nonteaching functions?

Finally, educators naturally believe that college makes a difference in the maturity of a student, in the kind of person he or she aspires to become. But the credibility of the academic enterprise is threatened, the advocate of general education claims, when the student finds that academics do not agree on priorities in education and that higher education suffers from a lack of common purpose. Without such a purpose to pull together the fragments of an educational experience, measurements of success in the university become superficial, even cynical. Scholars evaluate colleagues by counting the number of their printed pages; teachers seeking to be relevant confuse education in the classroom with group therapy or entertainment; and at one college students practice the marginal art of the handshake. "The job market today is so tight," the explanation runs, "that it takes much more imagination and ingenuity to get a job." From the general educator's perspective, the words *imagination* and *ingenuity* refer to an individual's overall intelligence, not to the way a person shakes hands.

The arguments against a renewed interest in general education are imposing, and current institutional arrangements, strengthened by individual skepticism, tend to favor the status quo. Opponents argue, first, that general education experiments during the last fifty years have been so diversified as to defeat the very notion of a core or whole. They point to the tangle of still unanswered questions surrounding general education. What knowledge is worth the most? Is general education preparatory to special education? Is it equal to but separate from a liberal arts concentration? Is it a continuing process always seeking to achieve a more unified integration of knowledge? Is it a superficial whole lacking detail and precision? Is general education accomplished by means of extensive or restricted distribution requirements, by means of great books, by surveys of civilizations, or by individual guidance and self-motivation? In view of all this confusion, say the detractors, general education might best survive in the practical world of higher education as a philosophical abstraction, a useful fiction, an experiment here and there—in other words, a platitude.

Second, many of the standard arguments for freedom in the curriculum, including electives, and in-depth study, are used to oppose general education. For many, "common" means not only equally shared but average, bland, and dull. Specialized courses can be as effective an introduction to learning as general ones; enthusiastic, interested students learn more in the courses and programs they select and design themselves than in required ones. Individual freedom is central to a definition of humanistic learning, the opponents of general education claim. The freedom of students during college permits them to receive new ideas that break with the past, to consider new and unconventional experiments, and to begin establishing an adult personality. Those who advocate this position point out that it would be unwise to impose a new authoritarianism on the curriculum when the last Victorian repressions in American society have finally been relaxed.

Third, education for its own sake—for human growth, mature judgment, and moral discretion—sounds like an admirable ideal, and it may well succeed as an adjunct of the educational experience. However, for most middle- and upper-middle-class American families, higher education is a considerable financial investment from which practical returns in the form of an occupation are expected. Historians, for example, became concerned both with the state of the humanities in America and with the college graduate's ignorance of historical traditions only when large numbers of students deserted history courses. Those historians who now deplore the "new barbarians" with their practical concerns might well remember that students of history formerly pursued the subject as part of an investment. They used the liberal arts training to enter careers in the educational establishment (one of the largest industries in the country), publishing, government service, politics, and the ministry. As higher education becomes more and more expensive, middle-class expectations will focus even more than before on careers, vocations, and results.

Moreover, why should career-oriented students be different from their professors? College teachers are specialized professionals, sensitive about their status and authority, jealous of their field of knowledge, concerned with the specifics of mobility and income, and protective of the freedom of their life-styles. Students cannot help but observe the intense careerism inside the American university, an institution structurally arranged so that individual scholars, departments, and administrators compete with each other for authority, promotion, power, and money. Quite naturally, students respond by pursuing their own utilitarian interests. After all, professionals in the American university reflect the practical society in which they live. Many academic departments, for instance, view general education courses as the least desirable to teach, courses unlikely to bring professional distinction. They are assigned to junior faculty who, in order to advance in their careers, must also satisfy research and publication requirements. Frequently, only after difficulty and stress does a career move forward once it has become involved in the time-consuming and difficult process of formulating basic themes, explaining them to uninitiated students, and teaching basic skills to unprepared students. The promising young scholar who takes this task too seriously might earn, in the managerial language of the university administrator, a "merit termination."

Finally, the most cynical argument against general education is that the current attention being paid to a core curriculum may simply reflect the latest fad among educators who watch the fluctuating American marketplace. The humanist's advocacy of general education, especially of required courses, may be merely an effort to stay employed in bad times. Administrators who present the core curriculum to the public as a concern with the quality of their product—the college graduate—are aware that their commodity has not received high marks in the marketplace recently and may increasingly be in oversupply. For the merchandiser of education, general education may be one economical way for colleges to package students attractively. For an academic community that lacks cohesion and often has a faltering sense of what it stands for and what it should be doing, general education provides a superficial unity for public view.

Whether pro or con, most of the arguments I have presented

here share a pragmatic flavor that reflects the current insecurity among educators. Many of the concerns are functional: Can a serious approach to general education work, given the current arrangements in higher education? Can one get support for a general education curriculum that is neither preprofessional, methodological, or a traditional survey—in other words, a program that does not recruit students for a specific discipline? Most educators would agree that problems that can be resolved pragmatically, without opening up basic issues of philosophy and institutional structure, are best handled that way.

However, in every historical era, the curriculum of American higher education has tended to reflect the more deeply held values of American society. One reason for this is that the purpose of higher education has been to draw out the higher mental talents of the individual and prepare him or her for leadership in a nation that, on the surface anyway, cannot draw on enduring structures of social class, tradition, history, or even ethnicity. By and large, schools have institutionalized the social values of the American middle class, and educators have given form to these cultural commitments in the curriculum. Yet, what seems to be missing from the current debate about general education are these very philosophical premises that have been at the heart of previous discussions.

Making significant choices in life requires confidence in one's mental ability to reason with the ambiguities of a complex existence without becoming cynical; to focus on a single issue without being distracted; to conceptualize an issue beyond particular examples without creating an unending thicket of detail. But such confidence in one's mental ability must be confirmed constantly by everyday experience. When individuals view their own society as corrupt, violent, and dangerous, and view themselves as innocent victims, it is not surprising that they lack confidence in their own rational processes. The modern hero is one who survives at the margin of society, a loner who succeeds by manipulation and violence and is victimized by success. Moreover, justice and merit cease to exist where every regulation and principle is seen as treacherous, suspended for special people, aggrandizing the power of a few, and adding to the bank accounts of the well-to-do. According to this view, life is a game of winners and losers, and to compete seriously the individual must not question the rationality of rules or admit publicly to the ambiguity of victory. Deepening the sense of cynicism is an awareness that the most venal people in America appear to be the best trained.

If we are to resolve the debate about general education, we must break through this cynicism to the more positive premises on which American democracy was formed. Only then will it be possible to understand the proper role of the humanities in education.

13

The Core
of Learning

Ernest L. Boyer

The time has come to reaffirm the purposes of liberal education and to recommit ourselves to a common core curriculum.[1] At this late moment in our history, we desperately need to rediscover the threads of common experience that bind us together. Our future on the planet Earth may very well depend on it.

The history of our search for a core curriculum is well known to most educators. Harvard College's early attempt to devise a core curriculum resulted in an inflexible, divinely ordained course of study that was pursued unquestioningly by both students and faculty. Exception to the academic rules at Harvard

---

[1]This chapter summarizes ideas originally presented in E. Boyer and M. Kaplin, "Educating for Survival," *Change Magazine*, 1977, *9* (3): 22-29. The ideas are developed further in a book of the same title by the same authors scheduled for fall 1977 publication by Change Magazine Press.

was rarely taken and even less frequently granted. But, as educators learned more about the educational process and the learning differences of students and as college doors began to swing more widely open, colleges began to offer more courses and more electives, and to allow more student independence. The idea of some sort of common core remained alive in experiments at Columbia, Chicago, and St. John's, but only barely. Overwhelmingly, the trend for the past several decades has been toward a free-elective system. Today a kind of "curriculum cafeteria" seems to dominate the scene. In fact, about the only safe generalization we can make regarding baccalaureate graduates is that they probably have been around the campus for about four years. We can be more confident about the length of a college education than we can about its substance.

In a true democracy, a healthy tension exists between self-interests and broader social interests. Similarly, in an academic context a healthy curriculum must focus not only on the individual but also on society. A curriculum that suggests that students have nothing in common is just as flawed as one that suggests that students are all alike. If we are educating toward isolation rather than independence, we are educating toward half-truth and ignorance. We need a common-core curriculum because as individuals we hold some very fundamental things in common.

What is the knowledge and what are the experiences that should form the new common core of liberal education? I have three suggestions—all of them embarrassingly simple in design and profoundly difficult to execute. First, *all of us as members of the human race share a common heritage.* I believe that one of the main obligations of higher education is to help the human race rediscover this heritage and maintain a collective human memory. If we fail to acknowledge our common heritage, we lose not only our past but our future too. One way to study our common heritage would be to choose a few seminal events in human history, study them with great care, and try to understand how they have helped to shape our world today.

The second part of the new core curriculum should *focus on the present.* It has always seemed curious to me that most of our experiments in general education have focused almost compulsively on the past. We seem to understand that there is a commonness *behind* us but fail to realize that there is a commonness that *surrounds* us. We have been remarkably inattentive to the crucial common experiences in our contemporary world. The new curriculum I propose would examine our existence here and now and focus on the common experiences that significantly shape all our lives. Three illustrations come to mind. The first is communication. The world would be chaotic and without meaning if we were not connected by the instruments and symbols of communication. We all engage in the sending and receiving of messages. I believe the messages we send one another today will substantially determine the nature of the world in days to come. So it is most important that students understand how our language has developed, how we use and misuse electronic and print media, and how we communicate—not just with words, but with mathematics, music, computers, and even with dance. All students should be able to communicate effectively. College curricula should move toward giving them an understanding of how our lives are shaped by the symbols we receive and send.

My second illustration has to do with our social institutions. As social creatures, we are caught up in a web of institutions— schools, banks, towns, cities, clubs, and so forth. We are creatures of our own bureaucracies. One of the most important duties of education is to make students aware of the extent to which they control and are controlled by these institutions. Related to this is understanding how institutions might be changed to serve social needs.

My third illustration is from the world of work. One of the most powerful commitments human beings make is the commitment to productive work. I believe we have been remiss in failing to recognize the powerful impact of work on our lives. Confronting this reality should be a central concern of the common core curriculum. Everything we know about society and about ourselves tells us that our choice of work, our vocation, is overwhelmingly important in shaping our values and in determining the quality of our lives. To a very great extent, our work influences our judgments of who we are. But for some reason we have encouraged students to treat this fundamental choice as if it were a negligible concern. Many educators have suggested that collegiate traditions are demeaned if courses prepare students for finding jobs. Such a view not only distorts the present but also denies the past. Formal education from its earliest days has been defined and defended on the grounds of its usefulness for the world of work.

Recently, I lived for several months in Cambridge, England. It is a bucolic spot with gardens and ivy-covered walls and quiet academic courts seemingly far removed from the corridors of commerce and the clang of industry. During this stay, I read *The Masters,* by C. P. Snow. In the appendix of the book, Snow talks about the history of Cambridge University and describes how 600 years ago the first students came to the little village of Cambridge to meet with tutors. They slept in dusty lofts and often went hungry. They faced poverty for months, and the reason they stayed was to improve their chances of getting jobs—jobs in the royal administration, jobs in the courts, jobs in the church, jobs teaching in the schools. Their training, according to Snow, was *vocational.*[2] Similarly, Harvard College was founded not only to defend the Christian faith but also to prepare young men for jobs in the ministry, law, medicine, and teaching.

In more recent years, the unspoken assumption on every campus has been that our graduates would get productive jobs, and the greatest embarrassment for any academic department is to discover that its graduates "cannot get placed." The realities of work have always been part of the liberal tradition simply because they are a part of the human condition. Educators should be honest enough to affirm this fact to themselves and to their students. It is ironic that often those who deny the importance of preparing students for meaningful work are themselves frantically engaged in securing tenure.

Educators do confirm the legitimacy of traditional, familiar, respectable jobs. But because of tradition, lethargy, ignorance, or snobbery, they make a mindless distinction between what is vocationally legitimate and what is illegitimate for college students. Thus, it is all right to be a doctor but less than all right to be a nurse. It is all right to be an engineer, but computer programming is off limits. Teaching elementary school is acceptable, but teaching college is honorable. Digging into the ruins of the past is a respectable occupation, but working with ruined lives in an urban jungle, a much more demanding task, is not quite so worthy. There is no logic behind these distinctions, but they are made all the time by educators who guard the portals of vocational choice by the curricula they offer. I am not suggesting that our colleges

[2]C. P. Snow, *The Masters* (Middlesex, England: Penguin, 1976), pp. 300-312.

become vocational but that as we rediscover the meaning of work and its powerful relationship to the human experience on earth we will rediscover the true meaning of liberal education.

The new common core curriculum I have discussed should deal not only with the heritage of the past and the commonly shared experiences of the present; it must also contend with the future. Educators all too often have failed to focus on the interlocking relationship of time past, present, and future. If we want to formulate a common core curriculum on the basis of the common bonds of humanity, we cannot afford to avoid the issue of the future because it *is* the present and the past. Tomorrow is being shaped today. Robert Heilbroner observes that "there is a question in the air, a question so disturbing that I would hesitate to ask it aloud did I not believe it exists in the minds of many." The question, Heilbroner says, is this: "Is there hope for man?"[3]

We are at a crucial point in human history and cannot afford to play games in the academic enterprise. I believe we must begin to probe our curricula with a sense of great urgency. We must begin to think about a world where basic human values are more widely recognized and where the future is more than a consequence of indulging in selfish satisfactions today. We must express conviction on a few fundamental issues. We must, in short, have moral courage. George Steiner reminded us that even when a man is intellectually advanced he can be morally bankrupt at the same time. And that is our dilemma. Steiner says that we now know that such a man, well-educated, can listen to Bach at sundown. He can read Goethe in the evening, and the next morning he can go to his daily work at the concentration camp to kill his fellow man.[4] In order to avoid such a grotesque mismatch between higher education and human ethics, we must not only teach the basic skills and protect academic freedom; we must help students understand the critical moral questions and choices they face.

The issues of the future can be phrased quite simply. Where will we get our food, and how can it be appropriately distributed? What about our energy supply? How can it be equitably shared?

[3]R. Heilbroner, "The Human Prospect," *New York Review of Books*, January 24, 1974.
[4]G. Steiner, *Language and Silence* (New York: Atheneum, 1970).

How can we reduce the poisons in the atmosphere and still stay warm and happy? Can we achieve a proper balance between population and the life support system of the planet? And, maybe more crucially, how can we live together, with civility, in a climate of increasing constraint? These are a few of the transcendent issues that need to preoccupy the students on our college campuses now. All of us must begin to think and talk about these issues with great care, not out of panic but out of concern.

At a recent seminar in the ancient Persian city of Persepolis, John Gardner said, "Our planet is but a speck of dust in the universe, and our life on it is but an instant in the long stretch of astrophysical time. Still, it is the only planet we have and our life on it holds great possibilities of beauty and dignity and meaning. Yet, if it were to be asked of us how we spend our instant of time on our speck of dust, we would have to say, 'We spend a good deal fighting one another and laying waste our earth.' Surely," Gardner went on to say, "all of us here believe that we can do better."[5]

Those of us in education, who have a hand in shaping the lives of others, and therefore in shaping the future of our world, have a special obligation to go beyond the issue of *where* we teach, or *how long* we teach, and confront the deeper issue of *what* we teach. It may be that, as we educate ourselves better and as we help to sensitize the human spirit, we will begin to build a more secure future for this fragile planet.

---

[5]J. Gardner, "The Modern World: General Perspectives," in J. W. Jacqz (Ed.), *Iran: Past and Present* (Palo Alto: Aspen Institute, 1976), p. 26.

14

Continuing Education and Licensing

Benjamin S. Shimberg

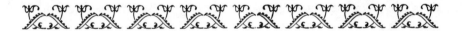

A confrontation is developing between the professions and the public over the matter of professional regulation. At issue are two closely related questions: What is the purpose of licensing? And to whom do licensing boards owe their primary allegiance—to the public or to the professional groups they regulate? There is a growing feeling among the public that the purpose of licensing has been subverted. Although licensing laws were passed initially with the promise that they would provide assurance of high-quality service and protect the public from incompetent practitioners, it is now alleged that the powers entrusted to licensing boards are often used to promote the interests of the occupational group at the expense of the public.

A study of licensing practices and policies has shown that licensing boards often seek to restrict the supply of practitioners by setting excessively high standards, by using exclusionary tests, or by creating arbitrary barriers to interstate mobility.[1] Reports from the Federal Trade Commission and the Anti-Trust Division of the Department of Justice have revealed that some boards have used their rule-making powers to restrict competition by prohibiting price advertising or by making it unethical to engage in competitive bidding. Consumer groups have charged that boards dominated by members of the regulated profession have often been insensitive to complaints from the public and have failed to discipline licensees for incompetence or for failure to fulfill their professional responsibilities.

Although such criticism has led to the passage of sunset laws in a number of states in an effort to get rid of unnecessary boards, relatively little has been done to correct the most serious and potentially explosive criticism of all—that licensing boards have failed to perform their primary function of protecting the public. They have consistently neglected to weed out incompetents successfully or to take steps needed to ensure the continued competence of those whom they have licensed.

The original justification for placing regulatory powers in the hands of boards made up of practitioners was that it was the best way to ensure high standards. It was argued that only qualified practioners would be able to establish minimum entry requirements and examine applicants with respect to their fitness to practice. Self-regulation carried with it the implied promise that these same boards would somehow monitor their licensees to ensure that each practitioner maintained his competence.

This last premise or promise—that boards will monitor the competence of licensees—has for the most part been a dead letter. American tradition holds that an individual's license is good for life. It can be taken away only for cause. This situation has arisen, in part, because boards have concentrated most of their attention on screening applicants for competence, making sure they have met training and experience requirements and have passed the necessary tests. Boards did not go out looking for evidence of incompetence. They generally waited for complaints to come in. Because there were few complaints and even fewer revocations, a myth was born: Once licensed, forever competent.

---

[1]B. Shimberg, D. Kruger, and B. Esser, *Occupational Licensing: Practices and Policies* (Washington, D.C.: Public Affairs Press, 1972).

This is a dangerous, self-serving myth. In a horse-and-buggy era, when the pace of change was relatively slow, the store of knowledge that practitioners brought with them from professional training might well serve for most, if not all, of their professional lives. As professionals, they were expected to keep up with new developments, and, given the pace of change, this was not an unreasonable expectation.

But today that expectation is no longer reasonable. In nearly all fields, but especially in those related to science and technology, the knowledge explosion has been enormous. What people learn during their years of professional training rapidly becomes obsolete. New knowledge, new techniques, and new materials have proliferated at an unprecedented rate. Professionals have narrowed their fields, thinking that in this way they might somehow manage to keep up. But even so, unless practitioners make strenuous efforts to stay abreast of developments, the probability is high that over time their knowledge of their fields will diminish.

This situation has troubled many thoughtful people in the professions, in legislatures, and in the consumer movement. While recognizing that many professionals were maintaining their competence through voluntary programs of continuing education, many people have felt that the voluntary approach might not be working as well as it should. It has been noted that not all professionals are equally conscientious. How is the public to distinguish between those who have kept up and those who have not? Accessibility to continuing education opportunities poses another problem. Opportunities for training are at present very unevenly distributed, so that what is accessible to a professional working in a metropolitan area may be inaccessible to a practitioner in a rural area. Leaving it to individual practitioners to determine their competence and to make their own decisions about maintaining competence does not appear to be in the public interest.

In 1967 the National Commission on Health Manpower took note of the problem of medical obsolescence and concluded that "simply making educational opportunities available will not assure their utilization . . . unless sufficient incentives are provided. One way of providing such incentives would be to relicense health professionals periodically on the basis of acceptable performance in programs of continuing education or on the basis of challenge examinations for those who choose not to participate formally in continuing education."[2]

In its 1971 report to Congress on the licensure of health manpower, the Department of Health, Education and Welfare (HEW) recommended that professional associations and states should include specific requirements to ensure a continued level of professional competence as one condition of the recredentialing process.[3]

It is always difficult to establish causality, but there can be little doubt that the 1971 HEW statement helped to trigger efforts by a number of professional groups and state licensing officials to make continuing education mandatory. New Mexico was the first state to enact mandatory continuing education legislation for physicians. Since then, fourteen other states have amended their practice acts to authorize licensing boards to require continuing medical education as a condition of relicensure. Other professions, such as nursing, optometry, pharmacy, and accountancy, have also worked hard to get mandatory continuing education laws on the statute books.

According to a recent American Medical Association (AMA) Continuing Education Fact Sheet, fourteen state medical associations and seven medical specialty societies have adopted a policy statement making continuing medical education a condition of membership.[4] Significantly, all twenty-two medical specialty boards have established policies that will require periodic recertification, and thirteen of them have actually announced specific dates when recertification will begin.

A whole new industry has been spawned to deal with the problems created by mandatory continuing education. Large numbers of educators and association officials are now developing and promoting continuing education courses, and machinery has been

[2]*Report of the National Advisory Commission on Health Manpower*, Vol. 1 (Washington, D.C.: U.S. Government Printing Office, 1967), pp. 41-42.

[3]U.S. Department of Health, Education and Welfare, *Report on Licensure and Related Health Personnel Credentialing*, DHEW Publication (HSW) 72-11 (Washington, D.C.: U.S. Government Printing Office, 1971).

[4]*AMA Continuing Education Fact Sheet*, Division of Education Policy Development, American Medical Association, 535 N. Dearborn Street, Chicago, Ill. 60610, September 30, 1976.

created for accrediting courses, recording participation, and maintaining cumulative records.

The headlong rush to mandatory continuing education has created problems. For example, while considerable effort has been expended to ensure that courses are offered under responsible auspices, that content is sound, and that individuals do, in fact, participate, there has been no comparable emphasis to find out whether those who take the courses have learned anything. The continuing education units (CEUs) awarded at the end of a course connote attendance. There seems to be a built-in assumption that, if an individual is physically present during a course, he or she must have learned something. It should be noted, however, that this criticism is not an inherent weakness of continuing education. Rather it is a problem that pertains to the way many programs are conducted at the present time. This weakness could be rectified by placing greater emphasis on evaluating the outcomes of the continuing education experience.

Another criticism of efforts to equate mandatory continuing education with competence is the lack of evidence that continuing education is necessarily related to performance on the job. People have asked, "How do we know that the continuing education experience is what the individual really needs to become more competent?" The present system relies on practitioners selecting from an array of accredited courses whichever ones they believe are most appropriate. Two assumptions seem to be operating here: first, that individuals know what they need, and, second, that they will take the courses that will be most rewarding from a professional viewpoint. The difficulty with these assumptions is that practitioners may not always know where they are weak, and the factors underlying course selection may be determined by considerations that have nothing to do with what will be most rewarding or beneficial professionally.

The lack of any demonstrated relationship between continuing education and competence has not gone unnoticed by legislators. During a series of regional conferences for legislators and other state officials conducted during 1975 and 1976, this point was frequently discussed. One legislator felt that "We should not try to mandate continuing education for everyone until we have a better feel for what it can accomplish." Another asked, "Is it worthwhile to subject a whole discipline to mandatory continuing education when only a small minority may need it?" A third legislator asked, "What assurance do we have that continuing education will provide the consumer with greater protection against incompetent practitioners?" Consumer officials frequently expressed concern about the cost of continuing education and the possibility that this requirement might increase the cost of services.[5]

In weighing the pros and cons of relying on mandatory or voluntary programs of continuing education to ensure continued competence, Ruth Roemer made the following observation: "Continuing education may entail the danger of introducing a pro forma proviso, whereby individual burdens in expenditure of time, energy and money are imposed on educational programs and practitioners without improving performance."[6]

Cohen and Miike, writing in the *International Journal of Health Services,* noted that "compulsory continuing education should not be oversimplified or accepted as a panacea. There are still basic questions . . . whether traditional forms of continuing education have any significant relationship to quality assurance."[7]

In a similar vein, William Selden, formerly the director of the Study of Accreditation of Selected Health Educational Programs, made the following observation during a conference on mandatory continuing education for the professions in Dallas, Texas: "Although continuing professional competence has been increasing in importance, we have not yet been able to define such competence with reasonable precision nor measure it with adequate accuracy. Despite these limitations, mandated continuing education is being established as a requirement for recertification and/or relicensure in a growing number of professions on the unproven assumption that mere participation in continuing education programs provides reasonable assurance of continuing competence."[8]

[5] B. Shimberg, *Improving Occupational Regulation* (Princeton, N.J.: Educational Testing Service, July 1976).

[6] R. Roemer, "Social Regulation of Health Manpower," in A. N. Charters and R. J. Blakely (Eds.), *Fostering the Growing Need to Learn,* DHEW Publication No. (HRA) 24-3112 (Washington, D.C.: U.S. Government Printing Office, 1973), p. 403.

[7] H. S. Cohen and L. H. Miike, "Toward a More Responsive System of Professional Licensure," *International Journal of Health Services,* 1974, *4* (2): 268.

[8] W. K. Selden, "Implications for Society of Mandatory Continuing Education for the Professions," address at Conference on Mandatory Con-

The *Proposal for Credentialing Health Manpower* issued by HEW in June 1976 alludes to the 1971 HEW report that had advocated specific requirements for recertification and relicensure. The authors of this latest HEW report state that the 1971 report had been "widely interpreted to mean that HEW endorsed the adoption of a mandatory continuing education requirement for relicensure or recertification." They say that this was not the intent of the earlier recommendation, that "it must be clearly understood that there may be other more efficient or effective models of attaining continued competence." They go on to say, "Instead of endorsing a single method such as continuing education, which itself is often unvalidated or of questionable relevance to continued competence, the subcommittee urges that additional support be given to the development of more sophisticated approaches to continued competence which ultimately can be tied into a mandatory recertification or relicensure requirement."[9]

Although such statements do not negate the value of continuing education, they do raise questions about the wisdom of relying exclusively on the mandatory continuing education approach to maintain continued competence or to assure the quality of service.

Periodic reassessment as a condition for relicensure is frequently mentioned as a more direct and more dependable way to determine whether or not practitioners have maintained their competence. Reassessment does not necessarily mean a sole reliance on written tests to evaluate competence. Peer review, case record review, and simulations could all be part of a reassessment process.

However, the idea of reassessment usually meets with strong resistance from practitioners, whose licenses could be jeopardized by failure to meet the competency standard set for renewal. It appears that many practitioners would prefer to go along with a relatively nonthreatening mandatory continuing education requirement of dubious value than face the perils of a meaningful reassessment process. This attitude is understandable. Nobody, least of all a professional, wants to risk losing a license on the basis of a

---

tinuing Education for the Professions in Texas, Southern Methodist University, Dallas, June 21, 1976.

[9] U.S. Department of Health, Education and Welfare, Health Resources Administration, *Proposal for Credentialing Health Manpower* (Washington, D.C.: U.S. Government Printing Office, June 1976).

test. Many hasten to point out, as Selden did in his Texas speech, that we have not yet been able "to define competence with reasonable precision or to measure it with adequate accuracy."

There is no doubt that the problems of defining competence and measuring it need further study before formal reassessment procedures can be introduced or used with confidence as a basis for determining who is and who is not competent to continue in practice. Fortunately, people are at work on these problems and some progress is being made in both areas.

Job analysis studies are under way in a number of professions to find out what practitioners actually do. From these analyses, an attempt will be made to determine what levels of knowledge and skill are required for satisfactory performance. Another approach being used is an analysis of critical incidents of physician performance. What is emerging from these studies of critical incidents is a better understanding of the importance of being able to integrate and apply knowledge in problem solving and in decision making. These studies are also highlighting the fact that competence involves noncognitive components such as interpersonal and communication skills, attitudes, and personal attributes such as ethics and responsibility. Defining competence, occupation by occupation, and then establishing meaningful standards is not going to be easy, but it definitely holds the key to future progress in this field.

The problem of measuring competency is equally challenging. What testing does best at present is measure the cognitive aspects of a field—a person's knowledge, skills, understanding, and, to some extent, the person's ability to use knowledge to solve problems. But measuring that knowledge is not enough. Practitioners need to know what is important and unimportant in given situations. They need to know what knowledge to apply and when to apply it. To this end, measurement specialists have been experimenting with simulations of real-life situations. Some simulations are very complex and require the test taker to interact with a computer. It is still too early to predict the future role of computers in the assessment of competency. While there is no doubt that computers have provided researchers with a powerful analytic tool, it remains to be seen if performance on computer simulations is significantly related to performance on the job and if their use can be justified in terms of cost effectiveness.

A less dramatic, less expensive, but equally fascinating approach that is already operational is called the "patient management problem." It is essentially a written simulation that presents a realistic problem. As the problem unfolds, the test taker can ask for more information, make decisions based on the information, and get feedback. In working on a patient management problem, the test taker uses a felt-tipped marker. A chemical in the pen causes invisible ink to appear in the response booklet each time the test taker seeks more information or makes a decision. From the pattern of responses, it is possible to evaluate the efficiency with which the test taker has managed both the diagnosis and treatment and to judge whether the treatment is satisfactory. As in the case of computer simulations, the validity and cost effectiveness of this approach have yet to be demonstrated empirically.

Progress is also being made in other areas. Peer review procedures—at least for physicians—are being sharpened under programs mandated by the federal government. Occupational therapists are one of the groups experimenting with methods to standardize and objectify the evaluation of case records. These nontest approaches are perceived by some as alternatives to formal testing, while others view them as supplements to written tests and simulations.

But, even as test and other procedures become more job related and more reliable, the anxiety generated by the prospect of reassessment is not likely to diminish for the practitioners, whose licenses would be at stake. If anything, it will probably increase because some of the arguments practitioners now use for rejecting tests and other reassessment procedures would become less tenable. One way to reduce the tensions associated with reassessment would be to provide practitioners with an opportunity to find out beforehand in which areas of competence they may be weak so they could "brush up" before facing the formal reassessment process on which license renewal would depend.

Such advance knowledge of possible areas of weakness can be acquired by a procedure known as "self-assessment" testing. This procedure is already well established and well accepted in a number of the health-related occupations. The self-assessment tests are prepared by experts using up-to-date job analysis data. Practitioners who elect to participate in the self-assessment process are usually advised beforehand which topics will be covered and by what standard their performance will be measured. Thus, the self-assessment enables practitioners to find out where they stand with respect to the competencies and standards.

A critical feature of self-assessment is the assurance of anonymity. The tests are taken in the privacy of the home or office. Test papers are scored centrally, and practitioners are advised of the results. They are assured that no one will be able to find out whether they did well or poorly in any areas.

Perhaps the greatest value of self-assessment is the diagnostic feedback that the program provides. For each question or problem, the test taker should be able to ascertain the correct answer, the rationale underlying the correct answer, and why other answers were incorrect or not acceptable. Bibliographic references are usually provided so that practitioners can go to source materials to get a fuller understanding of topics in which they display a weakness. If the content and procedures used in the self-assessment process were linked with those used in making the relicensure decision, much of the anxiety and uncertainty associated with relicensure could be eliminated. Practitioners would know beforehand what to expect from the relicensure procedure, where they were weak, and what corrective action to take.

The responsibility for overcoming deficiencies revealed during the self-assessment process should rest with the individual practitioner. The state should not prescribe continuing education or any other specific remedy. Indeed, the individual should be free to pursue continuing education in whatever manner best suits his or her circumstances and learning preferences. The entire process would thus be less ego threatening, since the likelihood of failure or "loss of face" among professional colleagues would have been minimized.

To date, the approach just described—linking self-assessment with some type of formal competency assessment—has not been used by any state for relicensure. But it should not be dismissed as visionary or impractical. The recertification program of the American Board of Internal Medicine (ABIM) incorporates virtually all of the elements set forth here. The current ABIM recertification program is entirely voluntary. However, if it proves successful and gains wide acceptance, it could become mandatory, as is already the case with the American Academy of Family Physicians. The ABIM recertification exam was offered for the first time in October 1974, and more than 3,000 certificate holders voluntarily took it.

There is a close tie between the ABIM recertification process and the self-assessment program sponsored by the American College of Physicians (ACP). The ACP self-assessment program was inaugurated in 1967. The exam included both multiple-choice and patient management problems.

As the first step in its self-assessment program, ABIM publishes a 300-page syllabus covering ten specialty areas and one subspecialty. The syllabus is not a textbook. It may best be described as a concise study guide of current information that can be superimposed on a framework of general medical knowledge.

Each subscriber receives a set of multiple-choice question testbooks and answer sheets. There are about eighty questions in each of the specialty areas. At about the same time, the subscriber also receives materials related to patient management problems, including a testbook, a response book, and pictorials.

Shortly after the papers are scored, the test takers receive computer-generated summary score reports. These reports provide a gross score for each of the specialty fields and give candidates a rough idea of their areas of weakness. A month or two later, candidates receive a ten-page computer printout showing results for every question in every area. A critique and reference book provide justification for the correct answers for each of the 800 multiple-choice questions. They also clarify why the other options were wrong or inappropriate.

Although the ABIM recertification program is voluntary, the one sponsored by the American Board of Family Practice (ABFP) is mandatory. When the ABFP was established in 1969, the founders decided that certification would be good for only six years. As a prerequisite to recertification, family physicians are required to take an average of fifty hours of coursework annually. The recertification examination consists of two parts. The first is a chart analysis in which the physician answers a set of detailed questions about how patients suffering from certain common ailments were treated. The practitioner is required to document the answers in this part by providing copies of office records with the names of patients removed.

The second phase of recertification consists of two written tests. One is a multiple-choice examination; the other, a series of patient management problems. A physician who fails any part of the recertification procedure is allowed to try again the following year. A second failure results in loss of certification.

If the examples cited represent the direction in which certification agencies are beginning to move, it is very likely that similar concepts will soon be applied in the field of licensure. One should not expect this to come about in the near future. However, as these concepts gain acceptance and demonstrate their usefulness in certification programs, it is reasonable to suppose that they will provide a framework for licensing procedures. The concept of re-certification and relicensure based exclusively on mandatory continuing education is not likely to survive as the procedures described here gain wider currency. In place of continuing education, we may expect to see the emergence of systems that use a variety of techniques—examinations, case-record analysis, peer review, and other approaches. Self-assessment procedures are likely to play an important role in directing the attention of practitioners to those areas of practice where their competencies fail to meet the standard.

What will these new approaches mean to the educational community? Clearly, there is an opportunity for the scholars and scientists who are generating new knowledge and new applications to work more closely with the practitioners who must demonstrate their continued competence. But colleges and universities should not assume that they can offer continuing education the same way they now conduct professional training. The prospective consumers of continuing education are busy professionals whose time is valuable. They want continuing education packaged so it can be absorbed in highly individualized ways—driving between home and office; early in the morning or late at night; alone or in the company of colleagues. Medical practitioners have been conditioned by drug companies and by commercial medical educators to expect not only high-quality material and production but also sophisticated packaging. They know all about audio and video cassettes, which are much more convenient than going to a medical school to listen to a lecture or watch a demonstration.

If higher education expects to play a major role in continuing education for the professions, it will need to research the market, as its competitors are already doing. It will need to display flexibility in the way its materials are organized and packaged. It will need to accommodate the varied learning styles and learning preferences of practitioners. Above all, it will need to take responsibility for making sure that what it offers is both efficient and effective in helping practitioners overcome the deficiencies revealed by self-assessment programs. The moment of truth will come when the practitioner takes the relicensure or recertification examination. Unless continuing education programs can prepare practitioners for that moment, whatever other merits the program may have will count for naught.

15

Licensure:
A Critical View

Daniel M. Kasper

Since at least 1910, when the publication of the Flexner Report led to the accreditation of medical schools, the standard explanation for accreditation and licensure statutes has been the protection of the public from incompetent practitioners.[1] The case for licensing physicians is the strongest that can be made for occupational licensure, and it is the example I will use throughout this paper as a proxy for the broader application of licensing and accrediting. An episode from the comic strip "The Wizard of Id" reflects the growing contemporary skepticism of the standard explanation. Rodney, the king's right-hand knight, drags a scruffy peasant before the throne and announces: "We caught this fraud practicing medicine without a license!" The obviously puzzled king responds: "So why bother me? Sell him a license."

---

[1]A. Flexner, *Medical Education in the United States and Canada* (New York: Arno Press, 1972).

The grounds for such skepticism are substantial. Kessel has shown that restriction of competition was a central purpose of the American Medical Association and traces its role in the Flexner Report.[2] Shimberg and others have revealed the efficacy of licensure as a tool for enrichment and protection of the licensed professions.[3] But questions of motive or purpose are perhaps the least serious challenges facing licensure, for motives can change and legislatures can rewrite statutes and reconstitute licensing boards to change regulatory directions. Two other basic questions, however, strike at the heart of licensure. First, even assuming that licensure's purpose is to protect the public, does the public need additional protection or are the normal range of consumer protections adequate? Second, if additional protection is required, is licensure the best means to that end? The first question strikes at the very reason for licensure's existence. The second challenges its effectiveness.

By far the strongest argument in favor of occupational licensure is that it (potentially) guarantees a minimum standard of practitioner competence in an area too technical for the average consumer to make an intelligent, informed decision. The absence of licensure, it is argued, would result in a lower average quality of care than consumers desire and would be willing to purchase.

But do consumers of medical services really need the purported protections of licensure? In addition to their normal common sense, patients are protected by the operation of market forces such as the doctor's desire for continued patronage and the availability of alternative physicians to supply services a doctor fails to provide patients. Further protections are provided by law. Incompetent or careless doctors can be sued for damages arising from malpractice or breach of contract. Civil and criminal prosecutions for fraud and other offenses are also used to police physician conduct. Finally, physicians undertake certain ethical obligations by virtue of their office, and these, too, afford some protection to patients.

Additional doubts concerning the need for medical licensure

[2] R. Kessel, "The AMA and the Supply of Physicians," *Journal of Law & Contemporary Problems*, 1970, *35* (2).
[3] B. Shimberg and others, *Occupational Licensing: Practices and Policies* (Washington, D.C.: Public Affairs Press, 1972).

are raised by the widespread adoption of third-party medical insurance. In the absence of licensure statutes, insurance companies could be expected to take a much more active interest in the quality of care received by those they insure. Screening of health care providers by insurers would provide additional information to the consumer without creating many of the undesirable side effects of licensure.

Finally, the growing role of large institutions in the delivery of health care services makes occupational licensure of individual health professionals increasingly anachronistic. It seems highly unlikely that the Mayo Clinic, for example, would fail to deliver quality health care in the absence of mandatory licensing of individual doctors.

In addition to its questionable conceptual foundations, occupational licensure, in practice, generates expensive operational costs. Some costs arise from the expense of operating the licensing and regulatory system. But the indirect costs are much more serious. Thus far, we have implicitly assumed that licensure actually increases the average quality of care, but that conclusion is not warranted. Since education to meet licensure standards is very costly, higher licensing standards tend to increase medical costs (and taxes), reduce the supply of doctors, and hence increase prices to consumers. This inevitably prevents some needy patients from obtaining physician services and thereby tends to lower the average quality of care for the population as a whole. The difficulty is that while licensure aims at producing uniformly high-quality doctors, many users would be better off with less qualified M.D.'s or even paramedics and midwives. In short, consumers would benefit from a wider range of price and quality choices than licensure provides.

Licensure also imposes other costs on society. In order to have any effect, licensure must define its scope of authority, for example, the practice of medicine. But defining and limiting the practice of medicine to licensed professionals generates costly side effects. First, it restrains innovation, such as the use of paramedics, by exposing innovators to criminal prosecution for practicing without a license. It is no accident that the armed forces, rather than the private medical community, pioneered the use of paramedics and other health professionals. Second, licensure frequently perpetuates a high-cost, overly standardized industry structure by defining acceptable practice so as to prevent the introduction of less-expensive technologies. Licensing for funeral parlors and embalmers is a classic example of this phenomenon. License restrictions that sharply limit the ability of charter airlines to compete with regularly scheduled airlines is another. The American Medical Association's use of its licensure and accreditation powers to limit the spread of low-cost competition from closed-panel health insurance plans (such as the Kaiser Plan) is a third example.

Problems such as these arise because licensure is essentially a static response to a dynamic process. It is, of necessity, directed to the past—like the proverbial generals who prepare for the last war rather than the next. The practice of medicine is, and should be, constantly changing. The more dynamic that change, the greater hindrance licensure becomes, for it shackles new developments to old concepts of "the practice of medicine."

Individuals also are hurt by licensure. Those excluded by licensure's restrictions are forced into lower-preference occupations. There is strong evidence that such restrictions tend to fall on minorities, which is the crux of the present controversy over the use of bar exams. Kessel, for example, finds evidence of anti-Semitism in medical licensure. Licensing restrictions on entry, as discussed earlier, reduce the supply and raise the price of medical services and may lower the average quality of care to individual users. Furthermore, to the extent that licensure restricts entry into an occupation, licensed members of that group can derive the economic benefits of lessened competition.

For those as yet unwilling to give up the "protection" of licensure let me pose the following question: If licensure is so valuable and useful to consumers and society, why is it a necessary prerequisite to consumption? Fruit and vegetables are valuable foodstuffs, but we do not (yet) require shoppers to buy only from licensed farmers. Consumers are not forced to eat only "Chiquita" bananas or "Sunkist" oranges.

Why is it that we, unlike the King of Id, assume the benefits of licensure lie in its power to exclude? A system combining required public disclosure of a practitioner's education, training, and experience, along with voluntary accrediting and certificating (such as is provided by current medical specialty boards) could extract the benefits imputed to licensure without incurring the added costs. The concept is best conveyed by a sign outside a bustling, prosperous medical office in a large Indian city: "Doctor A. Sethi, University of Tennessee Medical School (Failed)."

Perhaps even more urgent is the need to rethink the concept of what or who should be licensed, accredited, or certificated. The increasing complexity of medical treatment with the introduction of expensive, capital-intensive technologies requires the combined contributions of numerous participants. Who is the provider of medical services under such circumstances, individuals or the institution? Licensing only individual doctors, nurses, and other individuals in such an institutional setting is comparable to licensing tires and carburetors but not cars. In fact, it is much worse than that, for it prevents the institutional provider from experimenting with different combinations of medical personnel in order to find better ways to deliver health care services. In short, licensure focuses on the input characteristics of medical care (the training of doctors and nurses) when what is ultimately important is the output (healthy patients). At a minimum, licensure laws should be amended to permit the issuance of institutional licenses that do not restrict institutions in the manner prescribed by individual licensing statutes.

Alternatives to traditional licensure will require some social adjustments. More educational emphasis will be needed on preparing users for intelligent decision making under rapidly changing circumstances. Much less reliance will be needed on the elitist, guild-like mentality that substitutes the "better" decisions of experts for those of individual consumers. Likewise, the alternatives proposed require somewhat more humility about our collective ability as a society to improve the lot of consumers and somewhat more faith in the basic intelligence and educability of human beings. The proposals would require educators to do what they are already supposed to do: teach people how to think. The search for truth is just that—a search—and licensure, like other human creations, is not an eternal verity.

16

Too Many College Graduates?

Lewis C. Solmon

A recent review of changes in our society, recognizing the decline of the Puritan ethic, said: "In the mid 1970s, there is evidence of what might best be described as a 'no-risk ethic,' with everyone wanting assurance of what is coming to him or her and someone to blame and hold responsible if things go wrong. People increasingly want to be 'insured' against job loss, family breakup, inadequate or incorrect medical attention, and unsafe or faulty products."[1] It is not enough that education increases one's chances of finding a job; it is now argued that graduates are justified in demanding assurance of a "good job."

From current rhetoric, including vivid descriptions of a few Ph.D. holders driving taxis through the South Bronx, some people

[1] *A Culture in Transformation: Toward a Different Societal Ethic?* TAP Report 12 (New York: Institute of Life Insurance, 1975).

172

have concluded that the value of a college education is decreasing
and that Americans are "overeducated." This observation is also
based on the declining rate of return over the past few years from
a college education compared to the rate of return on less schooling. Although this decline has occurred during a recession, many
people view it with alarm. They observe that the increasing educational level of the general population—a development most of
them advocated only ten years ago—is evidence of an irreversible
oversupply of talented manpower that will lead to discontent and
possibly confrontation. These observers ignore the fact that the
college educated still earn more money than those with less education.

This is not to deny the existence of a supply-demand problem with respect to college-educated people. A much larger proportion of the population currently holds bachelor's degrees than
ever before, and as more people enter the labor force armed with
B.A.'s, they will be forced inevitably into taking jobs that have not
been traditional for college graduates. Although the job market
does not seem to have caused college enrollment to drop, it does
seem to have influenced students to move into fields with the best
employment prospects. The long period of growth in liberal arts
has been substantially reversed in recent years. In 1970, 3 percent
of entering freshmen selected English as their probable major field,
compared with only 1 percent in 1975. Some 12.7 percent of the
college freshmen selected other arts and humanities majors in
1970, but this percentage fell to 8.3 in 1975.[2] But this kind of
shifting in response to the job market is not unprecedented and
cannot, by itself, be taken as evidence of an oversupply of educated manpower.

To get a better fix on the issue, our recent study of the relationship between education and work, funded by the National
Institute of Education and the College Placement Council, surveyed people who had graduated in 1965 and who had been working about nine years.[3] This time frame enabled us to study gradu-

[2] A. W. Astin, and others, *The American Freshman: National Norms
for Fall 1970, 1971, 1972* (Washington, D.C.: American Council on Education). A. W. Astin and others, *The American Freshman: National Norms for
Fall 1973, 1974, 1975, 1976* (Los Angeles: University of California).
[3] L. C. Solmon, A. S. Bisconti, and N. L. Ochsner, *College as a Training Ground for Jobs* (New York: Praeger, 1977).

ates who had settled into their careers and to avoid the problem of new entrants, who are usually in temporary or experimental jobs or jobs they are still learning. Most new entrants to the labor market take positions that are not typical of those they will hold several years later. An analysis of this group might provide results unfairly biased toward dissatisfaction with, and nonutilization of, college training. The same individuals who are dissatisfied now because they are not using their training may very well get more satisfying jobs later.

If there is a value in analyzing new entrants, it is not in measuring the usefulness of college training or in comparing the job satisfaction of young workers with the job satisfaction of older workers. The proper comparison is between the youth today and youth of earlier generations. Some critics maintain that even when compared with earlier generations, current youth are more dissatisfied. However, a recent study that evaluated the job satisfaction of workers from 1958 to 1973 indicated that for the past fifteen years younger workers have been consistently less satisfied with their jobs than older workers.[4] The alleged decline in job satisfaction of younger workers has not been empirically substantiated.

Although few college graduates fail to find jobs, fear is growing that they are increasingly being forced into jobs in which they are underemployed. Inadequate thought has been given to the meaning and measurement of "underemployment." The most literal definition includes the concept that the individual is not working at the type of job for which he or she is trained. Our study has questioned whether even the most specific college major trains individuals for particular jobs. In many cases, college provides a way of thinking, communicating, and learning that makes the graduate an appropriate employee.

A broader but related question is how to utilize fully a graduate's skills and talents. In the past, a common assumption was that the skills of a college-educated person are not used fully if he or she has a job title that does not sound related to the college major. According to this view, to make the most of skills learned in the study of chemistry, one has to become a chemist. But our

---

[4]U.S. Department of Labor, *Job Satisfaction: Is There a Trend?* Manpower Research Monograph No. 30 (Washington, D.C.: U.S. Government Printing Office, 1974).

survey has shown that many people who work in jobs that might seem unrelated to their majors think they are using their college education frequently or almost always in their work. Although many individuals feel they use specific course content in their jobs, some of them also indicate they do not think all their skills and talents are used. Most perceive full utilization as the application of talents, both innate and learned, that go well beyond the specifics acquired in college courses.

About half the respondents in our study think they are working in jobs closely related to their majors; another 25 percent think they are in jobs somewhat related, while 25 percent think they hold jobs not at all related to their majors. Of those in unrelated jobs, about 90 percent hold these jobs voluntarily. That is, the majority of those not using their college training directly have not been pushed out of related jobs but pulled into more desirable situations.

Perceptions of job relatedness and the extent to which job relatedness contributes to work satisfaction and income vary substantially by major and by occupation. The percentages of respondents who use the major frequently or almost always include, by major: education, 61 percent; business, 55 percent; engineering, 49 percent; English, 44 percent; economics, 37 percent; and other social sciences, 24 percent. Overall, 10 percent report that they never use the content of major courses in the job, while 48 percent say they use the content frequently or almost always. Perceptions also differ substantially by sex. One reason for this could be that more women than men are in low-level jobs. Some 56 percent of the men and 37 percent of the women surveyed think their jobs fit their long-range goals.

Almost 60 percent of the respondents are very satisfied with their jobs. Those in jobs closely related to their majors are slightly more satisfied than those in unrelated jobs, but the difference is small. Only 5 percent of the respondents are not at all satisfied with their present jobs, and these are primarily individuals who involuntarily hold jobs unrelated to their majors. Aside from this, no clear pattern emerged to suggest that people with jobs related to their majors are more satisfied with their work or that those in unrelated jobs are less satisfied.

When one is interpreting data on the value of education, the distinction between a "large" response and a "small" response is somewhat arbitrary. For example, the survey of college graduates revealed that 48 percent think they use the content of their undergraduate majors in their jobs almost always or frequently. This figure can lead sympathetic commentators to argue that colleges and universities are doing well if almost half of those with bachelor's degrees find jobs in which they use the substance of their majors. But critics can argue that something is terribly wrong when over half of those with degrees are not in jobs that use their training. Most hard data are subject to at least two interpretations.

Added to the problem of subjective interpretation is the vagueness of the term *underemployment* itself. Taking it to mean insufficient use of one's training presents problems. For example, the bank president with a B.A. in classics is not, in the strict sense, using his college training in his work. However, who would say that, with a salary of perhaps $250,000 a year, he is underemployed? Has he been misled by the promise that college would provide him with a job without underemployment? This example suggests the need for some other definitions of underemployment. Perhaps those who are not satisfied with their work are underemployed. Research on the psychology of satisfaction with work and other aspects of life is inadequate. Perhaps some individuals feel dissatisfied with their jobs because they are generally dissatisfied with their lives. Similarly, those in the most menial or unpleasant jobs could feel satisfied if the sum of their lives was fulfilling and they were generally happy. Job satisfaction cannot be looked at in a vacuum.

The premise for much criticism of higher education has been that the purpose of college is to enable graduates to get good jobs. Yet there is no general agreement on what a "good job" is. Our study revealed that what is a good job to some people is not necessarily a good job to others. For example, only 8 percent of those in middle-level administration who graduated with degrees in the arts and humanities are satisfied with their jobs. However, 64 percent of those with bachelor's degrees in the social sciences and 87 percent of those with bachelor's degrees in history are satisfied with middle-level administration. Similarly, only 11 percent of those who have bachelor's degrees in English and who are communications specialists are satisfied with their work, compared to 70 percent of those with degrees in the social sciences. Specific jobs held by people with different majors may differ substantially, even though they fall under the same generic occupational heading.

It is traditionally accepted that high-paying jobs are better than low-paying jobs. However, the place of salary in the definition of a good job is by no means clear. The Department of Labor's 1969-1970 survey of working conditions found that pay ranked first in importance among twenty-three job facets to blue-collar workers but tenth to white-collar workers. More important to white-collar workers were having interesting work and developing special abilities.[5] In our survey, full skill utilization in work was consistently found to be a dominant influence on satisfaction. Although it has not been shown that a large proportion of people with high salaries would accept a pay cut to achieve fuller utilization of their skills, it seems that high salary alone often is insufficient to ensure high satisfaction. In any event, it is difficult to determine whether it is salary per se that makes workers satisfied or the internal characteristics of a job, such as the flexibility and independence associated with high-salaried positions.

Another definition holds that good jobs are those that are socially meaningful. But who can define socially meaningful work? Is a job meaningful if productivity is high—even though national income equality may be hindered by highly productive individuals making exceptionally high salaries? Is a job socially meaningful if it allows one to espouse liberal causes?

In still another definition, good jobs are associated with high status, and college graduates tend to go along with this definition. Unfortunately, there is little consensus about what a high-status job is. Our study shows that having policy- or decision-making responsibility and viewing one's job as professional are associated with status and contribute significantly to job satisfaction regardless of other factors. Yet a great many college graduates are highly satisfied in work they would not define as professional or work that carries no policy- or decision-making responsibility. Thus, one cannot say that jobs without these characteristics are inherently bad jobs.

The problem of defining good jobs is further complicated by a lack of consensus about what "professional" work is. Within most occupational groups, some workers view their work as professional, and others do not. Some people who are dissatisfied because they think their jobs have too little status may have been socialized into thinking that way. Graduates who have learned that

[5] U.S. Department of Labor, *Job Satisfaction: Is There a Trend?*

having a good job means being a doctor, lawyer, scientist, or college professor may feel they are underachievers if they are not in one of these fields. The sense of underachievement is often strong among students who have attended highly selective colleges, for they compare their occupational attainment not only with their own expectations but also with the career success of classmates who have entered the "choice" fields. If society continues to categorize certain jobs as low in status, college graduates who become middle-level office workers or who use manual or vocational skills will continue to feel unsuccessful.

Rather than measuring job status against outside standards, companies might find it more productive to develop a greater sense of occupational status within the firm. Perhaps internal responsibilities for low-level policy making or decisions on procedures and operations could be given to workers in lower-status jobs. If workers were allowed to contribute to their job development and to corporate policy, they might view their jobs as "good" even though outsiders might not classify the same jobs as high-status positions.

Good jobs may also include those that allow intellectual development and thinking. But if the *process* of thinking became respectable, rather than certain topics of thought, many jobs that we characteristically define as "manual" or "nonintellectual" could be redefined as good jobs. One manifestation of job snobbery has been an increasing shortage of people to fill manual and vocational jobs. Consequently, inflated wages must be offered to induce people to accept the low status such jobs confer.

A final consideration in defining the meaning of a good job might lie in the relationship between work and leisure. The person with an adequate but routine job may have chosen less demanding work in order to have ample time and resources to enjoy leisure or pursue other interests.

But the problems relating to underemployment and job dissatisfaction are more than problems of definition. To a considerable extent, they are connected with our assumptions about the purposes of education. As long as we believe that the main purpose of education is to prepare people for specific jobs, we are going to invite dissatisfaction and charges of underemployment. By narrowing our sense of purpose in this way, we deny the fluctuating realities of contemporary life.

The primary function of college should be to teach people how to learn. Most people do not pursue their original career plans throughout their working lives, and most will develop more skills after completing their formal education. Over 50 percent of the graduates in our study did not select their careers until several years after graduation. Useful vocational skills that are acquired in college are not limited to course content, but also include general knowledge, critical abilities, communication skills, and inter-personal competence.

The ability to socialize and the willingness to take risks and to innovate are other income-incrementing characteristics that might be gained from the educational experience. Specific values and attitudes demonstrated by graduates are probably of more use to employers than specific knowledge. College experiences that develop these might include extracurricular activities, dormitory living, fraternity or sorority life, or the disciplines involved in formal learning. There are many benefits of higher education other than providing students with specific job skills. Indeed, college preparation for work includes the ability to think, read, write, cal-culate, learn, and get along with people. It also includes the ability to use nonworking hours constructively.

Seventy-three percent of our respondents said college is very useful in increasing general knowledge, while 43 percent said it provides the ability to think clearly. Twenty percent indicated that college helped them choose their life goals. It has provided leadership ability for 22 percent and contacts that helped get a current job for 5 percent. Sixty-nine percent said college increased their chances of finding a good job, and 38 percent said college provided knowledge and skills that were useful on the current job.

Benefits from higher education also accrue to society. Col-leges and universities should not ignore these advantages in making the case for continued higher learning. Some benefits are shared by the student and society in general, while others accrue more to society than to the individual. There is evidence that the children of more-educated mothers, for example, ultimately become more successful than the children of less-educated mothers. In a sense, this is a social return. In a more-educated society democracy flour-ishes, violent crime is lower, and the gross national product (GNP) is generally higher. A high social return is also realized from the creativity, new ideas, and new products that grow out of the research programs in our best universities. Although poverty will exist regardless of GNP growth, it is difficult to argue that national income or welfare could be improved by educating fewer people.

This cataloguing of the social and personal benefits of higher education is not meant to obscure the need for changes in the ways higher education relates to employment. Colleges and universities must begin to provide students with specific information about employment opportunities. Students should know how to prepare themselves for jobs while they are in college. They need more guidance on appropriate curricula, and they should be told which aspects of college are useful in jobs. Students should also know that, despite their college education, most jobs will require additional preparation. At the same time, they should be made aware that flexible training and skills and broadly applicable experience are among the most important acquisitions of their college years.

The recent publicity about a declining labor market for college graduates may be misleading. When most people have degrees, the risks of not having one are great. At the same time, students should be informed about the probabilistic nature of the job market. A B.A. in chemistry does not assure the graduate of a high-powered research job, and a B.A. in classics may not guarantee any job at all. Students must be kept informed about the labor market with its shortages and surpluses. They must be knowledgeable about the employment rates of previous and current graduates, realizing that times may be quite different when they graduate in four or more years. Information about labor markets must be based on empirical evidence, not on anecdotes or personal biases. If students know about job prospects and the inherent risks of the job market and still choose to enroll in college, they will not be disillusioned later on, and they will derive the benefits—both work related and nonwork related—that a college education can provide.

There has been some debate about whether the filtering down of college-educated persons into jobs not traditionally held by graduates will be a liability or a benefit to the firm or to society. Some critics argue that worker discontent will cause higher turnover, absenteeism, and lower productivity. Others argue that brighter, more-educated people can work within the corporate structure to modify and expand traditionally lower-level jobs so productivity from those jobs increases. The growth potential of lower-level jobs appears to be a function of both the talents of those holding the jobs and the attitudes of supervisors and corporate managers. When these factors are positive, even low-level jobs can be satisfying and productive.

17

College and Jobs: International Problems

Beatrice G. Reubens

It may come as cold comfort to Americans that many other countries also find nowadays that the jobs and incomes expected by graduates of higher education institutions are not available for substantial numbers, especially at the outset of their careers. The discovery of an excess supply of graduates overseas has been all the more painful because the expansion of higher education there has been so recent, so deliberate, so rapid, and so full of promise of societal as well as private benefits.

Unlike the American mix of public and private institutions and the fifty independent state systems, higher education in Europe and Australia is almost entirely provided by government, which determines centrally the number, type, and location of institutions, the number of places for students, in total and by discipline, and many other aspects of higher education that influence its quantity and quality. One of the important decisions was that tuition should be free or very low and that government should cover a large part of students' living costs and expenses through grants and loans.[1] In shaping their expansion plans for higher education in the early 1960s, governments responded to the desire of individuals to prolong their education, a desire that was even stronger than had been anticipated and that frequently outran the provision. But governments also were motivated by other considerations as they consciously devoted more and more resources to education and especially to higher education.

The example of the United States was widely cited to demonstrate that economic growth, urgently desired by all these nations, was fostered by a more highly educated labor force. It became an article of faith that an increase in expenditures on higher education would be directly translated into economic growth, not least by ensuring the supply of highly qualified manpower required by an expanding economy. As they planned for their burgeoning higher education systems, some countries introduced manpower planning as an important element. Britain, for example, has stressed the provision of places in educational institutions for science and engineering students. To a greater extent than has been true in the United States, many western European countries tied together their educational and manpower planning.

Another motivation for expansion was the desire to reduce economic and social inequality. Instead of an elitist system, higher education was to become a mass movement, and, in the heady days of the late 1960s and early 1970s, visions of universal higher education appeared, again suggested by apparent American developments. By providing access to those from the lower socioeconomic classes, an enlarged higher education could improve "life chances" and foster upward social and economic mobility, enriching individuals and society. To the extent that earnings differentials between highly educated and less educated manpower could be reduced by increased numbers in higher education, the purposes of egalitarianism also would be served.

As a consequence of these several forces and the strong pri-

[1]M. Woodhall, *Review of Student Support Schemes in Selected OECD Countries* ED(76)7 (Paris: Organization for Economic Cooperation and Development, 1976).

vate demand, enrollments in higher education mounted rapidly in the 1960s. But because the starting base was so low, only a few countries have approached the North American enrollment of 40 percent of the age group. Still, the gap definitely has been narrowed since 1960.[2]

During the last few years, a reassessment of goals, achievements, and expenditures has begun abroad. While the aim of equality has never been satisfactorily or uniformly defined, it appears, as an Organization for Economic Cooperation and Development (OECD) report declares, "that achievement has fallen short of expectations and that the education systems have not had a great impact in raising the chances of upward mobility of children in the lower income groups, let alone trying to achieve some form of equality of result or attainment. Very limited data on participation rates by socio-economic classes indicate that large differences in participation at the secondary and higher levels of education continue to exist in nearly all countries.... For higher education...it appears, on the whole, that the benefits of expenditures have gone more to the middle classes than to less-privileged social groups."[3]

Not only were the results during the years of expansion disheartening, but the recent years of uncertainty about graduate underemployment and unemployment have intensified some disparities. Working-class youth have felt discouraged about attending higher education institutions because of the decline of employment opportunities in such fields as teaching. And females, whose participation rates during the expansive years generally were lower than those of males, have been retreating even more than males in countries where declines in enrollment rates are observed. Among German graduates from upper secondary education (*Abiturienten*), the proportion of boys desiring to enter higher education dropped from 90.3 percent in 1972 to 78.7 percent in 1976, but the girls' percentage declined even more—from 88.6 to 70.4.[4]

The impact of an increased flow of graduates on economic

[2]Organization for Economic Cooperation and Development, *Public Expenditure on Education* (Paris: OECD, 1976), p. 20. H. Werner, "Beschäftigungsprobleme von Akademikern," *Wirtschaftsdienst,* 1975, 3: 146-148.

[3]Organization for Economic Cooperation and Development, *Public Expenditure on Education,* p. 37.

[4]Federal Republic of Germany, Bundesministerium für Bildung und Wissenschaft, *Press Information,* October 21, 1976, p. 175.

growth has produced even more disillusion than have the social equalization results. As Ralf Dahrendorf, head of the London School of Economics and a former high official of the European Common Market, puts it, "Twenty years ago, the Organization for Economic Cooperation and Development in Paris began to spread the myth that the correlation observed between economic growth and the proportion of each age group going on to tertiary education had some causal significance: The more university students there are, the faster will an economy grow. . . . Today, few people would take such simple views. The relationship between educational expansion and economic growth is in fact much more tenuous. Once a country has reached, and crossed, a certain threshold of educational development—general literacy and numeracy perhaps, and something like 5 percent of each age group in higher education—the immediate economic effect of educational development may well be negligible. I can see no case for the assumption that further expansion of tertiary education would have a significant impact on economic development in Britain today."[5]

While acknowledging this line of criticism, a recent OECD report concludes that present adverse reactions may be exaggerated as earlier ones were unduly optimistic.[6] Yet a number of countries, especially those under pressures to restrain public expenditures, have reexamined the resources to be allocated to education as a whole and to higher education in particular.

Manpower planning as an integral part of the expansion of higher education has also yielded disappointing results, and it remains a contentious issue. Still, as it became clear that the demand for teachers was shrinking drastically, many countries deliberately closed the teacher training courses and converted the institutions to other courses, not waiting for the students to make their own discovery of the employment situation.

In its examination of its difficult economic position, Great Britain has engaged in a debate about the degree of responsibility of the educational system, which, it is said by many, including the Prime Minister, does not train enough engineers and scientists and fails to influence the best students to enter industry instead of

[5] *Times Higher Education Supplement* (London), November 19, 1976, p. 5.
[6] Organization for Economic Cooperation and Development, *Public Expenditure on Education*, p. 37.

research. One proposal has been that government grants to students should vary according to the importance of the study subject for manpower purposes; naturally, reactions have been varied and strong.[7] French indicative manpower planning sets up tables of the desired number of graduates from every level and type of education, but the choices of young people are not directed and do not correspond closely to the desires of the manpower planners. It is far more common in other countries than it is in the United States to declare shortages of highly educated manpower even in the midst of recession, as well as for the longer run.

A misleading impression of uniformity among all the countries may have been given by the foregoing general discussion. Some countries have committed themselves to admit to higher education all who qualify by completing the upper secondary level and even to provide all courses of study sought by individual students without regard to the total or specific needs of the labor market. Italy is a case in point. In 1968 Italy guaranteed each holder of a recognized school-leaving certificate the right to enroll in any university course regardless of the specific subjects studied in secondary school. Someone with a business studies background in high school could thus enroll in a classics course at college.

University enrollments have trebled since 1968 as young Italians opted for further studies instead of unemployment or low-level jobs in the weak economy, especially in the south. But the educational facilities and instructors required to maintain the quality of education for such a rapid increase have not been provided, and the overcrowding and dissatisfaction among university students are serious problems. Nor is the situation improved by the rising rate of unemployment among the increased numbers of university graduates.

In the medical faculties of Italy, the state of affairs is even more critical. Admitting all who seek entrance, the universities registered 150,000 medical students at the beginning of the

[7]Speech by Prime Minister James Callaghan at Ruskin College, Oxford, England, October 18, 1976. House of Commons, Select Committee on Science and Technology, Third Report, London, November 1976. "More Cash for Engineering Studies Proposed," *Times* (London), November 19, 1976. "Brain Power," *New Society*, August 26, 1976. M. Blaug, "The Uses and Abuses of Manpower Planning," *New Society*, July 31, 1976. R. Dahrendorf, "Universities and the Economy," *Times Higher Education Supplement* (London), November 19, 1976.

1976-77 academic year. (In the United States, with almost four times Italy's population, there are under 60,000 medical students.) The current Italian standard of training, especially the clinical portion, is generally regarded as dismal. Moreover, Italy cannot absorb so many doctors. Its existing 100,000 doctors already provide a ratio of 1 doctor to 300 inhabitants, one of the highest in Europe.

According to recent reports, the Italian educational authorities, like those in other countries, have reluctantly concluded that they should limit the number of entrants into the faculties that are most hard pressed. It is therefore likely that a *numerus clausus* will be introduced into the most overcrowded faculties, such as medicine, law, and arts.[8] But the pressures against such action should not be underestimated.

Sweden, perhaps most consciously determined of all western European countries to relate educational outputs to labor market needs, has had a quite different development.[9] Between 1940 and 1960, the number of students enrolled in Swedish higher education rose from 11,000 to 37,000. And then, in the next decade, the number more than tripled again, reaching 125,000 in the 1970-71 academic year.

It was not only the explosion in total numbers that called attention to higher education in Sweden. There also were sharp changes in the distribution of students among the faculties. In 1950 as many as 40 percent of the new entrants to higher education had been admitted to the faculties where numbers were restricted because of the costs of training, the needs in the labor market, or both. By the 1968-69 academic year, when new entrants reached a peak that has not since been equaled, the proportion in the restricted faculties was under 20 percent. Moreover, as has been the case since 1960 and like other countries with *nu-*

---

[8] "Numbers Crisis: Limits May Be on the Way," *The Times Higher Education Supplement* (London), November 19, 1976. "Overcrowding Reaches Breaking Point," *Times Higher Education Supplement* (London), November 19, 1976. "Italian Jobs," *New Society*, December 9, 1976, pp. 518-519.

[9] Sweden, 1968 Educational Commission (U68), *Higher Education* (Stockholm: 1968 Educational Commission, 1973). L. Kim, *Admission Policies in Swedish Post-Secondary Education*, DAS/EID/73.24 (Paris: Organization for Economic Cooperation and Development, 1973). Sweden, Arbetsmarknadsstyrelsen, *Vissa Data for Arbetskraft med Längre Utbildning* [Data on the Labor Force with Prolonged Education] (Stockholm: Arbetsmarknasstyrelsen: Meddelanden frän Utredningsenheten, 1974).

merus clausus, some of the available places in the restricted faculties were not taken up. At the same time, enrollments soared in
the unrestricted faculties, especially in literature, law, languages,
sociology, history, and similar subjects.

Fears that the latter students would have difficulty in finding
employment suited to their qualifications and expectations were
reinforced by the recession of 1968-1969. An effective information
program dealing with increasing graduate unemployment and the
types of jobs open to many graduates resulted in a decline in new
entrants in succeeding years, the introduction of more vocationally
oriented courses, encouragement to delay entrance to higher education or to accept older persons with nontraditional preparation, and
efforts to fill up the restricted faculties. The latter are somewhat
more extensive in Sweden than in other countries, since such fields
as technology, business administration, forestry, agriculture, social
services, journalism, and teacher training for gymnastics are restricted in admissions, along with the more usual fields of medicine, dentistry, pharmacy, and veterinary medicine.

A commission on higher education was appointed in 1968
to consider the long-run development of this sector. Taking account of the high level of prior public investment in higher education and the competing claims of other types of education and
other public services, the report of the commission in 1973 recommended limitations on the total numbers to be admitted to higher
education. It proposed two chief grounds: the potential for introducing educational alternatives, and the employment possibilities
for higher education graduates.

Although the commission accepted that higher education has
the goals of personality development, welfare development, democracy, internalization, and social change, it placed a special emphasis
on the preparation of "students for subsequent occupational activities. . . . Obviously, it does not imply that every study unit in a
university or college should be directly linked to an occupation. The
intention is rather that the individual's basic education as a whole
should prepare him for an occupation. In the opinion of the commission, working life should constitute an important source of renewal
for education, at the same time as education should function as an
important instrument for the development of working life."[10]

[10]Sweden, 1968 Educational Commission, *Higher Education,* p. 9.

Within the wide range of experience and views from Italy to Sweden, we find the remaining countries of western Europe along with other developed countries such as Australia and New Zealand. But all these countries differ from the United States, Canada, and Japan in their acceptance of a national policy responsibility for higher education and in the greater share of total costs borne by the public purse.

These facts do not make the other countries indifferent to the effects on individuals—the aspects of higher education and employment that most closely concern Americans. These effects include the rising unemployment rates, underemployment, and relative decline in earnings suffered by college graduates in recent years. As in the United States, the belief is growing that graduates face long-run employment problems, apart from the impact of the worldwide recession and the coming of age of the baby-boom generation. For some countries, notably West Germany and Austria, both the bulge of youth population and the peak of attendance at higher education institutions are still to come. Yet even these countries are feeling or considering the effects of the "student mountain." However, the differences in circumstances and attitudes abroad are interesting in themselves and give perspective to our own concepts of the "proper" jobs and incomes for graduates.

To begin with, the European discovery that graduates are in oversupply in terms of the economy's ability to absorb them has come at a point where those with higher education constitute a much smaller proportion of the total labor force and of new entrants to the labor market than is the case in the United States. The fact is that highly developed economies such as the German and Swedish function with a much lower percentage of highly qualified manpower than we do. Why should the absorptive capacity of such economies seem to be lower than ours? Three interlocking sets of reasons can be cited.

First, industry and business have recruited a relatively small share of their labor force from graduates. The latter have depended heavily on entering the public service—all levels of government, public enterprises, and education. Even Great Britain—which has moved closer to the American, Canadian, and Japanese patterns of graduate employment than have other European countries—still has a fairly high concentration of new graduates in the public sector. In West Germany, as the number of new graduates

entering the labor force rose from over 700,000 to over 1.1
million, the percentage employed in the public sector rose from
50.2 to 58.0. In Sweden, 68 percent of new graduates and 75 percent of all in the labor force who hold higher education qualifications were employed by all levels and agencies of government in
1975. A similar inquiry in the Netherlands in 1971, excluding doctors, found 62 percent in the public sector. A French survey in
1975 of 1970 graduates showed 60 percent in government-
financed jobs; an interesting spread appeared between the highly
selective *grandes écoles,* where only 28 percent of the graduates
were employed in the public sector, and the holders of diplomas in
the natural sciences, where 79 percent held government jobs, of
which 55 percent were in the education sector.[11] In all those cases,
and also in the United States, female graduates were more likely
than males to work for the public employers.

This employment pattern arises both from the slow acceptance of graduates by industry and from the earlier expansion of
public-sector opportunities, especially in teaching. Industry's
reluctance in several countries can be traced in part to the relative
absence of graduates among the present managers and recruiters.
Apparently, a process that began so long ago in the United States
that we can scarcely recall its beginnings has still to take root in
Europe. A German industry group recently reported that only 2
percent of its labor force were graduates and that it saw room for
only 1 percent addition.

A certain distrust on the part of industry toward the more
academic parts of the higher education system and its products is
visible in many European countries. Now that public-sector jobs
are increasing much more slowly or not at all, because of the decline in pupil populations and the financial crunch affecting government services and enterprises, a greater pressure is placed on
the private sector to accept graduates. Given the recession, the
reaction has been cautious and tends toward careful screening and
raising of requirements in light of the competition for jobs. The
longer-run developments may be more favorable, especially after
the numbers of graduates begin to drop off.

[11]Data from official, national sources collected and analyzed by the
West German Ministry of Education and Science and kindly made available to
the author.

Second, the traditional European university maintains a greater aloofness from the economy and its needs than does a similar American institution. The easy introduction of business and other professional schools, the ability of engineering courses wholly conducted in educational institutions to produce employable graduates, and the countless other examples of ways in which the American higher education system cooperates with the desires and needs of business and industry are not easily duplicated in Europe. Some argue, especially in Britain and France, that it is not the fault of the universities but rather of the broader society's low regard for technology. Whatever the cause, it is probably valid that European private enterprise should be somewhat wary of what goes on in the more academic universities, given their cultivation of research interests and disparagement of practical approaches. Part of the reason for policy direction of higher education at the national level lies in the independence and unresponsiveness of some universities and the power of individual professors. The American system adapts with fewer and less direct forms of national intervention.

Third, the employment expectations of graduates in Europe focus more on the type and status of the job and less on the amount of income or the income differentials among jobs than seems to be true of Americans. The high proportion of European graduates employed in the public sector is partly due to deliberate choice and to strong value judgments about the type of jobs that are proper and appropriate for higher education graduates. To some extent, the slow penetration of industry and business by graduates represents reluctance on their part, preference for other kinds of jobs, and a belief that the private sector does not know how to utilize the skills and interests of graduates.

Because of the narrower concept of what constitutes traditional employment for graduates, the Europeans regard as unacceptable many of the jobs that we have long accepted as suitable and usual for college graduates. We are talking about a coming wave of underemployment among our graduates—about O'Toole's reserve army of the underemployed[12]—but the Europeans look with wonder at what we have already accepted. The relativity to

[12]J. O'Toole, "The Reserve Army of the Underemployed," *Change*, 1975, 7 (4): 27-33, 63.

particular times and places of standards concerning traditional or suitable employment for graduates should make us wary of underemployment as an absolute concept.

Several consequences flow from the differences I have discerned between American and European attitudes and circumstances, remembering that any grouping under the heading "European" masks important differences among the countries. First, the earlier position of a small elite of graduates in Europe was so secure that even slight increases in graduate unemployment rates have been regarded with alarm; throughout recent years, including the recession, graduates have had a persistent advantage over lesseducated persons, expressed in terms of lower unemployment rates.

Second, the difficulty in obtaining traditional types of jobs has often brought a certain reaction, especially celebrated in anecdotal material, to accept the outrageous job, one that is well below the expectation rather than one that represents compromise and acceptance. Usually considered a temporary expedient, such actions also are a form of social protest. British statistics on the first destinations of graduates, taken six months after obtaining the degree, always have had a place for those who regard themselves as in temporary or stopgap employment. While American adjustment in the type of employment accepted by some graduates has always proceeded through individual action, a British government agency, after studying the American experience, felt it desirable to issue pamphlets advising graduates to change their views and broaden their job alternatives.

Third, changes in overall enrollment trends and in the composition of enrollments seem more responsive to signals from the marketplace in the United States than in Europe. Whether overall American enrollments do in fact move directly in response to changes in the relative earnings position of graduates, or are also importantly influenced in both directions by many other forces, is debated in the United States, but the case is made more strongly in the United States than elsewhere.[13] As Mark Blaug has ex-

---

[13]R. B. Freeman, *The Overeducated American* (New York: Academic Press, 1976). M. S. Gordon, "The Changing Job Market for College Graduates in the United States," paper prepared for the Conference on Youth in Contemporary Industrial Society, Ditchley Park, England, October 1976. E.

plained, the large private sector in education, and the emphasis on private sector employment and the size of earnings, give Americans a stake in human capital theory which they incorrectly extend to countries whose education and employment systems are not so privately controlled.[14]

In West Germany, which faces a youth population bulge well into the 1980s and foresees a somewhat uncertain economic future after a sustained period of overfull employment, educational planners are committed to a large expansion of higher education, along with every other type and level, simply as a means of absorbing the young people. Little attention is paid to the shape of the labor market or the returns that individuals will reap. The guiding principle is that more training and education are better than less. Accepting that everyone should be educated to the limit of his or her potential, most German policymakers concede that many higher education graduates are unlikely to find the jobs they now consider suitable and urge that information efforts be launched to prepare young people for a realistic view of the labor market. Some of the more optimistic hope that supply may create its own demand.

The greatest claims for American adaptability to changes in market conditions have been made with regard to internal shifts in the composition of enrollments. Cited evidence includes the movement from general subjects to the more professional courses, sharp declines in particular fields in slack times, increased preference for two-year occupational courses over the four-year general courses, and similar trends. In West Germany, by contrast, students are so affected by restrictions on admissions to particular courses of study that many end up choosing a course they can enter, ignoring both their personal preferences and the employment possibilities. French students are notably recalcitrant about adjusting their subject choices to market realities; many have said that the jobs should adapt to the students rather than vice versa.

The final issue, on which there is rather more agreement among the countries, concerns the longer-run outlook for higher

---

Rudd, "What a Falling Birthrate Will Mean to the Universities in 1982," *Times Higher Education Supplement* (London), November 19, 1976.

[14]M. Blaug, "The Empirical Status of Human Capital Theory: A Slightly Jaundiced Survey," *Journal of Economic Literature*, September 1976, *14* (3): 827-855.

education and employment. Many experts agree that, with the decline in numbers in the age group, shortages of graduates may again develop, perhaps in the late 1980s, and some of the earlier economic advantages of higher education may return. Nevertheless, the differences in the systems that have been described here suggest that many European governments will continue to exercise closer supervision over the higher education sector than we do, if only because their institutional rigidities and financial involvement demand it. Our adaptability, including our adjustment to underemployment, is a strength that permits a pluralistic system to operate, and allows less policy attention to be paid to the relation between education and employment than might be required in another setting.

18

Successful Careering

Adele M. Scheele

Critical career competences are skills that successful people have acquired and use. These skills make a difference in what such people pay attention to and think to do. They are demonstrated in successful interactions and dealings with people, but they appear as the result of casual, fortuitous circumstances in the course of everyday situations.

As a class of skills, critical career competences are different from cognitive or substantive skills, that is, they are apart from knowledge of a field or willingness to work hard. For the most part, they apparently are acquired "along the way." Because of their "everydayness," these critical skills have been largely ignored in professional training curricula. They are not always discovered or, once discovered, passed on as advice. Yet some of their characteristics are identified in our folk wisdom on how to succeed: for example, "It's who you know, not what"; "It's being the right person at the right time"; and "Success breeds success."

In a presentation to a graduate seminar for education administrators, I wanted to demonstrate these critical skills with regard to careering through three scenarios. I began by asking students how they would find jobs after graduation. Their responses were "go to the placement office" or "ask favorite professors for tips." When asked how they would design a national training program to sustain young adults during a depression, they could think only of tutoring ghetto children in reading. Their responses to what advice they would give to their brother, a recently unemployed stockbroker out from the East Coast, were, again, to go to the placement office and/or, worse, to the unemployment office. All responses suggested a low-level understanding of the way people get jobs or what training they need to think about getting them. These stock institutional answers revealed a passivity and dependence on a system that will only disappoint them.

People have varying explanations for what makes successful careering. At one extreme, life is looked at as a system of tricks and ploys. Any means is justified for getting ahead if you are not found out. "Making it" is equated with opportunistic hustling and using others as manipulative instruments. At this extreme, life is explained as a game. Independent action is required; knowledge presages success. This is the version academe presents. Yet both extremes are stereotyped views of what is supposed to produce success; both are equally unrealistic. Sooner or later, the hustlers lose, and the "good student" types are left behind.

One of the current problems in successful careering is finding some kind of behavior that will permit us to have the working lives we want. Success, as it looks now, is not only culturally defined (money and status) but also personally defined (satisfaction, peace of mind, and comparative values of work itself). A new conception of pragmatism and social consciousness is possible and needed.

Careering is the process of moving and growing not only within one's actual job but also within the series of jobs that constitute a productive life. The word *career* means "progress through life," according to the first definition in the *Oxford English Dictionary*. Ambiguity occurs within the term itself: In addition to meaning "life's trajectory," *career* also connotes *itness*—the specific and status-weighted job. By using the word *careering,* I mean to imply a process rather than things.

Careering includes a repertoire of known behaviors that are

situationally responsive—approaches, retreats, gambits, viewpoints, experiments, ventures, and so forth. These behavioral skills are quite separate from the factual content of careers but apparently are valuable to the successful negotiation of the everyday actions and transactions that move us through careers. With more and more students coming to (and returning to) graduate schools, and fewer and fewer jobs available relative to the number of competing persons, there is a growing demand to learn how to career—how to get into the right specialty, how to know what information is useful, how to find a particular clientele, how to become known within a specific professional group. On the other hand, my work in career and life planning suggests that critical career competences are derived from a sense of personal power and willingness to experiment with situations. Apparently, individuals who possess these critical competences view themselves as happening to things rather than persons to which things happen.

If these competences are identified, they can be taught, and students can be empowered to live full, satisfying, and expanding lives—the essential meaning of *career*. Such career skills, as well as the substantive skills on graduate and professional levels, should lead to a greater understanding of how to cope with the many realities we experience.

Generally speaking, teaching interpersonal skills is still considered "illegitimate" for education, outside the purview of what is to be learned in the university or the professional school. Yet, legitimization of such skills might change the pervasive feeling of "fraudulence" that is reported by those in the real world. To many, schooling not only brands, it also guarantees; A students think they get to stand in life's A line for careers, both personal and professional. It is time to teach the *process* of careering as well as its content.

In 1973, several informal surveys and panels conducted by Social Engineering Technology among well-known professional people elicited from their experiences those skills and strategies that led generally to their successes.[1] These surveys revealed spe-

---

[1] The results of these surveys appear in C. R. Price, A. Scheele, and D. S. Scheele, "Growing Up Aware: Initiatives for Employers in Supplying Comprehensive Career Education," a paper published by the Los Angeles Unified School District, 1972. Several ideas developed in this chapter were germinated during a panel discussion of "Successful Women" in which the author participated on KCET Radio in Los Angeles in 1970.

cific types of actions in critical career situations. These actions, which may be thought of as nontechnical skills, can be divided into three main areas: self-presentation, positioning, and connecting.

Self-presentation skills include an assessment of one's schooling and career skills both already attained and yet requisite, in order to shape and reshape self-image and confidence. Such assessments, some of which must validate and build on past successes and strengths, are particularly necessary for female late-entry students. Opportunities must be designed so that students can learn to build a repertoire of roles, an indication of healthy maneuvering in complex situations.

Positioning skills further develop appropriate behavioral roles in both personal and organizational settings. They teach concepts for ways to move and risk that open options and define possibilities.

Connecting skills are specifically rooted in the best use of the schooling experience. They are first steps in developing strategies to determine plans to meet goals by exploring the university for links with faculty as mentors and fellow students as colleagues, for research possibilities that can serve as apprenticeships, and for the bridges to the business and professional community that are necessary for living and the euphemistic "earning a living."

Within the three broad areas of successful careering, I have identified six critical career competences that were derived from an ethnomethodological study of lawyers. From experience in career management, I believe that these are generalizable to every career. The six skills are:

- To experience doing.
- To risk linking.
- To show belonging.
- To exhibit specializing.
- To use catapulting.
- To magnify accomplishing.

Although these categories are arbitrary, they are a first step in identifying what can be thought of as the hidden curriculum for most professionals. Some of the knowledge that is sought from higher education is not only about things—oneself, what is around us, and the relationship between them—but also about the use of knowledge in the course of one's life. These critical career competences have been included with the knowledge of group conventions and ability to confirm protocols as a social competence. More euphemistically, the social graces have served as subtle elitist and exclusionary devices as well as means for successfully handling interaction. The family, mentors, and, of course, "the right schools" served as well to impart many somewhat undifferentiated skills and modes of being. The artful use of a subset of what is often referred to as *social competence* to achieve career success is what I have attempted to define here.

Each of the six critical career competences is identified by a label that describes two separate processes. The first is a synergistic demonstration of the second—*doing, linking, belonging, specializing, catapulting,* and *accomplishing.* The gerund form rather than the noun, that is, *linking* rather than *linkage,* indicates the process toward completion rather than a completed state. The notion of process entails that of development. On two levels, these competences can be conceptualized as developmental. On one level, each is developmental from within. That is, each has endless capacity for continuing improvement—measurable only in progressive stages. In this sense, these skills are not to be thought of as results or outcomes, but rather as actions continuously being done or refined that may bring about the accolade of success.

On the second level, they can be perceived as being sequential, each critical career competence building on and leading to the next, and proceeding cyclicly. To experience doing leads to risk linking, which leads to group connectedness. Skills for displaying belonging and at the same time being special lead to recognition and enhancement beyond the group. To use catapulting can be built from any sequence while magnifying accomplishing is an ultimate competence. Then one is free to start again.

The following discussion can only briefly limn the definitions of the six competences. First, *to experience doing* is more than just to do either separate act. It is the combination of validating and being aware of the action. It means to recognize one's like or dislike of the doing. When one is acting, experimenting, or practicing, one creates an occasion for exhibiting skills that may not otherwise be available for development. An individual takes what he or she has to start with and makes something of it. To experience doing is then a way of knowing and confirming and creating part of one's identity. In terms of the card metaphor of Henry Adams, it is playing the hand dealt in the best possible way rather than waiting for a better hand or not playing at all. For many, this competence is as much a question of what to leave behind as well as what to build on. It involves learning to negotiate and feel comfortable with one's own personal world of actions, reactions, and assessments.

Second, *to risk linking* is more than to risk or to link as separate acts, but, taken together, these skills become an initial assertion of being able to chance connections. These connections are made with ideas, styles, organizations, and family, as well as with individuals. This competence is rooted not so much in a gamble, with explicit winning or losing as ends, as it is in an experiment. In this perception, life is more curious and exploratory than it is determining correct answers. Experiments carry with them an unexpectedness and a willingness to suspend judgments. *To risk linking,* then, is a skill in selecting what to risk where and knowing *what* to expect *when,* in order to successfully explore both concrete and abstract relationships. These experimental or tentative connections are made in order to develop the skills of associating, of forming with others, trying on styles of behaving, and incorporating other ways of thinking or doing. From the practice of this skill, one can experience either receptivity on which to continue to build, or else incongruence. Connections can be considered as ways to test potential and suitability. Willingness to leave situations or relationships without labeling the leaving as failure carries great significance for change within and between careers.

Third, *to show belonging* is to confirm affiliation to a group by demonstration of belonging. Going beyond the psychological notion of inclusion, this competence is comprised of actions of the individual toward the group to assert membership. Belonging is an essential process that only begins with an initial invitation or request to join; membership within any organization must be maintained. Skillful demonstration of belonging constitutes actions that are nonthreatening to those who aggressively protect the group from outside attack. Of all six skills, showing belonging is the least visible or obvious, but it is so essential that its absence becomes a serious affront that leads to negative action by the other members.

Fourth, *to exhibit specializing* is to develop and display unique talents necessary to the group. This critical competence is one of developing and demonstrating one's individual ways of functioning or connecting by making them visible and available to the group. Both *showing belonging* and *exhibiting specializing* involve demonstrated relational aspects between an individual and the group; the difference is in focus. In belonging, the individual seeks to fit into the group, to enhance the group. In specializing, the individual captures the attention and fills a need of the group. Yet, interestingly, acculturation trains females in showing belonging but not in specializing; males, conversely, are trained in specializing but not in belonging. Higher education can begin to teach what is being considered necessary for more successful living together.

Fifth, *to use catapulting* involves two actions: The first is a linking of one individual with another individual or a group and, within that connecting or linking, knowing, trusting, and maintaining some relationship. The second part of the skill is orbiting into a new world, a new idea, a new series of networks of connections that would not be there had not the first link been made. In careering, an individual can learn to link up with an important person who might serve as a mentor of some kind, can maintain the relationship with that person, and, through that person's connections and worlds, can have an entrée that would otherwise not be present. Unlike a synergistic approach, it is not the relationship between the individual and the other but rather the movement in the other's worlds.

Sixth, *to magnify accomplishing* is the act of enlarging, expanding, or broadcasting the group through the individual's actions. It is a skill to get recognition of the group and of self from outside groups. This enhancement is achieved by various maneuvers to publicly acknowledge contributions. Some contributions are valued by outside groups as participation through discovery or support. The getting of such notice carries with it a halo effect of glory or enhancement for the group as well as for the individual.

The six critical career competences come not only from accounts of successful lawyers in my dissertation but also from my own experience with what clients of my career management practice say they lacked. For example, many clients could not begin to plan or develop their careers because they could not recall any noteworthy experiences, nor could they point out any sources of self-identity. They reported having no connections or networks from which to proceed. When they probed, they could at least supply a preliminary list from which to start. When I recognized that lawyers used these skills, having built and experienced new connections, explored new ventures without the fear of failure, the critical career competences struck a harmony with my experiences. These competences seem to be congruent both with the lawyers' experience as fully as I can determine as well as with my own perceptions of lacks or deprivations of those who are not successful.

These six critical career competences can be integrated in higher education in general, in the humanities, the arts, and the sciences, including the preprofessional and professional courses of study. All of these fields of knowledge, in addition to their substantive curriculum, need the hidden one of careering. The notion of moving, succeeding, or heightening one's career in any subject, from philanthropy to politics, is a process of creating meanings, of establishing social agreements between oneself and another person, persons, or ideas in good currency. That these are agreements and arrangements made more on a daily basis than previously arranged by degree or decree is of vital importance for higher education to address.

Identifying these critical career competences then becomes a heuristic tool to help others to discover other kinds of skills to be interwoven in the life of any higher educational institution. This heuristic tool is based not on the external control that has been so much the purview of higher education but on the internal ones—the self-reflective and self-based controls.

The following matrix suggests ways of incorporating the six critical career competences in three areas of the normal higher education process—admissions, student work, and introduction to professions. I have made no attempt to suggest reforms for areas of higher education. Rather, I am showing how the critical career competences that comprise a hidden curriculum might be used within a higher education system. It would be better to incorporate these skills in this hidden curriculum than to compile them into one course, "The Hidden Curriculum," which would isolate them in a typical, "schoolized" fashion. Rather than separate careering from career skills, a better objective is to incorporate the two.

First, *admissions procedures,* in general, absorb a tremendous amount of time on both the students' and particularly the administration's part. That time might be put to better use, serving two functions. It would allow the college or university to have more information about whom it selects for students—not only those with academic promise but also those who indicate leadership, research ability, commitment to the field, and even potential alumni support. And for students, it would be a chance to practice self-presentation in new ways. Along with the other critical competences, admissions is a beginning process for revealing the student to herself or himself and to the university and for the university to reveal its own motivations and needs to itself and to the students reciprocally. Second, *student work* can be enriched to increase the potential for gaining more successful competences instead of only writing papers and examinations as demonstrations of a field or aspect of one. Third, *introduction to the professions* (preprofessional development) can be a systematic method of introducing students to the practical affairs of the life within their chosen profession. These suggestions are outlined in Table 1.

In conclusion, while only three areas of academic life have been explored, there is unlimited opportunity for higher education to include these skills in other aspects of college life. Some examples are research and teaching assistantships, student activities, testing, financial aid and work experience requests, the use of visiting lecturers and luminaries, and even student housing. Both subject fields and the extracurricular activities that surround the life of the university could be improved with the introduction of these critical career skills designed to teach students how to career. Their inclusion would be motivating. And professional societies, alumni groups, and "boards of visitors" are in a position to work with departments, schools, and colleges to develop ways appropriate to each setting to introduce critical career competences into curricula, not as isolated elements or courses but as integral parts of the total design for learning.

Table 1. Examples of New Practices Incorporating Critical Career Competences

Critical Career Competences	Admission-Orientation Phase	Student Phase	Professional Phase
To Experience Doing	extend admission procedure into first year to include workshops in responsibility, communication, values	explore comparative workstyles among students; design of effective work methods suitable to deliver personal styles	scenario writing of future roles in profession
	explore personal motives through imagery, projective tests and methods	focus on theory of practice, examining notions of practice held by professionals in light of direct observation of performance	specify procedures for acquiring skills and roles that do not yet exist
	detailed examination of role models and guided construction of ideal-model and ideal career outcome		interact and hold dialogue with mentors concerning emerging skills and scenario construction for future professional roles
To Risk Linking	establish proactive, expanding dossier as a guide to self-development and self-documentation	training workshops in group dynamics; guided experience in group collaboration with debriefing	ongoing informal seminars with professionals and exemplary students
	create a collaborator role: for professionals willing to sustain guidance function for students beyond referee role in admissions	structure opportunity to witness group efforts in the field; interviews with collaborators concerning their efforts	
	initiate early network formation among students and sharing of objectives		

To Show Belonging	document past associations of students with important schools, organizations, civic, political groups chart a socialization route for forming relationships with existing groups during the school career	work with outside interest groups applying training in group dynamics	serve as aides to professionals at conferences, conventions for work in collaborative mode
To Exhibit Specializing	organize ways for students to know each other through exhibiting individual attributes	develop cross-departmental teams of students to organize and perform tasks that involve specific elaboration of each individual's role	use extensive feedback and videotape playback to identify special strengths and to shape choice of areas of concentration
To Use Catapulting	use dossiers as a means of identifying important consultants on campus; extend to profession	develop ad hoc forces to explore significant new ideas, enter new realms of practice for both faculty and students	develop coaching role to link students with mentor
To Magnify Accomplishing	encourage students to identify articles for translation of themes for popular audiences; develop courses to be offered in local community	encourage students to work with media or media representatives course in journalism; public relations; marketing; management	explore professional development opportunities; examine relative advantages and disadvantages of initial, secondary, and tertiary trajectory

19

The Company and the Family

Jean R. Renshaw

Prior to the Republican nominating convention of 1976, Betty Ford made no secret of her personal preference to have a *former* President Gerald Ford, free of the burdens of the White House, giving more time to home and family. And in the middle of the campaign itself Nelson Rockefeller announced that he would not take a job in any new administration because he wanted to devote more attention to his wife and small children.

Thus were expressed, at the highest executive levels in the nation, the nature of the strains between work demands and family desires, between job requirements and home responsibilities, strains that are more visible than ever before in organizations of all kinds. The well-publicized growing resistance to company transfers —even at the risk of losing promotions and salary increases—is a dramatic example. My current research on the relationship of family life and work life has given me some new insights on a situation that, for the most part, is ignored in organizational policy making. However, ignoring the work-family interactions does not make them disappear.

To start the story, here are three vignettes from my research:

Scene 1. The manager of a large plant is worried. One of his brightest young executives is not living up to expectations. He has made erratic decisions and communications with his work team have been bad. As a result he has missed deadlines and there are signs of trouble with customers. What's the matter? The personnel manager suggests that the plant manager work around the young executive for a few months—because he is having family problems.

Scene 2. An international personnel manager is called into his superior's office for an urgent conference. A bright young supervisor in their company, only recently transferred to the United States for a two-year stay, a step upward in his career, has asked to be transferred back home at the end of one year—because his family is not happy in the United States.

Scene 3. The atmosphere is serious as three department heads meet to discuss a pile of complaints about travel from one important work team. Heavy travel during the summer season is vital for the project; but this year's complaints about extended family separations have been particularly bad, and sick days and postponed travel schedules have been rising alarmingly.

Such situations, not uncommon, affect an organization's ability to function properly. But the standard organizational response is familiar: "There's a problem all right, but it's the *employee's* problem with his family, and we cannot interfere in the personal lives of our employees. A good manager ought to be able to handle his own family."

According to traditional corporate mythology, the ideal family is a support system to help each employee carry out company policy. Each morning the executive emerges from his domestic cocoon, refreshed and ready to do battle in the business world. In the evening he returns to the family haven for solace, support, and refurbishment. If this was ever the reality, it is so no longer; and the illusion is becoming increasingly difficult to maintain.

Promotions, transfers, requirements for travel, demands for

creativity and innovation all subject an employee to new stresses. Correspondingly, each stress causes implicit demands for change in the supporting family. Promotions often require a different life-style and entertainment pattern for the family, transfers obviously uproot and change the family system, and extended business travel requires changes in family roles and functions.

At the same time that employees require more support, many families are moving away from the supportive role. Increased demands for self-determination by women and the changing roles of husband and wife are shaping new family patterns. While work and family sometimes support each other, at other times their goals and processes are in conflict.

Let us replay the three opening scenes from the viewpoints of the families involved:

Scene 1. Every night in this young executive's home, there are arguments and accusations about how much time he spends working and how little time he gives to his family. His wife believes they had agreed on joint responsibility for home and family. A decision had been made that she would go back to school after their baby was born, and she had expected her husband to give more time helping out at home. Invariably the nightly arguments lead to frustration and exhaustion.

Scene 2. The wife of the man transferred from abroad has a similar complaint, which is compounded by the stresses of being transplanted to an unfamiliar country: "I left my career and family to come to the United States so that you could be successful in your job. But it's too difficult for me. It's asking too much. I'm going home to have my baby."

Scene 3. In one of the families in which heavy travel was the issue, the wife went beyond complaints to make demands: "The teacher told me today that you must spend more time with our son. She thinks a lot of his disturbed behavior can be traced to wanting more attention from his father. He told her you're never home." The husband could only reply: "But you know I have to finish up this assignment. Things will be better in the fall, you'll see."

Although they may seem superficially different, there are striking similarities between the family arguments and the corporate meetings concerning such problems. Both scenes are full of impotence and regret; in each, the people feel powerless to change the situation; each group usually blames the other. The families believe that the troubles result from organizational policies and decisions that they were not consulted about and cannot influence. The upper-level managers think the troubles come from family problems that do not concern them and should not be allowed to interfere with running a business.

I believe that a double standard of participation has left families open to exploitation in such situations. On the one hand, their strengths are drawn on to help implement critical organization decisions—travel, transfer, training, promotion—that the employee cannot manage by himself. On the other hand, they are denied formal channels of participation in making the decisions and, therefore, cannot discuss or react to proposals that affect them. Management exploits the myth of the weak and insecure housewife, and husbands run the risk of being considered poor managers if they appear not to be able to "manage" or control their homes.

For several years, I have been conducting research on the relationships between work and family life, and I have developed a different perspective on the conflicts described in the preceding vignettes. Contrary to popular belief, I find that work organizations and families are independent social systems. But the two systems intersect at crucial points, and the interactions deeply affect both. Families and organizations have large stakes in finding creative and mutually satisfactory solutions to the problems in that relationship. It is no longer viable policy for management to insist that family matters be left at home.

Speaking privately, many personnel directors and managers understand these interrelationships. They are worried about the impact of family lives on such corporate necessities as travel, transfer, and entertainment. "But what can we do? We can't meddle." They are trained to come up with clearly assessed causes and recommended actions, not to get bogged down in the quagmires of off-duty private lives. A few major corporations take the trouble to have orientation and assimilation programs for transferred families, but there the line is drawn. Only one family issue is considered a legitimate area of concern for organizations—the "fit" of an executive's wife.

Families also have some understanding. But they usually shrug with equal eloquence and say, "What can *we* do? The company makes the decisions." As a matter of fact, this is not strictly true. Even without direct contact with company decision makers and operating without enough information, the wives of executives are often forced into decisions that have widespread and direct effects on company actions. The rising resistance to transfers is a case in point.

In the course of my research, I met families in a variety of work situations, including scientists engaged in chemical and agricultural research, civil and chemical engineers, and personnel transferred both from the United States to other countries and from other countries to the United States. All the husbands and wives I interviewed saw themselves as members of interrelated work and family systems. The employees considered themselves to be operating concurrently in both. The wives were family members first; but they also knew they were members of, and strongly influenced by, their husbands' work systems. "When we came to the company," they would say, or "when the company transferred us."

But, like the policy makers about whom they complained, they often operated as if the system they were in *at the moment* was the only one that existed. In many cases, while at work, both high-level policy makers and employees appeared to forget all about their families. At home, the families often ignored organizational realities. Over and over again this separation—out of sight, out of mind—created problems.

For example, one husband was offered a new position, a step upward that involved much more responsibility and meant that his family would have to move. He accepted it eagerly. But to his wife, the move was a disaster—it meant that she would have to stop her studies at the local college. At the same time, she found that she was pregnant. Eighteen months later, she was living with her parents. Her husband was bewildered, and the joy had gone out of the promotion for him.

In another family, the work system was the one ignored, at least at first. The wife felt trapped by domestic routine. So she and her husband decided that she would go back to her old profession, while husband and children took on more of the family responsibilities. The change exhilarated them, and although it meant much extra effort for the wife it also meant a great improvement in her life. But they had forgotten or did not consider that the husband was about to receive an important promotion; and when it came the simultaneously increased load on both work and family systems put great strains on all of them.

The potential friction between family and organization was most evident among families who were transferred to the United States from abroad. Thirteen families I interviewed were on temporary transfer (one to four years). Each had had its life disrupted and was attempting to restructure it in a new environment. At least at first, each wife was more dependent on her husband for basic family responsibilities: shopping, housekeeping, and handling medical and other everyday needs. This was particularly true of those women who did not speak English well. New schools had to be found; the children had to adjust to new buildings and teachers, to unfamiliar philosophies of education, and often to different languages. The men, of course, had to make adjustments on the job, but the new jobs usually had many things in common with the former ones. The family adjustments were the bigger ones, for all members.

All this was apparent to the department head and the personnel manager. In my interviews with them, they cited marital troubles and disturbed children as major problems for their organization. They were worried about the widespread resistance to transfers, even when they meant promotions. But how could they "interfere"?

When family stress reaches crisis proportions, it can no longer be ignored. The typical response then is to blame someone. A good manager likes to get to the bottom of problems, to find out what—or who—is the cause. The organization leaders speak about "family instability" and the "degeneration of the family" in these difficult times. The family blames "corporate policies" and unfeeling functionaries. The corporation, seeking "what is best for the family," puts pressure on the employee. At the same time, the employee's family is also putting on the pressure to get concessions from the company. Result? Frustration, dissatisfaction, and discontent leading to absenteeism and loss of efficiency. In this complex situation, blaming may well get in the way of understanding and useful action.

For instance, one couple blamed the wife's ulcer and her nervous stomach on the anxiety she suffered during her husband's business travels. But when she was interviewed alone, it developed that she had had these symptoms periodically all through their marriage. In fact, she had shown signs of psychosomatic illness since high school. Her husband knew all this, but he still took responsibility. He saw himself as the reliable center, the "Rock of Gibraltar" for everyone. These stances and methods of adjustment allowed them to maintain their accustomed ways of being together, but they did not deal with the underlying problems either of personal relationships or of interactions with company policies.

Another couple blamed their marital troubles on the husband's participation in a company-sponsored workshop that had triggered a personal change in him. Both chose to ignore the wife's return to work, after many years at home, at precisely the same time. Both events, one from each system, interacted, but only one was blamed.

Assigning the cause of the problem to the other system may not only be inaccurate but also may place any possible solution beyond reach. "The company makes the decision. What can we do?" The resulting tendency, therefore, is often for injured parties to give up trying for a solution.

In one case of transfer from abroad, the wife had to give up work, friends, and family to accompany her husband and further his career. At the end of six months, she returned for a "temporary" visit to Europe but kept extending it indefinitely. During the interview, the husband, left behind and not knowing when or if his wife might return, was having a very hard time. But he insisted that his family troubles and his wife's absence were irrelevant; his problems were caused by the job and company policies.

His supervisors and coworkers saw it differently; they blamed his problems, on and off the job, on family stresses. Both explanations had some validity, but neither was adequate, and neither helped lead to a resolution. The husband left after only one year of his two-year stay, with feelings of failure and resentment; as long as the fault was the company's, he felt he could do little about it. His superiors felt that he could not manage either job or family, although they had given him every chance. As long as the fault was not the family's, they felt they could do little about it and consequently did not have to reexamine company policies and norms on transfer and promotion.

The traditional model of work-family interaction can be

likened to a missile system with a command module (the company) and support system (family). Most theorists and practicing managers think this way about other people's families, if not their own. When queried, they maintain that families are primary, but in organizational actions and decision making the dependency model of families is implied. In this way of thinking, message direction is fixed: Control messages travel down; support and nourishment messages travel up. Inputs come from a common environment that is really the company's environment, not from feedback or from give and take between the two systems. The command module has the important information and "knows best."

In contrast, my research indicates that the real pattern is much more of an interacting open systems model. Message direction is not fixed, and control messages go both ways; relationships are more symmetrical; important information is held by both systems; relationships are recognized to be complex interactions, and inputs are understood to originate in different but overlapping environments of organization and family. One viewpoint does not predominate and set the standards by which the other system is judged, but each system operates under its own value structure.

If the command module concept is valid, then the organization must take complete responsibility for decisions about travel, transfer, and overtime without much information from the families. In the open systems model, the steady flow of information and interaction between the systems is essential to the efficient functioning of both. The research shows that managers ignore this model at their peril.

If the open systems model is essentially accurate, what can be done to decrease stress and resolve problems? At the beginning of my research, an attempt was made to create categories of family and career stages, on the assumption that people with similar family or job concerns—for instance, those with teen-age children, or with junior executive status—would tend to have similar stresses. This turned out to be wrong. No two families can be expected to react in the same way to a similar set of stressful events, whether in the family or the organization. For example, one husband found travel a pleasant way to escape from an unpleasant family situation; another found that exactly the same travel made such difficulties for himself and wife that he considered changing jobs. Some families on transfer from abroad found the experience an exciting challenge and opportunity to learn and travel; others found the experience traumatic. One family talked about the learning their children had picked up in the United States; another family could speak only of the disruptions and emotional problems endured by the children.

It became evident that the events in themselves could not indicate the response. A person's experience of stress is composed of two elements—the objective properties of the events involved and the subjective meanings they hold for him. One crucial subjective factor emerged consistently for all employees and all kinds of families: *The amount of influence a person perceives he has over a stressful situation—the extent to which, in effect, he feels he can control his own destiny—was key to effective functioning.* This explains why one individual can cope with the same events that defeat another; it explains why he can successfully handle certain kinds of stresses on some occasions and not on others.

The importance of perceived influence was strikingly demonstrated in one study that Sam Culbert (of the University of California at Los Angeles) and I conducted in a large, diversified organization the members of which frequently travel on business. Management recognized that travel placed pressures on personnel and had developed practices to ease the strain. Personnel were entitled to an extra round-trip air ticket on travel assignments lasting four weeks. They could use these tickets either to visit home for a weekend or to have their wives visit them at the work location. Management encouraged overseas travelers to rest a day before resuming business activity. Streamlined accounting procedures minimized the toil of preparing expense statements. In principle, management encouraged personnel to consider personal needs as well as their jobs when scheduling travel.

In practice, however, several forces subverted these human considerations. The organization's atmosphere put pressure on personnel to exercise individual prerogatives only under extreme stress. Following the "management way" meant accepting new assignments with a positive attitude. Thus, in many cases where travel was commensurate with new responsibilities or evolved naturally as a new part of an established job, staff members suppressed personal considerations. For example, they usually felt obliged to travel to overseas locations on weekends so that they would not waste a work day. If something had to give, it usually gave at home, not at work. They rationalized this by telling themselves that their families would eventually gain as a result of their job advancements.

We conducted a problem-solving workshop for several of the husbands and wives. Our original hypothesis had been that effectiveness in coping with the stresses of travel could be improved by a husband-wife seminar directed toward increasing their problem-solving skills. If the workshop were successful, we thought that travel patterns would change, and attitudes toward travel, the job, and the organization would improve. This presupposed that management would support the results.

After the workshop, participants, coworkers, and supervisory personnel reported improvements. A number of creative solutions emerged: sharing travel assignments, covering for other employees when a trip was necessary, better scheduling to reduce trips over the weekend, and so on.

But, although all participants reported greater family and organizational effectiveness, *attitudes about travel did not change.* Those who had considered travel a nuisance before the workshop still did after. Nor had the ways they valued their families and their organization altered. What had altered significantly was *their attitudes toward themselves.* They considered themselves more effective and influential. They saw themselves in a more positive light, with greater belief in their own strength and ability to make travel and work a better experience. In addition, the wives felt more important and influential because the organization had sponsored the workshop specifically to include them. The participants still felt this way three months later. (A control group that had not participated in the workshop did not have the same level of confidence in their ability to influence the work situation.) The family's role in plans for travel was strengthened and given legitimacy, and the wives' contributions toward effective problem solving were increased.

Travel was not the only area in which perceived influence made a difference in coping with stress. Transfer from abroad obviously involved many elements of stress, and there were dramatic contrasts in the abilities to cope with them among families that came to the United States for a two- to four-year assignment. I interviewed them during the first year.

In one particularly striking comparison, two families from the same European country, with the same number of children about the same ages and with foreign-born wives with similar proficiencies in English and with husbands at parallel career stages, nevertheless had opposite experiences. One family was the focus of concern for the whole work group; the supervisor was afraid that, because of continuing family problems, he would have to transfer the employee back long before the end of the scheduled three years. The other family was also having problems; but they were enjoying their stay and looking forward to what the remaining two-and-a-half years would bring.

What accounted for the differences? In the first family, the employee had known for years that he was to come to the United States and had prepared himself—but not his family. According to his wife, he had simply come home one evening and announced, "We must go to the United States in three months," and that was that. The results had been traumatic and catastrophic. The wife still spoke little English, the children were constantly ill, and the husband had to skip work to take care of domestic and medical crises his wife could not handle.

The second family had discussed and prepared for the move for two years beforehand. Together they decided that it would be an important step up in the husband's career and could be an important experience for all the rest, properly handled. And so it proved. After eighteen months, the wife spoke passable English and could drive a car; the children spoke English like Americans; all were looking forward to their summer vacation traveling by car through the United States. They did not feel isolated or unable to influence their own lives.

In all the groups studied, perceived influence was the determining factor in adjustment to stress. But emphasis should remain on the word *perceived*. No matter what formal or informal agreements people think they have with one another about the division of influence, each person makes his or her own estimate about how much influence he really has relative to the rest of the system. And that estimate, rather than the agreement or the objective situation, will determine his or her response.

To summarize, the organization and the family are two separate but interdependent systems intersecting at several places with the potential for either reinforcement or stress. There is a general tendency to ignore this interdependence, but after a time problems develop that force the interactions into consciousness. Stress is created because people live simultaneously in both systems, and the pressure can become cumulative. One system does not cause stress in the other; rather, it is caused by the interaction and by the accumulation of events occurring in the two. Ascribing blame to one system or the other is not only inaccurate but also interferes with resolution of the problems.

How may these problems be resolved? The key factor is the amount of influence that the people concerned perceive they have over the events that affect their lives and work. Although it may not always be possible to change the objective facts, it may be possible to reorganize them so that the individual may come to feel and assume greater control over events.

What are some specific things that we as educators can do to help students prepare for new and more productive styles of working and living? We can raise the issues of work and family systems interactions and legitimize the discussion in all subject areas of these life-style issues. When people think of their work and family as interacting systems rather than independent and dependent variables, different choices are made, and a wider range of alternatives becomes possible.

It is essential to create new ways of relating to both the work and family systems. On the one hand, it is important to increase awareness of the possible sources of stress between the worlds of work and family. Industrial organizations, government, and educators, as well as family members, must learn to recognize the danger signals that indicate stress overload, whether for individual, organization, or family—or all three.

On the other hand, it is important to help students take and feel more influence over their own lives and events in their lives. It is important to raise the possibility of making more conscious choices of life-styles in work, education, relationships, and families and to begin to create supports within the educational system for helping students make and implement these choices.

20

Breaking Down
Bureaucracy

Einar Thorsrud

When we started the industrial democracy program in Norway in 1962, we expected that our attempts to improve conditions for workers would soon be up against what some people refer to as the "machine theory" of organization and what others call "scientific management." Over the next ten years, a number of projects were undertaken on autonomous work groups and decentralized forms of planning and control. After the first projects in industry, we moved on to projects in banks, hotels, seafaring, and education, until finally we came to realize that we were up against something fundamental. What we were attacking was bureaucracy.[1]

Our work with different forms of organization gave us a bet-

---

[1] F. Emergy and E. Thorsrud, *Democracy at Work* (Leiden, Holland: Martinus Nijhoff, 1976).

218

ter understanding of what bureaucracy is all about. It is not only a way of organizing a large number of people so that they are easy to control from the top. It is more than a set of rules about how to carry out tasks and how to train, recruit, and promote personnel. It is more than a paper regime to prevent irrational treatment of problems and people. And it is more than a work culture where rules gradually become more important than the aims of the organization itself. The basic logic of bureaucracy is to split tasks into independent bits and then allocate the task bits to individuals or units of organization.[2] It is on the basis of this logic that persons and units within a bureaucracy are linked almost exclusively by a superior-subordinate relationship. Decisions about task performance are made by a superior level for a subordinate level, which in turn makes decisions for the next subordinate level. This leads to more and more decisions taken at the top and fewer and fewer at the bottom of the organization. Information and control is bureaucratized.

How bureaucracy works and how alternatives to it can be developed are perhaps best illustrated in one of the seafaring projects of the industrial democracy program. The project involved the crew of the *Balao,* a Norwegian Merchant Marine ship, and the point of departure was quite similar to that of manufacturing and service organizations in which we had redesigned work in Norway during the 1960s. First of all, traditional recruitment to the fleet could not be continued because the labor market was rather tight and the level of education had gone up so much that young boys, a traditional source of labor, could not qualify. The old career system was dead. Second, modern technology had reduced the size of the crew. This meant that some subgroups had become too small to function socially. Furthermore, in very large ships the new technology could not be handled safely and effectively by the old type of crew with traditional training. A third parallel with industrial and service organizations was that the seafarers, particularly the younger ones, no longer accepted a strict military type of work organization with rigid status systems (up to nine levels in one department of the ship). In one important respect, however, seafaring is very different from other occupations. The ship is a

---

[2] P. G. Herbst, *Alternatives to Hierarchy* (Leiden, Holland: Martinus Nijhoff, 1976).

twenty-four-hour society in which work cannot be isolated from leisure. Private and professional relationships overlap and merge, so that it is practically impossible to leave one's job "back at the office."

The following excerpts are from a summary of the research experience by the captain of the *Balao*.[3] Throughout the excerpts, "we" refers to the captain and the crew.

When we started the process of democratization on board Balao, we wanted first of all to train people better than before. We also wanted to remove the barriers between deck, engine, and catering. Thirdly, we had to get more stability among the people on board to be able to train them systematically. Stability among personnel can only be achieved if the ship has a high degree of control over the personnel policy. Stability depends not only on how release for holiday is arranged but also, more fundamentally, on a flexible manning system and a fixed salary system.

When we speak about the "ship environment," we include work, spare time, and living conditions. When we started what was called "project management" of the ship, we emphasized the improvement of the spare-time activities by improved welfare, by improvement of the living conditions, common dayroom, and so on. All of this would again have an impact upon the work environment. To a certain degree this was right, but it is impossible to go very far without directly changing the work environment itself.

On new concepts:

We had to change the known deep-rooted organizational structure of the past and introduce completely new concepts. Of particular importance was the building of mutual trust, particularly between the ship management and the rest of the crew. This we hoped to achieve by extensive meeting activity, by daily communication during spare time. To have something to cooperate about, it was natural for us to start with work planning.

On work planning:

Before we were able to clarify the objectives, we often disagreed about when the jobs were to be carried out. We felt that the size of the groups and the composition of the planning groups

---

[3]Quoted in R. Johansen, "Changes in Work Planning Increase Shipboard Democracy," *National Labor Institute Bulletin*, 1977, *3* (1).

were a problem. Gradually the ship management moved out of the planning group and left most of the planning to those who were to perform the work, to increase their independence as far as possible.

When we analyzed the work planning, it appeared that most tasks were of a technical nature, but we had rather few people able to do this kind of work. If, in addition, you are unfortunate enough to get people with poor training, the distribution of work will of course be difficult.

On an integrated crew:

We have come to the conclusion that we need a crew consisting of what we call ship mechanics and trainees on different levels. Initially we had only one man on board who was qualified as a ship mechanic. If we were to succeed within a limited time, we had to start recruiting people with better technical background. We found that trainees with one year from a technical-vocational school would be a good alternative. This is the basis of an integrated crew working across the old department barriers.

On safety and efficiency:

It is very important for the safety of the ship that ship mechanics and other trainees get technical as well as navigational training. Most of our people qualify for a boat navigation certificate. Because of this, they are generally well qualified for work on the bridge as well as in the engine room. In work-planning groups, all possible risks are discussed, and for each job specific requirements are stated in terms of equipment to be used, what safety equipment is needed, and so on.

Lifeboat and fire exercises are held regularly. We are training under very realistic conditions, and the planning is done by the crew itself. Stability has been very high, and this, of course, adds to safety. Everybody is well trained and is prepared to cooperate with others in taking care of ship and cargo. The crew is responsible for the whole ship.

On flexible manning and a fixed annual wage:

A fixed salary system combined with flexible manning has worked well, and it is now very easy also to plan holidays, and so on. It is important for the individual to know that he gets the holidays he deserves under good economic conditions. Secondly, this system is also an inspiration for efficient work. Efficiency must

*not be confused with more work. A rational distribution of work
is the main thing.*

On leisure time and education:

> *The quality of spare time is now much better and can be
used for studies or welfare arrangements and not simply for a comfortable relaxation in the cabin. The crew of* Balao *has been very
active in sports, shooting, swimming, and also publishing their own*
Balao Newspaper. *Adult education takes place in many ways,
mostly planned by the crew.*

On expectations:

> *As you can see, it has been a long process before we got to
where we are now. But we can also draw a clear-cut conclusion
which has been brought home to the shipping company.*

> *The way we have practiced increased participation through
1975 has fully met with our expectations regarding efficiency and
service to our customers. A good work and spare-time environment has been created. Very few accidents have occurred, and we
have had very few cases of illness. The motivation for training and
education has improved considerably. We judge all this as good
long-term economics.*

On hierarchy and communication:

> *The crew had made critical remarks regarding the hierarchy,
the organizational structure, where they find the root to most of
the evils hampering good communication. Within the hierarchy,
concepts like* information *and* communication *do not mean much.
Orders and directives are assumed to be enough. The rest is taken
care of by the "jungle telegraph." To get on any speaking terms at
all with the organization, it is necessary to break down the old
barriers. But simultaneously it is necessary to build up new types
of management and leadership. If this is not done, chaos may
occur. (These were the words of the crew.)*

On participation and open careers:

> *With this sort of ship democracy, we have chosen to start
from the bottom up and to make work more interesting. By improving the quality of jobs at the bottom, we are able to relieve
those better qualified and to have a much more even distribution
of jobs. To achieve this, the key concepts have been training and
education. It is very important for young sailors to learn something. And training and education have taken place ashore as well*

as on board. The work done on board needs people who are highly qualified. The sailor of today trained as a ship mechanic has very high qualifications not only for work on board but also as a mechanic ashore.

Captain Samuelson ends by saying that the process of change has been long and difficult. The old system was so deeply rooted that it was impossible to move forward too rapidly. To help ease this problem, the *Balao* and a number of other experimental ships have created their own network for exchange of experience. Each year they organize—with some support from the researchers, the authorities, unions, and branch organizations—a one-week workshop for evaluation, planning, and joint policy making.

By comparing the *Balao* experiment to the logic of bureaucracy, we can see that an alternative logic is emerging. First, instead of dividing tasks into bits, we can organize task elements into different patterns depending on the work situation. In the *Balao* case, the starting and stopping of engines and pumps during ordinary ship operations follow one pattern, while a different one occurs during safety drill and learning sessions. This means that one pattern may fit a *group* organization of the crew, while another pattern fits a *hierarchical* and *specialized* role system. A third pattern may fit a *matrix organization,* in which specialists rotate between their primary roles and other tasks that they are also qualified to perform as secondary roles.

Second, instead of having one single hierarchical structure of tasks and roles, we can have several structures changing over time, according to needs. If the tasks are to be carried out under great time pressure, one predetermined structure is established. If ample time is available and a different problem has to be investigated and different solutions tried out, then different structures of task and role relationships are set up.

Third, a uniform superior-subordinate relationship between people can be replaced by a series of different ones. In some cases, such as emergency situations on board *Balao,* relationships may be of the traditional type, but during ordinary operation a number of different work groups can be set up to function without any formal supervision. Instead of abolishing one hidebound system and introducing another, an organization can encourage flexibility. In many work situations, people in superior roles can switch into subordinate roles and vice versa to perform specific tasks.

Fourth, instead of a permanent and strict set of boundaries between organizational units, we may have several types of boundaries and sometimes almost none. On the *Balao,* strict segmentation and demarcations between departments and work roles began to disappear. This did not mean that responsibilities were not clearly defined. Nor did it mean that people lost their professional identity. The point is that they extended their technical and social responsibilities according to the needs of their ship and of their own career plans. In some work situations, they developed special skills, while in others they broadened their experience. During spare time, they interacted in open and flexible social groups. They ate in the same dining room and made a point of not keeping special seats. They played games, listened to music, and looked at television together irrespective of formal status. They studied together, drank together, and went ashore together. In other words, they related as people instead of as bureaucratic functionaries.

Finally, instead of isolated organizational units and individuals, we can have overlapping units and open relations between people. A remarkable thing about the *Balao* case, which we have seen also in some industrial and educational projects, is that the organization becomes more open to the outside world. Members are encouraged to build their own networks of relations in other work organizations, in educational institutions, and in professional and community associations. The relation between work and family life also becomes more open. And there is reason to believe that this same spirit of openness could help build bridges across the boundaries of a segmented society.

A review of emerging patterns in the quality of work life in Scandinavia reveals different trends leading to different scenarios.[4] Similar trends are apparent in Australia and in the United States. Which scenario prevails depends very much on the values cultivated in work organizations and schools.

The *technocratic scenario* is not likely to be the future context of work in Scandinavia. If nothing else, the new laws on work

---

[4] E. Thorsrud, *Perspectives on the Quality of Working Life in Scandinavia,* Research Series No. 8 (Geneva: International Institute of Labor Studies, 1976).

environment will put an end to the practice of first optimizing the technical system of work and only then considering the human and environmental effects. The way in which we counteract the technocratic trends may, however, lead us into new and doubtful areas of development. If social scientists, psychologists, and social workers become the new power groups in postindustrial society, we may exchange one sort of specialist domination for another. Neither is good for the democratization of work.

However, the *sociocratic scenario* is not likely to be the future context of work in Scandinavia either, despite some trends in this direction. The educational system has, over the past two decades, been invaded by new specialists from the social and human sciences. Educational policy has to some extent become a matter of translating rather sketchy research findings into new forms of education. Or, more often, a lack of research results has been accepted as a reason for not having an educational policy developed by those who are working in education. The health and welfare system has been subject to similar influences from the social scientists—ever since it became clear that human service systems cannot operate according to principles of mass manufacturing. I see no reason to believe these systems will function better if dominated by sociocratic specialists, who may be too eager to build their new professions. There has been a tendency to overestimate what can be done *for* people in situations where joint efforts on equal terms *with* people seem to be the only guarantee against specialist manipulation. New specialists may, even when they claim to have the opposite philosophy, become controllers rather than facilitators of communication and social change.

The *bureaucratic scenario,* almost by default, could become the new context of work in Scandinavia. This could be the case even though bureaucracy seems to be the opposite of what democratization has been about in work reform over the past twenty years. From the point of view of politics, it is understandable that new and rather elaborate systems of employee representation were recently introduced by law. The same applies to new laws and regulations regarding work environment and safe employment. And from the point of view of policy making, these reforms could improve the sanctioning processes in industry and in communities at large. But if work life itself continues to be dehumanizing, these reforms will be empty constructions. Only the introduction of nonbureaucratic forms of work organization in enterprises as well as unions, professional associations, and governmental agencies can prevent this. Meeting this challenge may turn out to be the critical test of democracy in Scandinavia.

If the challenge *is* met, the *local community scenario* will become the context within which work, education, and family life merge. During the recent economic recession, some basic social values have been tested in a critical way. Local employment has been supported as never before. Local schools and hospitals have been saved by community action in spite of cost savings claimed necessary by government. Highways and city reconstruction planned according to macroeconomic criteria have been stopped. Centralized mass education has been judged as a failure, and new decentralized forms of education have been tested. Adult education has been strengthened. The new feminism has made the most progress in labor-market family policy when the movement has been least centralized.

Just when we learned as social scientists to adapt to a network strategy of change in action research, we can see nonhierarchical movements take root in many parts of society. This may turn out to be a critical factor influencing people to quality not only in their work life but in their whole life.

21

A New Economics

Hazel Henderson

I t is said that Minerva's owl flies only at dusk, and that we become aware of the era in which we have lived only when it is in decline. I suggest that we are experiencing the decline of the industrial era—a very short period in human affairs, after all, that began 200 years ago in England and took as its main preoccupation the maximizing of production of material goods. The industrial era was geared primarily to utilitarian concerns. It gave rise to our current concept of "jobs"—a concept in which human beings are regarded as "commodities" to be bought and sold on labor markets. It also gave rise to the concept of training people for working in these various slots in the society, to be provided by the vagaries of the "invisible hand" guiding the so-called free market. One result of these concepts is that the majority of our population have been educated and socialized into the role of industrial peasants, passively waiting to be told by some business or government institution what to do with their lives.

In the emerging countereconomy, which I see already growing, the "industrial peasantry" of selling oneself as a commodity called labor—and I include in this intellectual labor and career professionals whose brains are for hire—will constitute a much less important fraction of overall productive activity than it does today. I think we will move toward the concept of what E. F. Schumacher calls "right livelihood," where labor is seen as an *output* of production.[1] In other words, this countereconomy is more concerned with labor as self-actualization.

L. S. Stavrianos, in *The Promise of the Coming Dark Age,* sees an interesting parallel between the present period of transition and the changes that took place in Europe centuries ago: "The Dark Age following the collapse of Rome was anything but dark," he says. "Rather, it was an age of epochal creativity, when values and institutions were evolved that constituted the bedrock foundation of modern civilization. It is true that this creativity was preceded by imperial disintegration—by the shrinkage of commerce and cities, the disappearance of bureaucracies and standing armies, and the crumbling of roads and aqueducts and palaces. This imperial wreckage explains, but scarcely justifies, the traditional characterization of the early medieval period as 'dark.' It was an age of birth, as well as death, and to concentrate on the latter is to miss the dynamism and significance of a seminal phase of human history."[2]

That which we call "our economy" is a continually changing, evolving system, with new enterprises growing at its advancing edge while older corporations and institutions die off and dissolve. In this decay process, they release their components of capital, land, human skills, and talents to be reabsorbed into the fledgling companies and new enterprises in the leading sector for their further development. Since an economy is also a living system, composed of live biological units—namely, humans in dynamic interaction with the energy and resources around them—it conforms to the basic laws of physics, as we know them, and the same entropy-syntropy cycles of decay and regeneration as do all biological systems.

This basic model of the entropy-syntropy cycle is crucial to

---

[1] E. F. Schumacher, *Small Is Beautiful: Economics as if People Mattered* (New York: Harper & Row, 1973).
[2] L. S. Stavrianos, *The Promise of the Coming Dark Age* (San Francisco: W. H. Freeman, 1976).

our understanding of the particular subsystem we call our economy and to helping us see current economic difficulties in longer time perspectives and may suggest ways to deal with the decline of industrialism. This decline, although it will undoubtedly prove uncomfortable, will likely affect only the unsustainable modes of production and consumption it has fostered. With leadership and foresight, it may release nutrients to spur the development of the already visible countereconomy now beginning to flourish in the interstices of the dying industrial system.

In mature, industrial countries—the United States, Japan, and the nations of Western Europe—the potential for economic growth is almost exhausted. Continued growth is constrained both by the internal structure and dynamics of these societies and by such external factors as the worsening planetary population-resource ratio, climatic uncertainties, the new and legitimate militancy of the countries of the southern hemisphere and the increasingly visible social costs of world trade. To those whose vision has remained unclouded by the mystifying jargon of economists, the transition to a new era seems obvious. It can be inferred from extremely simple sayings—for example, "There is no such thing as a free lunch" and "Nothing fails like success." The signs of death of the old industrial order can no longer be explained away. They have reached above the threshold of sensory awareness. Citizens can smell the foul air and water, hear the rising noise levels, and see the increasing urban disorder in slums, unsafe streets, and curtailed services.

In fact, it is fairly self-evident that mature industrial societies cannot continue expanding at past rates, simply because such rates are always in relation to the size of a *base*. Any citizen knows that, as a base grows, the rate of its expansion must sooner or later decline. This is as true for IBM or Xerox as it is for an oak tree. It is absurd for the United States to be alarmed about falling rates of economic growth (defined by gross national product) and falling rates of technological innovation and "productivity" (inadequately defined) when the base for calculating such rates, the giant U.S. sociotechnical system is the largest on the planet. So I am not impressed when U.S. rates of technological innovation and productivity are compared, with official horror, to the higher rates in Japan, which had a postwar base on an order of magnitude smaller than our own. I am not upset when warned that new "science and technology gaps" are widening. I am upset, however, when Congress is urged by science and groups promoting high technology to appropriate ever more tax dollars to save us from this fate.

The continuing crisis in economics, particularly the failure of macroeconomic management, is accompanied by crises in sociology, psychology, and even physics. Two insistent paradoxes are now almost unavoidable in any academic field relevant to policy making in industrial societies. First, advancing technological complexity systematically destroys free market conditions, making laissez-faire policies ever less workable. Second, advancing technological complexity also destroys the conditions necessary for democratic political governments to function, since legislators, and even heads of state, let alone the average voter, cannot master sufficient information to exert popular control of technological innovations. Some of these technologies—for example, nuclear power—are inherently totalitarian. This is a new idea for us: that some forms of technology may simply be *unconstitutional*.

And yet, intelligent or not, some form of control is inevitable. It is axiomatic that each order of magnitude of technological mastery and managerial control inevitably calls forth an equivalent order of magnitude of necessary government control in order to maintain our uneasy "social homeostasis." Any honest debate about deregulation must address this issue, for it concerns the entire direction of our technological societies. The question is this: Will we continue moving toward producer-oriented, capital-intensive, centralizing, and hazardous technologies, and accept the burgeoning risks and the price of government regulation and necessary control, or will we opt for simpler, cheaper, less violent, decentralized technologies that conserve capital, energy, and resources, that therefore require more people to own and operate them, and that, since they are benign, require less regulation?

The evolutionary dilemma summarized by "Nothing fails like success" can be restated in the terms of anthropology as "The law of the retarding lead." This law holds that the best adapted and most successful countries have the greatest difficulty in adapting and retaining their lead in world affairs under new conditions, and that, conversely, the backward and less successful societies are more likely to be able to adapt and forge ahead under changing times. Therefore, Western societies may have much to learn from the so-called less-developed countries and much to relearn from their own pasts if they are to become regenerative and sustainable societies.

Efforts to promote or pursue such learning are not likely to receive much "official" help. In any period of cultural transition, the dominant organs of a society often increase their efforts to reassure the public, while their leaders privately express doubt and fear. This is not surprising, since it is precisely these institutions of government, business, academia, labor, and religion that are in decline and whose leaders are threatened by a loss of power. A further obstacle is that we have been taught to measure the society's well-being in terms of the well-being of these existing institutions. Therefore, the growing shoots of alternative approaches are unmeasured, overlooked, and insufficiently monitored and studied as possible new social models. But we cannot afford to wait until the conceptual wreckage of industrialism is sifted and composted. We need to study the countereconomy at the same time that we are examining the gross national product, unemployment statistics, and measures of productivity and efficiency, all of which are now generating dangerous illusions.

I think it is premature to envision a planetary countereconomy, since much pragmatic experimentation will be needed before the ancient and now irrelevant dogmas and conflicts over capitalism versus communism can be transcended. Nevertheless, a sense of the character of the emerging countereconomy is conveyed by the following developments.

The first is the growth of countermedia and alternative publishing ventures, which are sort of a measuring rod for the countereconomy. In the United States, these include *Prevention* magazine, which has a circulation of 2 million; *Organic Gardening*, 1 million; *Rolling Stone*, 1.5 million; *Mother Earth News*, about 500,000, and the spectacularly successful *Whole Earth Catalog*. In addition, we see the proliferation of regional magazines dealing with ecological life-styles and appropriate technology, some eighty publishing ventures operated by feminists, the rise of the black press, and the emergence of hundreds of small, often cooperatively owned book stores, publishing houses, and distributorships.

Then there are the alternative marketing enterprises. The "Alternative Christmas Catalog" offers, instead of materialistic goods and junk gifts, a vast selection of "psychic" gifts, such as subscriptions to counterculture magazines and newsletters and memberships in various citizen organizations. Organizations have been created to market rural crafts such as quilts, embroidery, clothing, and toys to urban department stores, often on a non-profit basis. The counterculture media also perform a marketing service through their inexpensive advertising rates and well-defined audiences. Highly professional public-interest advertising agencies, such as the Public Media Center of San Francisco, eschew ordinary commercial clients but "sell" citizen organizations and their social causes. Other groups, such as Oxfam's Bridge in Britain, catalogs and links small, rural producers of handcrafted goods and art in the Third World with affluent, concerned consumers. Unlike the large multinational export enterprises, these groups operate in a small-scale, nonprofit, people-to-people mode.

Another increasingly popular development is the staging of both rural and urban "fairs," where various sectors of the counter-economy can nucleate and cross-fertilize, featuring their own commune-made arts and crafts. A good example is the Toward Tomorrow Fair in New England, which last year hosted five acres of alternative technology exhibits by small businesses in solar, wind, and bioconversion, and attracted 7,000 people. Another example is the Cousteau Society's Involvement Days, which have been held in various urban areas the past two years, attracting crowds of several thousand people. These are some of the new natural linkages and networks operating outside traditional industrial merchandising. They are based on emerging value systems that are impervious to the old, materialistic, Madison Avenue "hard sell."

There is a growing interest in household economics, that is, in the economics of use value, rather than market value. A survey in 1969 by Ismail Sirageldin on "Non-Market Components of National Income" found the total value of all goods and services produced by the household sector in 1965 to be about $300 billion.[3] The increasing protest at the statistical blackout perpetrated for so long on the household economy is, of course, being spearheaded by women. Those who work at home but receive no income have been consistently ignored by economists' definitions of "productivity" and "value," and have been excluded from the gross national product and their rightful access to retirement security.

[3]S. Burns, *Home, Inc.* (Garden City, N.Y.: Doubleday, 1975), p. 35.

Another sign of the emerging countereconomy is the rebirth of populism and cooperative movements. This includes neighborhood and block development projects ("sweat equity urban renewal"), land trusts, and the increased bartering of skills and home produced goods and services. The Cooperative League of the United States, in its 1975 review, states that more than fifty million Americans now belong to cooperatives of one kind or another, from co-op banks and credit unions to co-op food stores.[4] A bill to establish a national cooperative bank came close to passage recently in Congress and will no doubt pass during the new administration. Many local organizations, in order to make credit available to small farmers and co-ops, are campaigning to set up state-owned development banks modeled after the successful state Bank of North Dakota. The Massachusetts Community Development Finance Corporation may be one of the first of these community-type financial instruments. It is already authorized with an initial appropriation of $10 million, and it will buy stock in enterprises owned in common by the residents of any geographical area in the state.[5]

Worker participation and self-management movements are also on the rise. Although more prominent in western Europe and Canada, these movements are beginning to take root in the United States as well. The newly formed Federation for Economic Democracy is a network that is helping develop some of these ideas, and worker-owned enterprises such as Washington's International Group Plans, which sells $60 million of insurance annually, are providing new models.

The global ecology movement and the feminist movement are also providing unique roles in social transformation, since they operate in all industrial societies. These movements are so pervasive they are impossible to ignore. The wives of corporate and government bureaucrats become their uncomfortable social consciences, and many decision makers must now face their own sons and daughters to defend their daily decisions.

Meanwhile, the building of new coalitions in industrial countries between formerly fragmented citizen groups is continuing. In the 1960s the convergence of citizen movements occurred

[4]The Cooperative League of the U.S.A., *Co-Op Facts and Figures* (Washington, D.C.: The Cooperative League, 1975).
[5]Institute for Local Self-Reliance, *Self-Reliance* (Washington, D.C.: Institute for Local Self-Reliance, June 1976), p. 8.

around the concept of corporate accountability. When the consumer and environmental advocates, the civil rights, women, and student movements joined the antiwar and media access groups, they all found that a major cause of their grievances was the profit-hungry practices of large corporations. Today's coalitions bring together many of these existing forces with new and older elements of the labor movement, rural voters, small business people and farmers, grass-roots and neighborhood groups, and appropriate technology advocates.

Perhaps the most convincing statistics so far on the dimension of the emerging countereconomy in the United States is the recent estimate, made by the Stanford Research Institute (SRI), that approximately four to five million adult Americans have now transformed their personal life-styles to what they call *voluntary simplicity*. They have reduced their incomes drastically and withdrawn from their former slots in the dominant industrial consumer economy. SRI estimates that another eight to ten million adhere to and act on some, but not all, of the basic tenets of the voluntary-simplicity approach, which embraces frugal consumption, ecological awareness, and a dominant concern with inner, personal growth. SRI claims that these statistics on the adoption of material frugality and "psychic riches" are important because they may augur a major transformation in the goals and values of Americans in the coming decades.[6]

In other countries, such as Canada, the voluntary-simplicity theme emerges officially. A recent study commissioned by the Canadian government challenges the assumption that Canada can continue as a mass-consumption society.[7] It examines five scenarios:

1. Status quo, or "doing more with more."
2. Growth with conservation, or "doing more with less."
3. High-level stable state, or "doing the same with less."
4. The Buddhist scenario, or "doing less with less."
5. The squander society, or "doing less with more"—in other

[6]D. Elgin and A. Mitchell, "Voluntary Simplicity," *Guidelines* 1976, 104.

[7]GAMMA Study Group, *The Conserver Society: Blueprint for the Future?* (Montreal, Canada: McGill University and the University of Montreal, October 1976).

words, extravagant consumption, waste, manipulative advertising, planned obsolescence, and self-destructing goods.

Three of these scenarios—2, 3, and 4—require legislative action to ensure conservation, durability of products, recycling, use of renewable resources, full-cost pricing, and the internalizing of all social costs of production. Other specific changes that are called for are flexible time schedules for work and more intensive use of existing capital and productive facilities.

To foster the kinds of positive changes taking place in the emerging countereconomy, educators need to recognize that they must change too and that their institutions have in some cases become obsolete. In media-rich cultures such as our own, it makes sense to move toward more noninstitutional learning, more apprenticeships and internships, and more learning in the context of communal production modes and self-managed enterprises.

More than ever, educators will be called on to teach values for human development and ecological harmony. They must teach a broader, more realistic definition of self-interest: as coterminous with group interest and, indeed, on our little blue planet, with concern for all species. We humans are self-organizing systems. We have, in our collective history, developed many examples of stable, self-organizing communities, based on psychic structures, concepts of reverence and transcendence and the sacred, that permitted voluntary internalization of behavior control. This ability to self-organize is encoded in our DNA. We *know* how it could be: the vision of empathy between humans and their harmony with the ecosystem. This vision is our commonest myth: the Elysian Fields, the Kingdom of Heaven, Nirvana, the Great Oneness. We know the hologram: "Do as you would be done by." For the first time in our history, morality has become pragmatic.[8]

[8]This chapter is excerpted from the author's forthcoming book, *Creating Alternative Futures* (New York: G. P. Putnam's Berkley Paperback, 1977).

22

Future Work,
Future Learning

Willis W. Harman

☙☙☙☙☙☙☙☙☙☙☙☙☙☙

I want to invite you to think freshly and fundamentally about the complex subject of future work and future learning. Several basic observations frame our inquiry:

- There is a high correlation in industrialized society between *employment* and *resource utilization.*
- Characteristic of the development of industrialized society has been a steady increase in *labor productivity,* premised on the continued presence of cheap and plentiful energy (mainly fossil fuel).
- Growing *environmental and resource problems* will tend to have a negative impact, both on employment and labor productivity.
- With increasing labor productivity come the virtual elimination of crafts and *reduced intrinsic meaningfulness* of much work.
- Increasing educational levels, together with this reduced meaningfulness of work, have led to problems of *underemployment.*

How serious are these problems? Are they chronic problems? If so, what is the role of education?

The usual approach to these questions is heavy on statistics. Because most of those who will be entering the labor force between now and 1995 are already born, projections can be made with fair confidence. Between now and 1990, the labor force as conventionally defined is expected to increase by about 22 percent, while the overall population will increase by only about 9 percent. (This discrepancy is due partly to a drop in the birthrate from the "baby boom" peak of twenty-five per thousand population in 1955 to below fifteen per thousand in 1973, and partly to the continued increase in female participation, which has grown from 39 percent in 1964 to 46 percent in 1974). Annual growth of the labor force has been around 2 percent; it is projected to slow to approximately 1.1 percent in the 1980-1985 period and to drop below 1 percent after that. To produce new jobs at the rate required to accommodate these increases and simultaneously bring national unemployment down to somewhere near the 4 percent level by 1985 (assuming the historic rate of productivity increase of around 3 percent a year) would require a sustained real gross national product (GNP) growth rate of around 5 or 6 percent (whereas the real GNP growth rate was about −2 percent per year for 1974 and 1975). Thus, the existence of a serious near-term unemployment problem seems clear. What the longer term holds is more in dispute.

There are those who assure us there is no need to worry. As Daniel Bell argues, the fraction of the work force in the services sector (government, professional, trade, finance, insurance, real estate, miscellaneous services, transportation, and utilities) is increasing steadily in comparison to the fraction involved in the agricultural, extractive, and manufacturing industries.[1] The services sector does not encounter the same limits to expansion caused by resource shortages and environmental impacts; thus there is no compelling reason to assume that the economy cannot grow at a sufficient rate to meet demands for jobs a decade or so from now. (The Bureau of Labor Statistics projects that the number of jobs in the services sector will increase by over a third by 1985.) Then there is still the expanding "knowledge sector" described by

[1]D. Bell, *The Coming of Post-Industrial Society* (New York: Basic Books, 1973).

Kahn and others as being capable of almost indefinite expansion.[2]

Thus, the main reasons given for not being concerned about future prospects for employment are as follows. First, current unemployment statistics are misleading, partly because of the temporarily high rate of growth of the labor force, and partly because of the temporary recession. Second, the shift to the services sector will provide jobs; consumer investment patterns are shifting from durable goods (saturation effects in appliances, automobiles, and housing partly caused by decreasing family size) to education, health, miscellaneous services, and leisure activities. And, third, we can expect more people to leave the work force or to work less. Since people are, on the whole, hedonistic, consuming, and work avoiding (so it is claimed), more and more opportunities for leisure will be taken, including earlier retirement. Already much of the youth unemployment is voluntary; as Feldstein notes, young workers tend to have a casual attitude toward work, holding many jobs briefly, with spells of unemployment in between, and prefer this as a way of life.[3] In other words, much unemployment seems to be "voluntary" in that jobs are available but are deemed undesirable, resulting in high job turnover and unemployment rates.

There are also conflicting opinions, holding a much more pessimistic picture. In 1976 more than seven million adults were looking for work, and unemployment insurance benefits paid out totaled roughly $18 billion. To keep unemployment down to 5 percent by 1980 would require creation of around twelve million new jobs in five years, more than have ever been generated so quickly in peacetime. (The number of jobs created in the preceding five years was less than seven million, and that was accompanied by inflation rates that ranged into two-digit figures.)

The 6 percent real GNP growth that would be required to generate jobs at such a high rate will probably not be approached (except for a possible postrecession recovery period) because of various limiting factors. Among these are environmental and resource limitations and the threat of high inflation. Another limit-

[2]H. Kahn and others, *The Next 200 Years* (New York: William Morrow, 1976).
[3]M. Feldstein, "The Economics of the New Unemployment," *The Public Interest*, 1973 (33): 3-42.

ing factor is the looming capital needs of large energy projects, which reduce the capital availability for other expansion. Costs relating to increasing regulation, delays stemming from environmental protection demands, and increasing labor and material costs all conspire to slow down and cause cancellation of job-generating projects. An uncertain business environment, to which fluctuating government policy and unpredictable court actions contribute frightens away investment.

Computer processors and cybernetic production processes, their attractiveness increased by rising labor rates, are contributing to the elimination of many blue-collar jobs. Reevaluations are being made of capital-intensive, automated production methods, including dramatic thrusts toward sophisticated material-handling devices—even robots.

Meanwhile, white-collar clerical work is undergoing a technological revolution, and systematization, computer power, and word-processing equipment are being more widely employed. Further automation and productivity increases will contribute to the technological obsolescence of large numbers of persons who have been led to expect work opportunities commensurate with their academic degrees.

Another development apparently contributing to unemployment in this country is the increasing migration of assembly work to less economically advanced countries. This is only in part caused by prospects of cheaper labor. It is to a greater extent a consequence of the unwillingness of American workers to accept dull, routine work.

In spite of these indications of trouble ahead, by no means everyone shares a perception of future chronic unemployment. In part this lack of consensus stems from the extent to which the seriousness of the work problem is concealed.[4]

Various estimates have been made of the "real unemployment," taking into account nonworking women who desire jobs, the young and the elderly who are squeezed out of the job market, the involuntarily retired, the despairing who no longer seek work, those who are quite clearly in a featherbedding or make-work

---

[4]B. Gross and J. Straussman, " 'Full' Employment, Growthmanship and the Expansion of Labor Supply," *The Annals* of the American Academy of Political and Social Science, 1975, *418* (March): 1-16.

situation, and those dropouts in "holding institutions" such as reform schools and mental health facilities. These estimates range
from 25 to 35 percent of the potential work force. "Subemploy-
ment" rates in a number of cities are estimated at well over 40
percent.[5]

U.S. society's underlying anxiety about unemployment
shows up in pressures on older employees to get out of the work
force by retiring early (a form of "age discrimination" now being
challenged), in inflated age and education criteria for job entry, in
delayed automation of routine operations because of the job-
eliminating effect, in subtle forms of featherbedding, and in panic
reactions when there is talk of canceling a defense contract or
space project or reducing the U.S. role as arms supplier to the
world. Fear of unemployment is a key factor in the energy policy
issue—the most compelling reason that moderation of energy use is
feared is our inability to handle the unemployment that presumably would accompany it.

Underemployment—the undcrutilization of skills, training,
and education of workers—is fast becoming the major source of
work place problems in the United States and in other industrially
advanced nations. As the levels of educational attainment of the
workforce rise, discontent and alienation spread among more
qualified workers who are forced to take jobs easily performable
by workers with lower qualifications (and lower expectations).
The proportion of the adult labor force with one or more years of
college rose from 19 percent in 1960 to 27 percent in 1970. But
the proportion of total employment represented by managerial,
administrative, technical, and professional jobs was rising more
slowly. It went from 20 percent in 1960 to 22 percent in 1970 (as
contrasted with nearly 50 percent of young adults who *expect*
these kinds of work). In sum, the future work force will be better
educated and will be making more demands for interesting and
meaningful jobs that satisfy their requirements for challenge,
growth, and self-fulfillment. And more of them will be disaffected,
because too few fulfilling jobs will be available. "There is no *expanding* area in the occupational structure to take care of the large

[5]W. J. Spring, "Underemployment: The Measure We Refuse to Take,"
New Generation, 1971, 53 (1).

number of people with the new aspirations of high-income, high-status, and high-'meaning' jobs."[6]

So much for the statistics. In spite of the ambiguity and disagreements, their message can probably be summarized somewhat as follows:

1. In the short term, there is a serious unemployment problem and a continuing underemployment problem.
2. In the mid term (that is, in the mid 1980s), there may be a respite as regards unemployment, because of demographic changes, but there will still be a persistent underemployment problem.
3. In the longer term, there may be both a chronic unemployment and underemployment problem, but the statistical projections are equivocal.

These work-related problems have their counterparts in education. Society views education essentially as job preparation—notwithstanding much rhetoric to the contrary. Viewed in that framework, education has two problems—the "overeducated" (or the overcredentialed, or perhaps the overexpecting); and the ill trained (or perhaps the ill motivated). In some sense, these are both pseudo-problems. The first is a fundamental failure of the social order to provide enough satisfactory social roles to match the changing characteristics of the citizenry. The second problem could, under other circumstances, be handled by commerce and industry. (In World War II, when there was a severe labor shortage and when job applicants were motivated by a sense of purpose in it all, industry found training of even the poorly educated to be a problem it could take in stride.)

Now, having looked at these four problems—unemployment, underemployment, "overeducation" and the ill trained—in a rather conventional way, let us try to step back and see them in a more fundamental light.

The French historian, Fernand Braudel, in his introduction to *The Mediterranean,* explains that in treating the Mediterranean

---

[6] B. Berger, "People Work—The Youth Culture and the Labor Market," *The Public Interest,* 1975, *38* (Winter): 67-79.

world in the age of Philip II he has to write three histories.[7] First is a history at the level of events—accessions to power, revolutions, treatises, laws, and wars. As he says, "We must learn to distrust this history," because of the illusion that actions cause events rather than both being manifestations of a deeper flow. The second history is at the level of institutions and institutional change. But this too fails to deal with all the forces present, so Braudel writes a third history, at the level of those enduring factors and patterns—climate, geography, and basic cultural characteristics—that change only very slowly through the centuries but nonetheless shape the changes at more rapidly varying levels.

Following Braudel's lead, I would like to look at the future of work and education in terms of what has been happening at that third level. The problems of work and education we were examining earlier are essentially problems of success. They are problems that result from our fabulous past successes in technology, industrial management, and in raising educational (and expectational) levels.

To understand them we need to examine that long, multifold trend (eight to ten centuries in western Europe and less in other parts of the world) that Robert Heilbroner calls the "Great Ascent"—the trend of modernization and economic development that contains within it such stages as medieval capitalism, the growth of empirical science, and the industrial revolution.[8]

In premodern society, most people were involved in work to meet their own needs and those of a limited community. There was some long-distance trade, but not much. The money economy was not central; most exchanges were outside the money economy. Behavior fell largely into traditional roles.

The economic development multifold trend includes several important components:

- Increasing secularization—that is, rational organization of society's activities and institutions around impersonal, utilitarian values, in place of the traditional cultural and religious shaping values.

---

[7] F. Braudel, *The Mediterranean and the Mediterranean World in the Age of Philip II* (New York: Harper & Row, 1976).

[8] R. Heilbroner, *The Great Ascent* (New York: Harper & Row, 1963).

- Increasing industrialization of human activity and inclusion of an increasing fraction of activity in the primary economic sector.
- Increasing dominance of economic rationality in decision making.
- Increasing "scientification" of knowledge, with special emphasis on the utility of knowledge in generating manipulative technology.

Some societies (ours included) have been on this path for many centuries. Others are just starting on it. The tensions between these two groups of nations will dominate the globe in the decades to come. Almost all the serious societal problems are associated with positions along this path. In the "advanced" societies, there has come to be a questioning about how much further in this direction it is advisable to go. Resistance is evident with regard to continuation of each of the four component trends just mentioned and to numerous derivative trends, including:

- Increasing scale of environmental impact of human activities.
- Increasing rate of use of "nonrenewable" natural resources of minerals and fossil fuels.
- Increasing urbanization and growth of megalopoli.
- Increasing centralization and concentration of economic and political power.
- Increasing destructive power of military weaponry.
- Increasing manipulative power of science and technology (for example, behavior modification techniques, genetic engineering, and weather modification).
- Increasing gap between the affluence of the world's richer populations and the impoverishment of the poorer groups.

The future is predominantly a matter of what happens with this fundamental multifold trend—whether it will continue and effectively overrun the counterforces or whether the counterforces will prevail and societal evolution turn in some new direction.

The main point of all this for our purposes is that we may come to understand the problems of work and education differently if we see them as deriving to an important extent from this fundamental systemic trend. We shall do this by examining four functions of work-education institutions and seeing how these have been changing as society proceeds along the "Great Ascent."

Four main functions have involved our institutions of education and work in the past:

1. Promoting the education and development of the individual citizen.
2. Accomplishing certain service needs of the society (for example, production of goods and protection of life and property).
3. Distributing the total income of society in a way that is generally perceived as equitable.
4. Providing the individual with a role to play in the activities of his society; with an opportunity to gain a sense of contribution, belonging, and being appreciated; and with the consequent opportunity to develop a healthy self-image and sense of self-affirmation.

In the past, these four functions of *education, production, income distribution,* and *social roles* have been largely delegated to schools (for the first function and during childhood for the fourth) and jobs (for the latter three). But this delegation is working less and less well.

Education, for numerous reasons, is coming more and more to be considered a lifelong activity. The work place, as well as the school, is a learning place. But the economy has difficulty accommodating to this concept and providing an adequate number of suitably challenging work roles for the workers on ever-increasing educational levels.

As society evolves along the economic development trend, industrial production depends to an increasing extent on technology and capital, and decreasingly on labor. This has several consequences. For one thing, the economy no longer needs all the able-bodied and able-minded workers who produced all the goods and conventional services to fill previously felt needs. This has led to the abandonment of the frugality ethic of early capitalism and to its replacement by a consumption-and-waste ethic. Because limitless consumption (even of services) runs into difficulties associated with physical planetary limits, there is the future threat of chronic unemployment. To disguise this, planetary limits are in effect denied and various forms of featherbedding and make-work and exclusions from the workforce are tacitly accepted.

Because labor is less important in production, the rationale of using productive jobs in the economy as the primary income distribution mechanism has broken down. Because jobs have been the main legitimated roles in industrialized society—that is, having a job in the primary economic sector, being married to someone who has one, or preparing to get one—to be jobless is to be a marginal person.

A more basic approach, then, to the problems of education and work, involves reassessing the institutionalization of the four functions of education-work institutions. If they are considered separately, this may suggest new approaches. The importance of taking such a fundamental look is that the sustained threat of unemployment and grievances about underemployment will bring pressure for responses. If the problems are misperceived, the responses will be wrong. And wrong responses may (1) exacerbate other problems (such as inflation, welfare ills, and alienation and such related problems of crime, drugs, and social disruptions) and (2) lead to more dashed expectations.

It is unquestionably true that industrialized society does not need all the potential workforce to be engaged full-time in producing goods and services in the mainstream economy. The solution to the unemployment problem does *not* lie, however, in making production more "labor intensive," so as to use up all the people doing routine production jobs, nor in imposing restrictions on the number of hours a person can work. Both of these directions have the smell of absurdity about them. The solution lies, rather, in the direction of asking what kinds of useful social roles can be made available other than production in the conventional economic sense. The solution lies in the direction of making economic production *secondary to productive activity* in the humanistic sense. (This is *not* the same as "job enrichment," wherein the product is still the goal and labor the means.)

If society moves in this direction, it is likely that production of many types of goods will become more decentralized, with a significant proportion of it returned to the household and the community.[9] Emphasis would be on the quality of productive

---

[9] S. Burns, *Home, Inc.* (Garden City, N.Y.: Doubleday, 1975). See also L. S. Stavrianos, *The Promise of the Coming Dark Age* (San Francisco: W. H. Freeman, 1975). J. Robertson, *Power, Money and Sex: Towards a New Social Balance* (London: Marion Boyars, 1976).

work rather than the quantity of production. Grass-roots entrepreneurship would probably flourish. After all, highly sophisticated technology is not restricted to the large, centralized factory; it can be adapted to household and community production as well. (These decentralization arguments do not apply to all production, of course. Centralized production is more appropriate for some goods and services, such as appliances, automobiles, and insurance. For some services, such as telephones, utilities, and energy supply, quasi-public institutions are probably more appropriate.

As I have argued, job enrichment is not the solution to having sufficient and satisfactory social roles. A society that is learning and consciously evolving does not need to run out of constructive, participative roles. Only if the attempt is made to get these roles all from the activity of economic production does the problem become insoluble. There is unlimited potential for generation of creative and satisfying social roles in the voluntary sector. The potentialities of nonprofit organizations in this regard have scarcely been tapped. (Simple observation of the flourishing new enterprises in the voluntary sector will demonstrate the fallacy of the conventional argument that entrepreneurship is driven exclusively by the profit motive. A revised approach to the economic distribution task could release a flood of entrepreneurial activity in the voluntary and nonprofit sector.)

As regards meaningfulness of occupation, an apocryphal story is pertinent. Two medieval stonecutters were working on the same public works project. Asked what he was doing, one answered, "I'm squaring up this bloody stone." The other replied, "I am building a cathedral." The first was underemployed; the second was not. Occupation in even a menial socially useful task has meaning if the overall society has meaning. Lack of meaning in many jobs today translates into lack of a sense of meaning in the hedonistic consumption-and-waste frenzy of modern industrialized society.

We mentioned that vitalization of the voluntary sector requires an altered approach to income distribution. Basically there are five bases for distribution of gross income:

1. Payment for specific services (employment in the usual sense).
2. Membership (for example, right by virtue of being a member of family or tribe).

3. Social investment (for example, competitive scholarships and research grants).
4. Conditional need (for example, some scholarships and Local Initiatives programs).
5. Unconditional need (for example, welfare, unemployment aid, and assistance to the aged).

The Canadian Local Initiatives Programs, now renamed Canada Works, are a particularly promising approach to avoiding the problems typically attaching to the fifth of these bases—the "welfare mess." In these programs, monies that might otherwise be used for welfare and unemployment payments are instead made available for projects initiated by persons who then receive wages for carrying them out. The projects typically involve such socially useful tasks as neighborhood improvement, environmental cleanup, neighborhood child care, and assistance to the infirm and handicapped.

Of these five basic types of income distribution, some sort of basic income maintenance of the last type will undoubtedly be necessary for the disabled and aged. The majority of adults will probably receive their income via the first route. But we have hardly begun to explore the potentialities of the other three types, none of which appear to carry the social disadvantages of transfer payments of the fifth type. An example will illustrate the possibilities.

One group of underemployed could be characterized as overqualified and underchallenged. Its members have capabilities that they find no opportunity to use. To obtain needed income, they retain employment assigned to tasks that could be performed by persons with far less endowment and training. As a result, morale is low and performance inferior. However, many of these persons are attracted to socially desirable contributions of other sorts if giving up their routine employment were economically feasible. Examples of these alternative employments include a multitude of kinds of nonprofit entrepreneurship, such as experimental schools, holistic health care centers, legal aid organizations, enterprises for the handicapped, and teams to preserve and beautify the environment. Other persons might want to undertake study and research or to prepare themselves for new careers. The essential point is that here is a group of persons who have jobs but who wish for a kind of income maintenance that would allow them to pursue other creative activities. But there is among the unemployed another group, composed of individuals less inclined to be entrepreneurial or self-defining, who want jobs, routine or otherwise. They may be supported by unemployment payments and welfare. Just the reverse of the first group, they have income maintenance but want jobs. This situation suggests the approach of providing the transfer payments, not as welfare to the second group, but as enhancement income maintenance to the first— allowing them to move out and free up jobs in the economy for the second group. This is not an approach likely to be politically acceptable in the near future. However, it exemplifies the kind of thinking needed to free us from the sterile approaches of the past.

For it is fresh thinking, more than any other factor, that is needed to resolve the work dilemma. In an age when production of sufficient goods and services is a matter the society can handle with ease, an adequate economic system must emphasize a sufficiency of work roles that foster growth of self-esteem and actualization of potentialities, facilitating movement toward self-actualization. Employment in such a society is primarily the activity of self-development and only secondarily the production of goods and services.

Thus work is self-development, is education. It is *not* true that work is for production and education is for preparation for a job. But the doctrine that the goal of industrialized society is production has become so deeply embedded in the culture that it is difficult to even imagine how things might be otherwise.

Two scholars who have thought deeply and written about the kind of society and the kind of education that seem to make sense in human terms are Lewis Mumford (describing "biotechnic culture")[10] and Robert Hutchins (in *The Learning Society*). Both stress the ancient Greek concept of *paidea*. As Hutchins describes the humane society, learning, fulfilling work, and becoming human are the primary goals and "all its institutions are directed to this end. This is what the Athenians did. . . . They made their society one designed to bring all its members to the fullest development of their highest powers. . . . Education was not a segregated activity, conducted for certain hours, in certain places, at a

---

[10]L. Mumford, *The Transformations of Man* (New York: Harper & Row, 1956).

certain time of life. It was the aim of the society. . . . The Athenian was educated by the culture, by *paidea*."[11] The educating matrix of the society, involving all its institutions, was *paidea*. (It is perhaps worth noting, particularly in view of the contemporary interest in exploring inner expeience, that the highest and central theme of *paidea* was the individual's "search for the divine center.")

We noted earlier the basic long-term trend toward economic development and the fundamental transformation involved in each society as it has embarked on this path. Four components were identified—secularization, industrialization, dominance of economic rationality, and "scientification" of knowledge. Significantly, each of these component directions is increasingly challenged today. Secularization of values has left society without goals that can command the deepest commitments of its citizens—and there are indications of a new search for transcendent meanings. The industrialization of more and more of human activity —from horticulture and animal husbandry to health care, education, food preparation, leisure, aesthetic enjoyment, tourism, and computerized dating—has led us to ask what is happening to quality of life in the process. Dominance of economic rationality is charged with having made means—the economy and technology— into goals that fill the vacuum left by the secularization of values. The "scientification" of knowledge is accused of having contributed to the imbalance between our fabulous ability to manipulate the environment and our impoverished understanding of how to seek and achieve humane goals.

These fundamental challenges, appearing in a multitude of forms—emphasizing "appropriate technology," environmental concerns, personal liberation, becoming a "conserver society," or a new religiosity and search for meanings—together constitute a powerful modifying force to the long-term economic development trend. Satisfactory resolution of the perplexing dilemmas of education and work seem more likely to lie with these forces for systemic change than with the familiar mélange of curricular innovations, welfare schemes, and programs for job creation, job enrichment, job rationing, and job sharing. Most importantly, we need to ask our questions about the future of education and work in a more fundamental form than they are usually heard.

[11]R. Hutchins, *The Learning Society* (New York: Praeger, 1968).

23

Cyclic Life Patterns

Barry Stern
Fred Best

F or most Americans, the activities of education, work, and leisure are distributed in a "linear life plan."[1] Stated simply, this means people go to school in youth, work during their middle years, and retire in old age. This pattern of lifetime scheduling is the product of the natural dynamics of the human life cycle and the opportunities and constraints that have emerged within industrial societies. In terms of the life cycle, it is natural for a person to acquire physical and mental skills during youth, to assume a productive work role during the peak strength of middle life when

---

[1] This chapter is an abridgement of a paper entitled "Lifetime Distribution of Education, Work, and Leisure: Research, Speculations, and Implications," January 1977, available from the Institute for Educational Leadership, Washington, D.C.

family responsibilities are usually greatest, and finally to withdraw from work demands as physical and mental vigor decline in old age. The impact of industrial society on lifetime patterns is more complex. However, it can be generally stated that the prevailing "linear life plan" has emerged as a result of two developments: the expansion of nonwork time as a proportion of total lifetime and competition for work between age groups.

For the past one hundred years, the tremendous growth of economic productivity brought about by industrialization has allowed tremendous increases in nonwork time as a proportion of total lifetime. Some rough estimates computed by the New York Metropolitan Insurance Company of the years of total lifetime spent on major life activities during different stages of societal development serve to dramatize this growth of nonwork time. These estimates show that only 13.5 percent of a person's total lifetime during the industrial era is spent on work, compared to 28.6 percent of a person's lifetime during the agricultural era, and 33 percent of a person's life during the primitive era.[2]

A large measure of the added nonwork time has come in the form of the reduced work week. Specifically, the average U.S. work week has declined from approximately sixty hours to thirty-nine hours over the past one hundred years.[3] However, for the past three decades the work week has remained remarkably stable,[4] and much increased nonwork time has come in the form of longer vacations and more holidays.[5] In addition, nonwork time has taken the form of more years for education in youth and more for retirement in old age.

The increase in nonwork time during youth and old age has also been fostered by industrial forces that have caused job shortages and a growing competition for available work between age groups. Put differently, those in middle life, who are at the peak of their skill competency and political influence, have competed

[2] J. McHale, "World Facts and Trends," *Futures,* 1971 (September): 260.

[3] Significant portions of this reduction came from the decline of agricultural work. See J. Hedges and G. Moore, "Trends in Labor and Leisure," *Monthly Labor Review,* 1971, *94* (February): 3-11.

[4] For an informative discussion of work week stability, see J. D. Owen, "Workweeks and Leisure: An Analysis of Trends, 1948-1975," *Monthly Labor Review,* 1976, *99* (August): 3-8.

[5] Hedges and Moore.

more successfully, thus pushing young persons back into school and older persons into ever earlier retirement. Thus, both the added leisure time and the added job competition brought on by advanced industrialization have led to a compression of work into the middle years of life and to the pronounced development of the linear life plan.

Just how extensive has the linear life plan become? Figures computed to show the average lifetime spent primarily on work and nonwork for U.S. males for the years 1900, 1940, 1960, and 1970 reveal some interesting trends.[6] First, the percentage of the average U.S. male's lifetime spent primarily working or looking for work has decreased from 66.6 percent in 1900 to 59.7 percent in 1970. Second, computations based on average life longevity, years of school and average age of retirement indicate that the time spent primarily in work activities has been increasingly compressed into middle life, and nonwork time has increased substantially in the earlier and later years of life.[7] Projections from the Bureau of Labor Statistics indicate that if current trends continue, the proportion of lifetime given to work during middle life will decline to 55.8 percent by 1990, leaving 44.2 percent for either education or leisure at the extremes of the life cycle.

The trends of lifetime distribution of education, work, and leisure raise some important questions. First, are we approaching or perhaps past a point of diminishing returns for the linear life plan? Second, are we beginning to move toward an alternative way

[6] Figures were computed for U.S. males only because of fundamental differences in the current lifetime patterns between men and women which made consolidation of figures for both men and women inadvisable. Time limitations made comparable computations for women impossible, but these figures will be computed and published at a later date. Parenthetically, when "homekeeping" and "child rearing" are considered as "work," the life pattern differences between men and women become more similar. We expect that a number of trends will reduce still further these life pattern differences between the sexes.

[7] "Work life expectancy" (number of years in which a person is in the labor force, either working or looking for work) figures obtained from H. N. Fullerton and J. J. Byrne, "Length of Working Life for Men and Women, 1970," *Monthly Labor Review*, 1976 (February). "Life expectancy" (at birth) figures obtained from *Statistical Abstracts of the United States—1974* (Washington, D.C.: U.S. Government Printing Office, 1975), p. 55. "School years" (completed for persons over age 25) obtained from the *Digest of Educational Statistics for 1975* (Washington, D.C.: U.S. Office of Education, 1975), pp. 14-15.

of distributing education, work, and leisure throughout our lives? The most likely alternative to current linear lifetime patterns is a more cyclic life plan. The basic idea of this alternative is that current time spent on education and retirement, as well as any further gains in nonwork time, be redistributed to the center of life in the form of extended periods of leisure or education. The likelihood and feasibility of more cyclic life patterns will be discussed later, but first it is important to confront another more timely question: Is the continued widespread pursuit of the currently prevailing linear life plan feasible?

The issue of whether or not the linear life plan is dysfunctional for society requires that this pattern be analyzed both as a cause and a result of numerous social problems and trends. The number one human resource problem in the United States today is the shortage of jobs, especially jobs that fit the educational attainment and vocational aspirations of our labor force.[8] The problem goes beyond the current recession. For the past fifty years, society has not been able to provide jobs during peacetime for everyone able and willing to work. High unemployment has given rise, in part, to a variety of social ills, including crime, mental illness, and a large, expensive, inefficient, and degrading welfare system. These ills have been borne disproportionately by minority groups, women, youth, and older people. Although employment discrimination against these groups is still a problem, some progress has been made in eliminating it for minority group members and women. But the job prospects for youth and older people have deteriorated steadily during the past several decades.

The progressively inequitable distribution of work, especially preferred or career-type work, among the three age cohorts is perhaps most vividly illustrated by what has happened to the youth labor market in the past few years. Between 1960 and 1970 in the United States, the proportion of jobs falling in the lower third of the earnings distribution increased from 36 percent to 46

---

[8] For a current discussion of the shortage of jobs, see E. Ginzberg (Ed.), *Jobs for Americans* (Englewood Cliffs, N.J.: Prentice-Hall, 1976). For discussion of overeducation and unfulfilled job aspirations, see J. O'Toole, *Work in America* (Cambridge, Mass.: M.I.T. Press, 1973). I. Berg, *Education and Jobs: The Great Training Robbery* (New York: Praeger Publishers, 1970). R. Freeman, *The Over-Educated American* (New York: Academic Press, 1976).

percent. These lower-level jobs went disproportionately and increasingly to mature women and youth under the age of twenty-five. During the same period, mature males maintained their share of the high- and middle-level jobs, and minority-group workers maintained their extent of overrepresentation in the lower-level jobs.[9]

The poor or dead-end jobs in the society, then, are being assumed principally and increasingly by women, youth, and minority-group members. Indeed, these groups are competing with each other for the same jobs.

Getting a fair share of the preferred, career-type jobs is a problem that affects not only youth, the elderly, and minorities. Even *within* the cohort of middle-aged workers (age twenty-five to sixty), there are great inequities. Obviously, not all or even most middle-aged workers can be expected to get high-status, well-paying jobs. But the ones who hold the low-status, unskilled, low-paying jobs are the ones who have the least leisure time and educational benefits as well. Highly skilled, unionized, or professional persons who work for large companies experiencing continual technological development have the best of all worlds: They find their work challenging and secure, and they receive better vacation and education benefits than other workers.

A good example of the progressive inequality in the distribution of leisure and education among adult workers is that the greatest share of the increase in the participation rate of workers in adult part-time education between 1969 and 1975 was accounted for by workers who were well educated already or who were in occupations requiring a high level of education, such as the professional-technical occupations.[10] Moreover, the increases in opportunities to participate in education and training went overwhelmingly to workers in industries that have experienced continual technological development and accordingly have programs to upgrade and keep skills current.[11] Thus it may be said that par-

[9]M. Freedman, *Labor Markets: Segments and Shelters* (New York: Allanheld, Osmun, 1976), p. 75.

[10]National Center for Educational Statistics, Department of Health, Education and Welfare, published and unpublished data from "Triennial Adult Education Survey" (Washington, D.C.: U.S. Government Printing Office, 1969, 1972, 1975).

[11]S. Lusterman, "Education for Work," *Conference Board Record*, 1976 (May): 39-44. Bureau of Labor Statistics, *Characteristics of Agreements*

ticipation by adults in part-time educational activities is as likely to *result* from the kind of work that one does as it is to *lead* to such work. It is quite plausible, in fact, that economic opportunity is a better predictor of educational opportunity among adults than vice versa.

The problems and frustrations that result in part from the linear life plan and the inequitable distribution of work are getting worse. First, vertical career mobility is decreasing within the large, well-educated "baby-boom" generation (born between 1947 and 1961). These young workers are experiencing more difficulties than their counterparts from previous generations in moving past the lower rungs of the occupational ladder.[12] More young people are simply available to compete for the relatively stable number of preferred jobs. Competition for these jobs is increased further by young, better-educated members of minority groups seeking the job opportunities denied their parents and by more women re-entering the labor force to become full-time career workers. All are competing for the same entry-level career-type jobs. Thus, compared to previous generations, a smaller proportion of the baby-boom generation is getting the preferred jobs, thereby increasing the inequitable distribution of work between age groups as well as within the younger age group.

A second factor inhibiting a more equitable distribution of work, especially the preferred career-type work, is what appears to be an ever-present job shortage problem, aggravated further by a sluggish economy. Public employment programs *might* increase the number of jobs, but so far they have been unable to satisfy the demand for career-type jobs. And holders of preferred jobs are less likely to give them up (to seek new work or to leave the labor force temporarily) in today's highly competitive labor market. One vivid example of job tenacity is the greatly decreased turnover in the teaching profession during the past few years.

Third, while demographic and economic forces have re-

Covering 1,000 or More Workers, July 1, 1973, Bulletin 1822 (Washington, D.C.: U.S. Government Printing Office, 1974), Table 47. *Training and Retraining Provisions,* Bulletin 1425-7 (Washington, D.C.: U.S. Government Printing Office).

12"Changing Patterns of Occupational Opportunity," *Manpower Report of the President 1975* (Washington, D.C.: U.S. Government Printing Office, 1975), pp. 104-130.

duced the possibility for a more equitable distribution of work, other social forces are heightening the desire for greater parity. People today have higher occupational aspirations than ever because of greater affluence, higher levels of educational attainment, and declining family obligations. Parents want their children to be better off than they were, and the children, who have been nurtured by considerable amounts of schooling and greater financial resources, agree. Moreover, because of the increased penetration of the mass media, people are more aware of the desirable jobs that exist, especially the ones glamorized by television. Another factor that is increasing the desire among more people for a greater share of the preferred work is the increased personal freedom resulting from changing patterns of family life. Americans marry later, have fewer children, live in nuclear families, divorce more often, and are more financially self-reliant during old age. Also, in a growing number of families, both husband and wife work.

Economic and demographic constraints for the rest of this century are probably too strong to permit a degree of occupational mobility that will satisfy the desire for a more equitable distribution of work. If the constraints are allowed to run their course and nothing is done to restructure or redistribute work, we can expect a deepening and widening of the problems commonly associated with the linear life plan: first, a progressively inequitable distribution of work among the three major age cohorts of the population, with the middle-aged group monopolizing even more of the preferred jobs in the society, while forcing older people to retire earlier and younger people to defer even longer their entry into career-related work, and, second, increasing amounts of job stagnation, boredom, and underutilization of skills and education.

Already there are several strong indications that Americans perceive these problems and are favorably disposed to alter the current distributions of work, leisure, and education. Women and students, who traditionally have not been workers, now want more work. Prime-age full-time workers, about two thirds of whom are men and who are working about as many hours per week as they did thirty years ago, indicate that they would like more free time. A sizeable proportion of retired workers would rather continue working, although perhaps for fewer hours per week, than retire completely. Finally, many adults of all ages appear to want additional and more varied education opportunities.

Given this disposition to change, are the problems and shortcomings of current lifetime patterns great enough to move us toward alternative patterns? If so, what suitable alternatives exist? What are the forces that can converge to move U.S. society toward more cyclic patterns of life?

Clearly, the *demographic variables* of population size and the distribution of characteristics within the population represent one powerful force. As noted already, the post-World War II baby boom has given rise to an inordinately large proportion of persons now aged sixteen to thirty. Many of the people of this age group have deferred their entry into career-type work while prolonging their education, in part because of the fierce competition for jobs. As these people move into middle age, they will experience more difficulty than previous generations in getting career-type work, and they will find it more difficult to get promoted or to change into some other occupation providing similar status and pay. This lack of mobility will work to the disadvantage of workers from the *post*-baby-boom generation, who will not be able to dislodge the experienced workers "stuck" above them. For the next thirty years, the increased competition for work, especially preferred work, will bring pressure for earlier compulsory retirement, more jobs, and greater sharing of existing jobs.

If the current linear pattern of life persists, we can expect even further social tensions when the baby-boom generation begins to withdraw from the labor force around the year 2000. Since the next age cohort is significantly smaller, there may be an inadequate number of persons to fill the jobs developed by their predecessors. As a result, younger persons are likely to be drawn out of schooling and older persons detained from retirement to fill the demand for labor.

So, on the basis of demographic forces alone, the problems associated with the linear life plan are likely to worsen dramatically, with new problems abruptly taking their place around the year 2000. To deal with these problems, we may have to scrap linear lifetime patterns in favor of a more cyclic model.

Life longevity and health may also affect lifetime patterns, although less dramatically. With the current lifespan in the United States at about seventy, workers may be less willing to delay extended leisure until retirement and more willing to engage in middle-life training. Furthermore, improved health in old age is likely to decrease the desire of older workers for earlier retirement. Healthy workers will likely want to work more, not less, and, because work in the future probably will be less physically demanding, older workers will be *able* to work more. The ability to continue working in old age will bring pressure for gradual, not earlier retirement. Thus, longevity and health are, if anything, likely to be conducive to more cyclic patterns of life.

Changes in sex roles and family structure will be another critical force fostering more cyclic life patterns. The rise of women workers, particularly working wives, may enable males to spend less time earning an income and more time sharing family duties or pursuing leisure activities. At the same time, the need of employed mothers to take at least some time away from their work activities for pregnancy and child rearing will likely have the effect of increasing the flexibility of work hours and work years for both men and women. Husbands and wives are becoming increasingly flexible in exchanging work, household, and child-rearing responsibilities. While past sex roles froze men into the "breadwinner" duties and relegated women to the role of "housewife," increasing sex-role flexibility is likely to expand the opportunity for spouses to rotate roles and thus free each other from the linear life patterns of the past.

A third influence on life patterns is suggested by emerging theories on the developmental stages of adulthood. Over the last few years several scholars have proposed that adults pass through developmental stages the same as children and adolescents do. While these developmental theories are highly speculative and empirical research is inconclusive, there appears to be some consensus that most adults progress through successive phases of stabilization and consolidation followed by change and growth as they pursue new goals and confront the changing crises of different ages. If periodic realignment of values and life-styles are indeed traits of adult development, it is probable that cyclic life patterns would correspond more to the needs and rhythms of adulthood than do linear patterns.

Current *methods of education* are another force following the development of cyclic life patterns. Until recently, our society thought it proper to administer education—from elementary through advanced graduate levels—in one massive dose. Education was for young people—and beyond a certain point for just certain young people. And the whole process was best accomplished with little or no interruption. Teachers provided lectures, read assignments and graded tests within a classroom setting. Although there were rare exceptions to this model of education, it was not until the massive democratization of education during the 1960s that educational research and the political pressures fostered by a larger and more diverse educational constituency forced a widespread recognition that different individuals learn best under varying methods and time frames. The result has been a wave of educational innovations such as student-initiated courses, nongraded studies, academic credit for work and other experiences, vouchers and learning contracts, residential colleges, decentralized campuses, ethnic curriculums, programs for the elderly, and equivalency examinations. In terms of future life patterns, these "nontraditional" approaches to education will be generally conducive to more cyclic patterns. Their continuance and likely growth will tend to increase the scheduling flexibility of schooling and therefore to foster increasing departures from current linear life patterns.

The failing link between educational attainment and occupational advancement is another factor that could lead to more cyclic life patterns. For many years, schooling was the central avenue for social mobility. It represented the "meritocratic" ideal: The rewards and valued positions in society were distributed largely on the basis of educational certification. Today we are beginning to realize that the developed skills and the undeveloped potentials within our population are considerably greater than the demands of our labor market. Nonetheless, young people are continuing to stay in school longer in order to avoid and then overcome competition with older workers and each other. As a result, more and more education is required for jobs of relatively stable skill requirements. In the absence of other channels of opportunity, the true meaning of education for both occupational achievement and human fulfillment is being lost as those seeking advancement try to compete by pursuing ever higher levels of "overeducation."

The proportion of professional and technical jobs as a percentage of all employment will remain about the same in 1985 as it was in 1975 (about 15 percent). But over the same period, the proportion of college graduates in the labor force will increase from about 17 percent to 21 percent.[13] This translates to a labor-market surplus of millions of college graduates. Even the rather conservative estimates of the U.S. Bureau of Labor Statistics project a surplus of 1.6 million college graduates in 1985. Other analysts project an even greater oversupply. Joseph Froomkin, for example, assumes lower demand for professional-technical and managerial jobs than does the Bureau of Labor Statistics, because of technological advances and automation, and assumes a greater supply of college graduates, because of the increased labor force participation and educational attainment of women. His figures project an oversupply of from 6 to 8 million college graduates.

In future years, we may have to develop new channels, and perhaps new definitions, for social opportunity and personal achievement. In looking to this task, we should recognize that schools cannot be blamed for failures of society to provide opportunities for economic and occupational achievement. If a society reaches a point where human capacities for achievement surpass the opportunities, then the opportunities need to be expanded or redistributed. Otherwise, that society confronts stagnation. The structural realities of the U.S. labor force are not likely to allow a significant expansion of opportunities, but we *can* redistribute opportunities by moving toward a rotational system for sharing not only the number of jobs but also the quality of work. In this sense, a cyclic life pattern, in which work and advancement opportunities would be created by people periodically leaving their jobs for extended periods, may well become the next step in America's traditional pursuit of achievement and equal opportunity.

The overall rate of social change is a sixth factor that will have a crucial impact on lifetime patterns. Empirical indicators such as the shifting structure of the labor force, the rate of technological advancements, travel and communications, and popular perceptions suggest that overall social change is occurring at a rapid pace that will likely continue if not increase. In any society

[13]These are unpublished projections by the Bureau of Labor Statistics, U.S. Department of Labor, and by J. Froomkin, "Supply and Demand for Persons with Postsecondary Education," Policy Research Center paper prepared for the Assistant Secretary for Education, U.S. Department of Health, Education and Welfare, Washington, D.C., 1976.

experiencing rapid social change, we can expect that individuals will be constantly confronted with new problems and opportunities requiring adjustments and major life junctures. These adjustments and junctures will likely move more and more people toward cyclic life patterns.

The preferences of American workers between time and income may be another determinant of future lifetime patterns. While we have no conclusive data on this topic, there are a number of indications that the American worker may prefer time-income trade-offs and work-scheduling reforms that will foster more cyclic life patterns. A comprehensive review of behavioral, attitudinal, and consumer data indicates that worker trade-off preferences between income and free time may be shifting toward more free time.[14] This study reached five major conclusions. First, the income level of the average American worker allows enough discretion to forego income for more free time. Second, income remains a higher priority than free time. Third, people are not as inclined as they have been in the past to prefer income over free time. Fourth, future gains in free time are preferred in the form of extended time away from work such as vacations. Fifth, and most important, the way potential free time is scheduled is an important determinant of whether or not workers are willing to give up existing or potential income for more free time. Other studies indicate that if workers are asked to rank their choices between equally costly options such as a 2-percent pay raise, fifty minutes off the work week, and an additional week of paid vacation, they commonly choose vacation first, income second, and shorter work weeks last.[15] The implications of this data are that those currently employed are willing to give up work time during middle life for extended periods of free time.

[14]F. Best, "Changing Values Toward Material Wealth and Leisure," Policy research paper (Contract No. P00-75-0221) prepared for the Office of the U.S. Assistant Secretary for Education, Washington, D.C., January 1976.
[15]S. M. Neally and J. D. Goodale, "Time-Off Benefits and Pay," *Journal of Applied Psychology*, 1967, 5. B. Chapman and R. Ottemann, "Employee Preferences for Various Compensation and Fringe Benefits," *The Personnel Administrator*, 1975 (November). F. Best and J. Wright, "The Effect of Work and Full-Time Scheduling Upon Worker Time-Income Trade-Off Preferences," to be published in a forthcoming edition of *Social Forces*. F. Best and B. Stern, "Education, Work and Leisure—Must They Come in that Order?" *Monthly Labor Review*, 1977 (July).

Preliminary findings of a recent survey of a limited sample of workers provide a more direct indication of overall lifetime scheduling preferences.[16] A nonrandom sample of 151 workers from manual and nonmanual occupations were presented with three broad options for scheduling education, work, and leisure throughout life. The options can be described as the linear life plan, a moderate cyclic plan, and a fully developed cyclic plan. The workers were asked to rank these options in terms of their own personal preferences. The moderate cyclic plan was the first choice of 37.7 percent, the fully developed cyclic plan was chosen first by 29.8 percent, and the linear plan by 21.2 percent (11.3 percent did not give preferences). Next, the respondents were asked which plan they thought other persons would prefer. The results of this question suggest that people tend to think that everyone else prefers the type of life plan we currently have. Specifically, 37.1 percent thought others would prefer the linear life plan, 37.7 percent thought others would choose a moderate cyclic plan, and only 15.2 percent thought others would prefer the full cyclic plan. When the respondents were asked which life plan would be best for the overall well-being of society, most chose one of the two cyclic plans. Thus, in terms of both personal preferences and overall societal well-being, over 67 percent of the respondents chose one of the two cyclic life plans. Although these data are not representative of the U.S. labor force, the heterogeneity of the sample supports the speculation that American workers may prefer more cyclic life patterns.

The final factor that needs to be discussed as an influence on lifetime patterns is organizational constraints. While the other forces that have been discussed tend to foster or allow movement toward more cyclic lifetime patterns, institutional inertia could make the emergence of more cyclic life patterns more fantasy than reality. Among the obstacles to more cyclic patterns that might be expected from such organizations and those who manage them are problems of organizational discontinuity, threats of losing trained

[16]Data are from survey pretests before questionnaire was administered by F. Best to a varied sample of 791 employees of the county of Alameda, California. The final study is being prepared for publication in the researchers' forthcoming book, *Recycling People*. (Further information available from Quality of Life Research Associates, 925 25th Street No. 220, Washington, D.C. 20037.)

personnel and possible business secrets to competitors, administrative costs of coordinating noncontinuous employees, and fears by employees of all levels that they may lose jobs or organizational influence. Of course, more cyclic life patterns may also have positive impacts on organizations. Extended nonwork time may allow both self-renewal and retraining of employees; worker morale and productivity may improve; nonproductive or "dead-ended" workers may find new and more suitable jobs to the benefit of themselves and their old organization; and tax burdens for unemployment and welfare services may be lowered.

In evaluating the adaptability of work organizations to cyclic life patterns, one must recognize that their constraints and options vary tremendously. The product type, size structure, and stability of organizations are important considerations. The work-scheduling flexibility of organizations concerned with continuous, year-round mass production is different from the scheduling flexibility of organizations concerned with seasonal or batch production. A small firm will face different constraints and options from those faced by a large corporation. The level of capital investment and the nature of technologies will also influence organizational flexibility, as will the ways in which employees are organized, the overall stability of the organization, and the "accepted" rate of organizational change.

While it is difficult to generalize about the adaptability of work organizations to cyclic patterns of life, there are a number of indications that suggest widespread adaptation may be possible. The growth of progressively longer vacations is an important case in point, suggesting that large numbers of organizations are finding it possible to adapt to extended absences by their employees. On a more limited scale, organizations have been adaptable to a wide variety of work-scheduling innovations such as flexitime, four-day work weeks, leaves of absence without pay, extended vacations sometimes approaching three months, "cafeteria" time-income trade-off options, a variety of sabbatical programs, and job-rotation schemes. These trends and innovations suggest that institutions of work are gradually adapting to work arrangements that are more compatible with cyclic life patterns.

Americans appear to want to diminish the inequities in the distribution of work, leisure, and education, but there is little consensus about how to do it. Some would redistribute more equitably the amount of work (and hence leisure) that people have by introducing a shortened work week (four days, thirty hours), limiting the work year, or prohibiting forced overtime. Others would effect such a redistribution by expanding the total amount of employment through government-subsidized public works and public service employment. Still others would redistribute more equitably the preferred career-type jobs through such schemes as job sharing and the creation of more part-time jobs in highly skilled occupations. Schemes to redistribute leisure include guaranteed minimum amounts of paid or unpaid annual vacation, extended vacations as reward for length of service, greater opportunities to take leave of absence without pay, and the laying off of workers (when that is required) in reverse order of seniority with supplemental unemployment benefits. Finally, schemes to redistribute education more equitably to adults include a variety of entitlement or voucher plans, paid or unpaid educational leave, work sabbaticals, and the use of unemployment insurance to support job-related education and training.

Obviously, there is considerable overlap among proposals to redistribute work, leisure, and education. Redistribution in one area is almost certain to mean a redistribution in the other two. People who work less will have more leisure and hence more time, if not money, to engage in further education. Those who continue their education will become somewhat more likely to obtain work, especially more highly skilled work. And those who get more highly skilled work are likely to get more opportunities to participate in further education.

Despite general agreement that the present system of progression from school during youth to work during adulthood to retirement during old age is too rigid, there is little agreement about which of the redistribution schemes noted earlier are most likely to result in a more cyclical or rhythmical life pattern. People concerned with full employment tend to focus on proposals to expand the number of jobs and to redistribute work. People concerned with the arts and other cultural activities tend to be more attracted to proposals that increase the amount of discretionary leisure time. And educators, naturally, look favorably on proposals to promote education among adults who have had lesser amounts of it.

While the evidence is mixed, it does tend to favor the point of view that if you have enough jobs, most of the other human resource problems are going to take care of themselves. And most people would agree that the best way to provide jobs is through a faster rate of economic growth. What happens, however, if the economy does not expand and jobs are not created fast enough for all who want them? What if the unemployment rate does not go down? What if the public jobs created by new legislation are the same kinds of public jobs that we created in the 1960s—dead-end jobs that have no career potential and tend to disappear as soon as the federal subsidy for them disappears? What happens if we have increasing amounts of job stagnation and boredom due to economic and demographic forces that prevent an increasing number of workers from getting promoted ("stepping up") or changing occupations ("stepping out")? Finally, what if the extent of featherbedding increases, where two people are paid to do the work that one can do? These are very serious problems that are likely to become even more entrenched and solidified if the linear life plan—the current system for distributing work among the three major age groups—is allowed to continue unchecked.

Although it is premature to recommend specific public policies and programs to foster more flexible or cyclic patterns, there is evidently sufficient public concern to warrant extensive research and experimentation in this area. Various redistribution plans should be compared and contrasted in terms of their likely impact on the economy and the political structure. Some of the more feasible ones could be tried out experimentally in several locations. We believe there are four plans which merit increased attention and developmental efforts. In order of progressive degrees of federal commitment, they are as follows:

1. Time-income trade-offs and work-scheduling options. Labor and management in both the public and private sector could negotiate plans to allow individual employees more control over their workloads and time schedule. The range of options is wide enough to allow both employees and employers considerable choice in suiting their respective needs. The federal government might apply this idea internally as a "demonstration case" as well as investigate the use of tax and other incentives to foster more flexible work time within the private sector.

2. Extended leaves of absence. Public policy to guarantee employees the right to take temporary leaves would increase work-

life flexibility. Eligibility and length of leave might be made contingent on the seniority of individual employees. The federal government could provide incentives to industry (for example, tax credits) to carry out such policies or pass legislation guaranteeing all workers leave-of-absence rights.

3. Work sabbaticals with income support provisions. Such programs would guarantee workers the right to leave their jobs for extended periods and return, as well as provide partial income support during periods of absence. Generally speaking, workers would not be eligible for sabbatical until they had worked for about five or six years consecutively. Length of leave and income support would likely be determined by job seniority and earning level. Such programs have been and can be implemented for select groups and organizations in ways similar to private pension arrangements. If demonstrations of this idea are successful the federal government might also provide monetary incentives to employees to take sabbatical leaves and possibly initiate a national, voluntary sabbatical program for all government workers.

4. Integrated income maintenance and transfer payments. The goal of increasing the flexibility of working lives could be met by an integrated system of income maintenance and transfer payments. Income-support programs, such as social security, unemployment insurance, food stamps, aid for dependent children, and other welfare programs, would be combined into a single system. New income transfer programs, such as a guaranteed minimum income (negative income tax) program, would be included as they were implemented. So would a work-sabbatical program designed to provide partial support for persons leaving or reducing work activities for the purpose of education, self-renewal, or retirement. Such an integrated system would be more comprehensible to users, would eliminate needless program overlaps, and would minimize administrative and other costs.

Whereas work sabbaticals, integrated income maintenance, and transfer-payment programs are unlikely to become widespread public policy in the near future, other activities with public- and private-sector support could be pursued which would contribute toward making working life more flexible, while at the same time providing valuable information for future program planning. Taken together, these activities could move us closer to neutralizing the economic and demographic forces which inhibit risk taking in changing one's career or life direction.

One advantage of a policy that incorporates cyclic life patterns is that it can be structured to deal with a number of social problems simultaneously, particularly inadequate access to leisure and education throughout life and the need to ease the "lockstep" progression from school to work to retirement. Achieving the goal of making work more accessible, while making education and leisure more accessible as well, merits high priority on the nation's policy research agenda.

24

Education for What?

Willard Wirtz

For some five to ten years now, both in this country and in others with which we compare notes, the problem of under-employment among college graduates has been worsening. The first reaction, both here and abroad, was to attribute this unhappy development, which we had not anticipated, to a malfunction in the educational system. The convenient explanation was that young people were being prepared for the wrong occupations.

Because this "manpower-needs" theory had just enough justification to make it plausible and because it involved no questioning of sacrosanct economic premises, it gained immediate and general currency. So did the solution it suggested—namely the building of new bridges between the worlds of education and of work. And so we set about the fairly intensive building of these bridges. In general, this meant shifting toward a more technically and vocationally oriented emphasis in the educational system.

Although the solution implied a reciprocal effort, the work of building the bridges was all assigned to one side.

That proved insufficient. It has become increasingly clear that even a perfect matching of preparation and identifiable employment opportunities would leave a serious gap. The sterner truth has emerged: There is not today and will not be as long as we stay on our present course enough employment to absorb all the young people whose training was based on the prospect of a particular kind of employment. The demographers' consoling assurance that this will be better five or ten years from now offers too little, too late. The one-dimensional view that "labor-market" needs, as presently perceived, are the controlling determinants of what higher education should offer leads logically only to the conclusion Sweden has now officially adopted, which is to ration higher education.

A deep-rooted American allergy to that kind of answer has led to a renewed emphasis on a second dimension of education-work policy, centering on the reminder that higher education has higher purposes and values than preparation for employment. We hear more and more today about the merits, if the need for philosopher statesmen and erudite professionals is satisfied, of blue-collar workers cum laude, clerks and taxi drivers capable of broader contemplations, and a people better able to improve on the uses of leisure. This is not to belittle the importance of this second view of the matter. Every teacher worth the name believes deeply in the value of education not only as preparation for life's broader pursuits and purposes but as an end in itself. Yet very few would believe or argue that this case for education can stand alone. It would be enough answer, although there is more, that the continued underemployment of college graduates gives those who do not believe in education's higher values and those who give priority to other items on tight budgets too strong a hand in appropriation committees and other exchequers, private and public alike, where education's resources are allocated.

A two-dimensional education-work policy—bowing to education's manpower training obligations on the one hand and then, on the other, pleading its broader values to those who cannot find jobs that use it—is not going to work. These two dimensions take work virtually as a given and education as the variable. I would therefore like to explore the validity of a third dimension of education-work policy—not as substitute for the other two but as a supplement and complement to them. This third dimension involves an inquiry into whether there are elements in the changing amount, nature, distribution, and quality of work that are relevant to any effort to integrate these two central life processes better. It goes beyond that to consider the possibility that a different integration of these two processes could itself contribute to the value of education and work. It makes no assumption that either process is an end in itself or that either takes supremacy over other activities that give the human experience meaning. It does not think in terms of two worlds—separate institutional sovereignties—but in terms of one—the world of life. This third dimension needs an identifying phrase, and, since the only legitimate purpose of any system of things or pattern of institutions is to provide as many people as possible with the maximum practicable opportunity to make the highest and best use of the human experience, we can call this dimension the "highest-and-best-use" policy.

With this brief shooting of the stars of ultimate purpose in order to get our bearings, what would a "highest-and-best-use" concept suggest with respect to meeting the problem of the underemployment of fully qualified college graduates? I believe it suggests moving broadly and boldly in three directions: first, to recognize that the difficulty regarding youth underemployment is actually only one manifestation of a developing problem—and a parallel prospect—affecting the entire life span, so that it cannot be effectively dealt with separately; second, to realize that this broader problem will yield only to the development of what amounts to an essentially new economics and politics—built, in E. F. Schumacher's phrase—on the premise that only people matter; third, to encourage people to accept more responsibility for handling their common affairs than they have recently been exercising, and this means acceptance by teachers of primary responsibility for qualifying people as architects of change.[1]

To suggest, first, that the underemployment of college graduates is only one part of a much broader situation may appear a counsel of discouragement. Not at all. And it is not a matter of

[1] E. F. Schumacher, *Small Is Beautiful: Economics as if People Mattered* (New York: Harper & Row, 1973).

offering misery the consolation of company. It is a matter of allying the forces of those who can accomplish together, if their common interests are identified, what separate contingents of them cannot do.

Each year, as one group of Americans receives college degrees, another—about equally large—receives retirement notices. Members of both groups are eating their hearts out now because there are no uses to be made of talents they have worked hard to develop. Add to these two classes the millions of American women for whom equal employment opportunity has proved counterfeit because of the obstacles to combining career motherhood with a career in anything else. Add, too, all those in the middle of their careers who are stuck in jobs using only a little of what is inside them. If these huge segments of our population can be pulled together to form a coalition, they will have an impact far beyond that of a youth employment program alone.

The second element of this highest-and-best-use policy relates to economics and politics. Here again, we have to think comprehensively or we are going to be in trouble. Critically important as it is to do everything possible to revitalize the economy by appropriate fiscal and monetary measures, I do not believe many people really believe that this will ever again lead to anything worth calling *full employment*. It is time to recognize that the only way the employment figures are being maintained at even tolerable levels in this country—if 7.5 percent unemployment can be counted tolerable—is by turning more and more older people out to pasture earlier and keeping more younger people in school longer.

The view that any conceivable countercyclical economic measures will ever create a renewed need for all the higher education young people will be taking ignores the fact that the causes underlying the present circumstance are in no major respect cyclical but are the consequence of forces that have been gathering for a long time. The only way to make adequate use of developed human resources is to develop a new economics that takes that human potential as its starting point. This means an economics and a politics that put people in the first place instead of someplace else on down the line. Such an economics would recognize behind all the apocalyptic talk about limited growth two important facts: One is the limitless amount that needs to be done in this country and in the world; the other is that while some *natural* resources are in critically short supply, the *human* resource is boundless.

The new economics would start from a commitment to make the fullest practicable use of the most highly developed form of whatever talents are inside people instead of starting from a consideration of the most profitable use, or misuse, of the elements inside the thin and fragile crust of the planet. Such a policy would measure all major enterprises in terms of their comparative drain on dwindling natural resources and their comparative use of the highly developed—meaning educated—human resource. This would present a hard question in determining, for example, the socially desirable balance of various uses of motor vehicles. But the *Concorde* would be seen immediately as a monstrous absurdity. The new policy would require also a review and redefinition of which kinds of human activity should be compensated and properly included in the gross national product—which would probably be renamed the *net national strength*. Many things that people used to do—housework, for example, and bearing and raising children—would be reckoned as productive. A system designed in this way would still have to be self-supporting and to provide for and depend on growth, but the notion of growth would include different elements from those reflected in the grossest national product in history. It would center rather on those elements of growth that coincide with our human purposes and our underlying ideals as a civilization.

Starting from a fuller identification of individual and societal needs and desires and hopes than comes from gambling on how many people will pay how much for whatever is widely enough advertised, a new economics based on the limitless human resource would center increasingly on services. But this would not mean any diminution of the authentic American model of private enterprise. There is no proven basis for the assumption that people would be less willing to pay for those things contributing to life's quality than they are for those detracting from it. We are still reeling from the lesson that so many millions of people would watch ten hours of *Roots* and that so many tens of thousands would stand in line for sometimes seven hours to get a glimpse of King Tut's treasures.

Such a new economics would include a complete rethinking

of the time frames into which we cast our work lives. Any current assumptions about how much of people's lives most advisedly goes into work and when and in what units would be completely re-examined. No presumption of validity would be attached to the notion that the right answer is eight hours a day, between 8:00 and 5:00 P.M., five days a week, between the ages of about twenty-five and sixty-five or less. The alleged advantages of full-time over part-time employment and the disadvantages of flexi-time, lucratively speaking, would be considered in the brighter light of what such changes would mean in human terms.

This matter of alternative work patterns is integrally related to the development of a coalition constituency in support of a highest-and-best-use education-work program. For the considera-tion of a new economics "as if people mattered" would include, perhaps most centrally, a deliberate and thorough review of what is today's reality only because it was once necessity and then sur-vived only as custom: that life is divided into three time traps—youth for education, maturity for work, and older age for denial of both of these opportunities. It would probably be decided that sixteen or more years of education at one long, uninterrupted sit-ting is not the best answer for nearly as many young people as are following this course today. For many, a preferred approach may be continued education and retraining—through tuition refund and similar plans and perhaps by extending the practice of paid sab-batical leaves far beyond the teaching profession, possibly to everybody.

The third element of the highest-and-best-use policy is con-nected with ways and means, particularly as they involve the func-tions of education. In other words, where and how can a three-dimensional education-work policy, a new economics, develop and gather its strength? Surely not through legislative enactment. Nor is the corporate world likely to promote change of the kind and magnitude involved here. Although some of it will come through collective bargaining, there are elements of understandable ambiv-alence in organized labor's reaction to both the quality of work and the youth employment initiatives. Where then does this kind of change originate, and where does it gather its force? When the only proven catalyst of significant social change is dramatic crisis, who is going to develop a "new economics" in the absence of such a crisis? If there is an answer to this, it lies in one word: *people*.

It is perhaps naive to suggest that there is some force in people that can bring about such change without institutionalized support—except in education. But there are signs that the people are a more potent source of change than was imagined a few years ago.

One such sign is the fascinating experiment in government going on right now in the national capital. Stated too simply, a new president has decided to go over the heads of the political establishment and to take his case, not as candidate but as executive, to the general membership: in walks down Pennsylvania Avenue, fireside chats, New England town meetings, and all the rest. He is talking principally about human rights, the quality of life, and underlying ideals. If the usual measures and sources are to be relied on, the consequence of this so far is that the president's stock is going rapidly up with people in general and equally rapidly down in the Congress. So far, he has only *talked* about most things, making it pretty plain that he is deliberately developing a support base to be used in the future. The question, of course, is what is going to happen when the proposals for *action* come along. Are people in general going to accept what the president does as fully as they have accepted what he is saying? Some observers of the Washington scene are predicting that the answer to this is going to be that the people will drop off the rhetoric someplace along the hard road. I'm guessing the other way. I think we have been selling people's idealism terribly short.[2]

I find the same kind of encouragement in the emergence across this country of an insistence on the part of people generally to take a larger direct part in the handling of their own common affairs at the local community level. There is no question but that there is a yeasting of community in America today, but there *is* a question of what form this movement will take or how responsible it will prove. One person's volunteer is going to be somebody else's vigilante. Much of the planning going on at the community level is aimed at improving the quality of life, and it is heartening to note that the many young people involved in community projects are

---

[2] By the time these statements are in print, the president's energy package will have been debated in Congress and in public and private places for several months. I can only hope at this point that developments will bear me out.

working together *for* something instead of *against* something. I suspect that if an effective education-work policy does evolve, it will depend only in small measure on congressional enactment or federal action. It will come largely, I think, through the development of collaborative processes at the local level—involving representatives of educational institutions, business, labor unions, and the community at large. It may well prove that the development of education-work policy will permit the long overdue experimentation in this country with the ideas of pluralism on which it was founded.

And what is education's role in shaping and adapting to this new policy? One product of a professional lifetime's nomadic wandering back and forth between higher education and higher and lower politics has been a complete reversal of my earlier understanding of the comparative roles of these two processes in the dynamics of change. I used to think of politics as the moving agent of change and of education as exercising a stabilizing, in some ways restraining, influence. I do not think so anymore. It seems to me now that it is in the educational process alone that the seeds of change are planted and grow; and that elections, legislative debates, and executive councils only decide when the harvest is to be taken—which is too often after the frost. Whether any higher and better use will be made of the life experience depends ultimately on what people decide on the basis of the education they get.

These days, when young people ask, "Education for what?" the cynicism of the question strikes home. Our generation played a brutal shell game with theirs in the 1960s—with a war we said was not there when it was. We are coming very close in the 1970s to playing another—with talk about jobs we say are there when they are not. The stakes are higher than we yet realize.

Index

A

Academic disciplines, nature of, 40ff
Accurate empathy, 105-106
Achilles, 44
Adams, H., 89, 200
Adler, M., 5, 46ff
Adult education, 116; in Great Britain, 75
Alternative work patterns, 74ff
Alverno College, 120
American Academy of Family Physicians, 163
American Board of Family Practice, 164
American Board of Internal Medicine, 163-164
American Center for Quality of Work Life, 90
American College of Physicians, 164
American Council on Education, 115
American Federation of State, County, and Municipal Employees, 76
American Management Association, 81
American Medical Association, 157, 168, 170

American Vocational Journal, The, 15
Aquinas, T., 57, 61
Associated Colleges of the Midwest, 120
Astin, A., 173

B

Baby boom, 255
Balao, 219ff
Bayer, C., 118
Beane, K., 108
Beard, C., 94
Becker, G., 68
Bell, D., 12-13, 19, 92, 237
Benderly, B., 92
Berg, I., 253
Berger, B., 241
Best, F., 250ff
Bisconti, A., 173
Blakely, R., 159
Blaug, M., 74, 186, 192-193
Bledstein, B., 141ff
Bowen, H., xi, 5, 22ff
Boyer, E., 148ff
Bradford, L., 108
Branscomb, L., 83
Braudel, F., 241-242

Brown, J., 2
Buddhist economics, 89ff
Bullock report, 74
Bureau of Labor Statistics, 237, 252
Bureaucracy, alternatives to, 218ff
Burns, S., 232, 245
Byrne, J., 252

C

Callaghan, J., 186
Cambridge University, 151
Canada Works, 247
Canterbury Tales, 126-127
Carkhuff, R., 108
Carnegie Commission on Higher Education, 3, 23
Carnegie Corporation of New York, 79
Carter, J., 2, 93
Chapman, B., 261
Chaucer, G., 126
Chicago Urban Corps, 118
Chickering, A., 5, 125ff
Citizens Policy Center, 118
Cognitive initiative, 107
Cognitive skills, 103-105
Cohen, H., 159
Coleman, J., 117
College Placement Council, 173
Colleges of Further Education, 73-74
Columbia University, 149
Common core curriculum, 148ff
Communist Manifesto, 51
Competence, problems in defining, 161ff
Competency-based education, 109
Concorde, 272
Conference Board, 79-80
Constitution of the United States, 24
Continuing education, 154ff; mandatory, 157ff
Coomaraswamy, A., 62
Cooperative Assessment of Experiential Learning, 115
Cooperative League of the United States, 233
Corporate education. *See* Workers, education for
Counseling for education work, 113-114
Countereconomy, 227ff

Critical career competences, 195ff
Cyclic life patterns, 250ff

D

Dahrendorf, R., 185-186
DeCharms, R., 109
Declaration of Independence, 24
Democracy and Education, 101
Department of Health, Education and Welfare, 157
Department of Justice, 155
De Paul University, 113-114
Descartes, R., 57
Dewey, J., x-xi, 14, 16ff, 35, 38, 96, 101
Distributive Workers of America, 116
Drucker, P., 92
Dylan, B., 93

E

Earned idle time, 91
Economics, new directions in, 227ff
Economy, theory of, in the United States, 24ff
Edgerton, R., 5, 110ff
Education, purpose of, 58
Educational brokers, 113
Educational leaves of absence, 69ff, 265-266; union pressure for, 76ff
Educational Testing Service, 115
Elgin, D., 234
Eliot, C., 15
Emergy, F., 218
Empire State College, 113-114, 128
Employment, future prospects for, 236ff, 268ff
Energy crisis, x-xi
Enzer, S., 8
Esser, B., 155
Extended admission, 72

F

Faure, E., 23
Federal Trade Commission, 155
Federation for Economic Democracy, 233
Feldstein, M., 238
Ferris, W., xii
Fink, N., 115, 122
FIPSE. *See* Fund for the Improve-

ment of Postsecondary Education
Flexner, A., 167
Florida State University, 120
Ford, B., 206
Ford, G., 2, 206
Ford, H. II, 93
Fraser, R., 61
Freedman, M., 254
Freeman, R., 192, 253
Fromm, E., 93ff
Froomkin, J., 260
Frost, R., 139
Fullerton, H., 252
Fund for the Improvement of Postsecondary Education, 110ff

G

Gardner, J., 153
General education, 141ff; arguments against, 143-145; arguments for, 142-143
General Motors, 76, 99-100
Gerzon, M., 23
Gibb, R., 108
Gilmore, P., 83
Ginsberg, E., 130-131, 253
Good jobs, 176ff
Good work, 55ff
Goodale, J., 261
Graduates, supply of, and demand for, 172ff, 182ff
Graphic Arts International Union, 78
Gray-collar workers, 77-78
Green, T., 5, 12-13, 36
Gross, B., 239
Guilds, 126

H

Hall, J., 128
Harman, W., 6, 236ff
Harman International, 76
Harper, W., 19
Harvard College, 151
Haynes, E., 38
Heard, A., 24
Hedges, J., 251
Hedonistic paradox, 36ff
Heilbroner, R., 152, 243
Henderson, H., x-xi, 5-6, 227ff
Henderson State University, 119

Herbst, P., 219
Hesiod, 129
Higher education: benefits of, 179-180; future of, 2; purposes of, 1ff; value of, 4, 6
Hofstra University, 116
Homer, 44
Houle, C., 126
Hutchins, R., 11, 248

I

Individualism Old and New, 17
Industrial age, xi
Industrial democracy, x, 20, 99, 218ff
Industrial Training Act of 1964, 73
Industrial Training Boards, 73
Interdisciplinary education, 40ff
International Journal of Health Services, 159
International Labor Organization, 65
Interpersonal skills, 105

J

Jacobsen, L., 106
James, W., 141
Jamestown (NY) Labor-Management Committee, 78
Jefferson, T., 35, 53
Jesus, 31-32
Job satisfaction, 174ff
Jobs, in relation to work, 42ff
Johansen, R., 220

K

Kahn, H., 238
Kaiser Permanente Medical Care Plan, 77
Kaiser Plan, 170
Kaplin, M., 148
Kasper, D., 167ff
Keniston, K., 23
Kepler, J., 56
Kessel, R., 168
Ketcham, R., 29-30
Kim, L., 187
Kimberly-Clark Corporation, 77
Klemp, G. Jr., 102ff
Kruger, D., 155
Kurland, N., 75

L

Laboratory School, 18
Labor force, composition of, 80
Laissez-faire, 24, 27
League of Voluntary Hospitals, 76
Learning Society, The, 248-249
Leisure, 46ff
Le Mont St. Michel and Chartres, 89
Lerner, M., 12
Levine, H., 67
Levi-Strauss, C., 89
Liberal arts, usefulness of, for vocations, 125ff
Liberal education, 33
Licensing, 154ff; arguments against, 167ff; costs of, 169ff
Lifelong learning, 66
Lifetime Learning Act, 66
Linear life plan, 250ff
Little, T., 118
Lone Mountain College, 116, 118
Lusterman, S., 75, 79ff, 254

M

McClelland, D., 108
McHale, J., 251
Macy, F., 123
Management, worker participation in, 70
Marx, K., 31, 51
Marxism, 31
Massachusetts Community Development Finance Corporation, 233
Master, The, 151
Mayo Clinic, 169
Mead, G., 18
Mead, M., 89
Mediterranean, The, 241
Middlesex Community College, 113
Miike, L., 159
Mills, T., xii, 6, 87ff
Minnesota Metropolitan State University, 113-114
Mitchell, A., 234
Monroe Doctrine, 128
Moore, G., 251
Morris, G., 99-100
Mother Earth News, 231
Motivation, 106
Mumford, L., 248
Mushkin, S., 66

N

National Association of Manufacturers, 14
National Commission on Health Manpower, 156-157
National Conference on Higher Education, xii
National Council of Negro Women, 122
National Institute of Education, 173
National Society for the Promotion of Industrial Education, 15
National Union of Hospital and Health Care Workers, 76
Neally, S., 261
Net national strength, 272
New Jersey Educational Consortium, 123
New Republic, The, 16
New York Health and Hospitals Corporation, 76
New York Times, 93
Newsweek, 2-3
Newton, I., 56
Nollen, S., 65ff
Northeastern University, 115

O

Ochsner, N., 173
Ontario Institute for Studies in Education, 125
Oregon Career Information project, 112
Organic Gardening, 231
Organization for Economic Cooperation and Development, 65, 184-185
O'Toole, J., xii, 1ff, 191, 253
Ottemann, R., 261
Overeducation, 172ff
Owen, J., 251
Oxford English Dictionary, 196

P

Pace College, 122
Paidea, 248-249
Parkersburg Community College, 116
Pepperdine University, 120, 123
Plato, 22, 32, 35
Prevention magazine, 231
Price, C., 197
Problem solving, 6ff

Promise of the Coming Dark Age, The, 228
Proposal for Credentialing Health Manpower, 160
Prosser, C., 15

Q

Quality of Work Life Program, 76

R

Rakoff, J., 116, 118
Read, J., xii
Recertification, 160ff
Recurrent education, 65ff; in Great Britain, 72ff; in Sweden, 70ff; in the United States, 75ff; in West Germany, 67ff
Regional Educational Consortium for Women, 113
Regional Learning Service of Central New York, 113
Relicensure, 160ff
Renshaw, J., 206ff
Reubens, B., 182ff
Robertson, J., 245
Rockefeller Brothers Fund, 79
Roemer, R., 159
Rolling Stone, 231
Roots, 272
Rosenthal, R., 106
Rudd, E., 192-193
Rush Medical Hospital, 120

S

St. Paul, 59
Sakharov, A., 93
Sanford, N., 23
Scheele, A., 195ff
Scheele, D., 197
School for New Learning, 113-114
Schumacher, E., x-xi, 5-6, 8, 12-13, 55, 89ff, 228, 270
Seeman, A., 9-10
Seeman, M., 9-10
Selden, W., 159
Self-assessment testing, 162ff
Sengenberger, W., 67
Service Employees International Union, 77
Shimberg, B., 154ff, 168
Sirageldin, I., 232
Small Is Beautiful: Economics as if People Mattered, xi

Smith, A., 24, 30
Smith, R., 125
Smith-Hughes Act, 15
Snedden, D., 15ff
Snow, C. P., 151
Social Darwinism, 15ff
Social efficiency, philosophers of, 14ff
Social Engineering Technology, 197
Society of Automotive Engineers, 99
Socrates, 22, 129
Solmon, L., 172ff
Spring, W., 240
Stanford Research Institute, 234
Stavrianos, L., 228, 245
Steiner, G., 152
Stern, B., 250ff
Stewart, A., 108
Straussman, J., 239
Strömgvist, S., 70
Success, attributes of, 102ff
Successful careering, 195ff
Sumner, W., 14

T

Technology, consequences of, 230
Textron, 116
Thorsrud, E., 20, 218ff
Toffler, A., 92
Training Opportunities Scheme, 73
Training Within Industry Program, 73

U

Underemployment, 172ff, 240, 268-269
Unemployment, x
United Auto Workers, 76
United States Postal Service, 77
University for Action, 117
University of Chicago, 18, 149
University of Massachusetts, 114

V

Values in education, xii, 22ff
Vermilye, D., xii, 66
Vermont Community College, 113
Vickers, D., 123
Vietnam War, 2
Vocational education, 14ff, 126-127
Voluntary simplicity, 234-235

W

Webster's New Collegiate Dictionary,
   128
*Webster's New International Diction-
   ary,* 89
Weiner, M., 115, 122
Wells, H. G., 35
Whole Earth Catalog, 231
Winter, D., 108
Wirth, A., 12ff
Wirtz, W., xi, 6, 268ff
Women workers, 258
Women's Opportunity Research Cen-
   ter, 113

Woodhall, M., 183
Work: characteristics of, 48ff; future
   of, 236ff; as a learning experience, 87ff; meaning of, 129;
   national policy for, 268ff; purposes of, 12ff, 60ff, 88ff; in
   relation to family life, 260ff;
   in relation to jobs, 42ff
Work Improvement Program, 76
Workers: alienation of, 43; education
   for, 69ff, 79ff; sabbaticals for,
   266
Worklife, quality of, ix-x, 101
Wright, J., 261